BLOOD RED MOON

GRANT RUST

Blood Red Moon
© Grant Rust

All rights reserved. No part of this publication may be reproduced, stored in a retrieval system, or transmitted in any form or by any means, electronic, mechanical, photocopying, recording or otherwise, without the prior written permission of the author.

National Library of Australia Cataloguing-in-Publication entry

Author: Rust, Grant.

Title: Blood Red Moon / Grant Rust

ISBN: 9780992511500 (paperback)

Subjects: To be completed

Dewey Number: To be completed

Published with the assistance of www.inhousepublishing.com.au

AUTHOR NOTE

All of us carry around a personal body of knowledge, some factually based, some based on our own perception of truth and some embedded in folklore and legend handed down, often without question, through the generations.

Donald Rumsfeld summed this concept up in a philosophical speech.

"There are known knowns. These are things we know that we know.

There are known unknowns. That is to say, there are things that we don't know.

But there are also unknown unknowns. There are things we don't know we don't know."

Donald Rumsfeld, US Secretary of Defence

As I contemplated Rumsfeld's intriguing words, I toyed with the idea what if the things we had always considered irrefutable truth were, in fact, based on ancient folklore.

I wondered if the entire basis to my Christianity was based on traditionally accepted anecdotes, folklore and half-truths. On the other hand, what if the facts presented in the New Testament were in fact absolute truths and the folklore was being retold by vested interests? Could any of our preconceived notions be regarded as true without any real basis?

Intrigued by the whole concept of what is truth and how do we know when we have found it I embarked on a quest to test the hypothesis on the book at the heart of the Christian religion, The New Testament.

Blood Red Moon is the result of my journey to find *the truth* in what most of us have traditionally regarded as irrefutable as contained in The New Testament. My reading of the Bible coupled with years of extensive research including cross-referencing dates, times, places and events, has irreconcilably altered my perception of what is commonly regarded as the story of Jesus in the New Testament.

Blood Red Moon delves into some of the accepted notions of Jesus' family life and times, into the political and personal intrigues current at the time. The perceived concepts of Heaven and Hell as understood by ordinary people who lived at the time of Jesus and the perplexing notion of Virgin Mary's Immaculate Conception.

I unravelled some of the accepted terminology and concepts inherent in The New Testament as well as Jesus' traditionally accepted demise by crucifixion, Jesus' resurrection from the tomb and specified the time period of his prophesied second coming.

Grant Rust.
March 29th 2014.

Table of Contents

AUTHOR NOTE	1
PROLOGUE	5
CHAPTER 1: The Holy Spirit	9
CHAPTER 2: Virgin Mary	55
CHAPTER 3: Heaven and Hell	91
CHAPTER 4: The Quest	129
CHAPTER 5: Flight to Safety	187
CHAPTER 6: The Family Reunion	235
CHAPTER 7: Armed Conflict	283
CHAPTER 8: Titius and Paul	331
CHAPTER 9: The Word of God Spreads	377
REFERENCES	409
LIFE OF JESUS - BIRTH TO CRUCIFIXION	410
LIFE OF JESUS – RESURECTION TO REVELATION	414
THE PROPHESISED SECOND COMING OF JESUS	416
IMMEDIATE FAMILY OF JESUS	417
PROVINCES, KINGDOMS, COUNTRIES	418
RELIGIOUS GROUPS	419
GLOSSARY	421

Book cover designed by Radika Nayar.
Book cover photograph by Grant Rust.
Layout and light editing by Libby.
E-book formatted by Peter.
Blood Red Moon is based on the New Testament.

PROLOGUE

The Israelite and Judean Kingdoms situated west of the Mediterranean Sea covered an area of approximately one hundred and seventy miles long by seventy miles wide. The inhabitants were periodically attacked by hordes of tribesmen from neighbouring kingdoms. The area was conquered by several ancient world powers including the Babylonians 586 B.C., the Persians 539 B.C., the Grecians 332 B.C., and the Romans in 53 B.C.

The two small kingdoms became client states of the Roman republic and were broken up into several provinces. Herod was appointed King of the Jews by the first Emperor of Rome, Octavius Augustus and given client king control of the provinces of Judea, Idumea, Samaria, Perea, Galilee, Decapolis and Gaulantis. The Roman Senate named the collective provinces as the Kingdom of Iudaea.

The Israelites were the first known race of people who believed in one almighty God in heaven that created the whole world and every living thing on earth. The Romans were pagans, believing in many types of Gods and myths. The Jewish citizens of Iudaea believed that under Roman rule they were losing their religious beliefs, autonomy, freedom and being taxed into a state of slavery.

Control of The Promised Land was slipping away and the two main religious sects were at odds with each other to which path to take to keep the Kingdom from collapsing into anarchy. The aristocratic Sadducee sect chose political alliance with the Romans, whereas the Pharisee sect preached strict observance of Jewish laws, traditions and religious ceremonies. Many Pharisees and other small sects believed Roman authority and control should be met with armed aggression.

The new Kingdom of Iudaea was reaching a crisis point where ambitious men and women clashed, with politics in turmoil, autonomy contested and religious beliefs and alliances tested to extremes. The dethroned descendants of King David and Solomon rose out of the wilderness to fight the might of Rome with devastating effects on the known world.

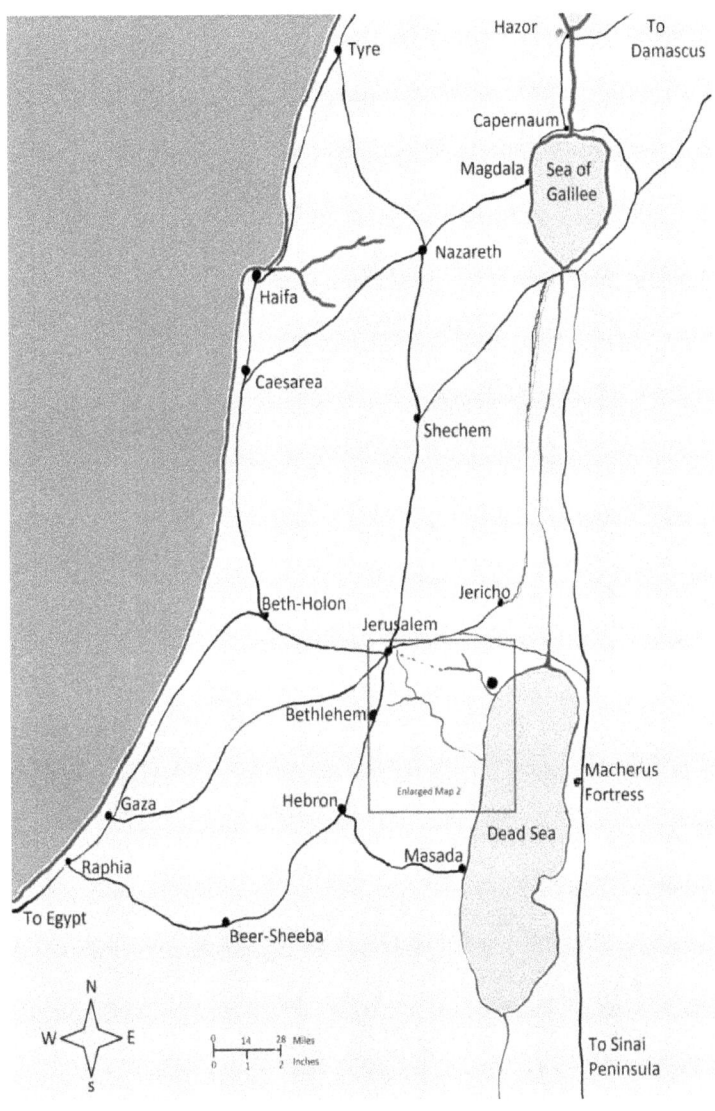

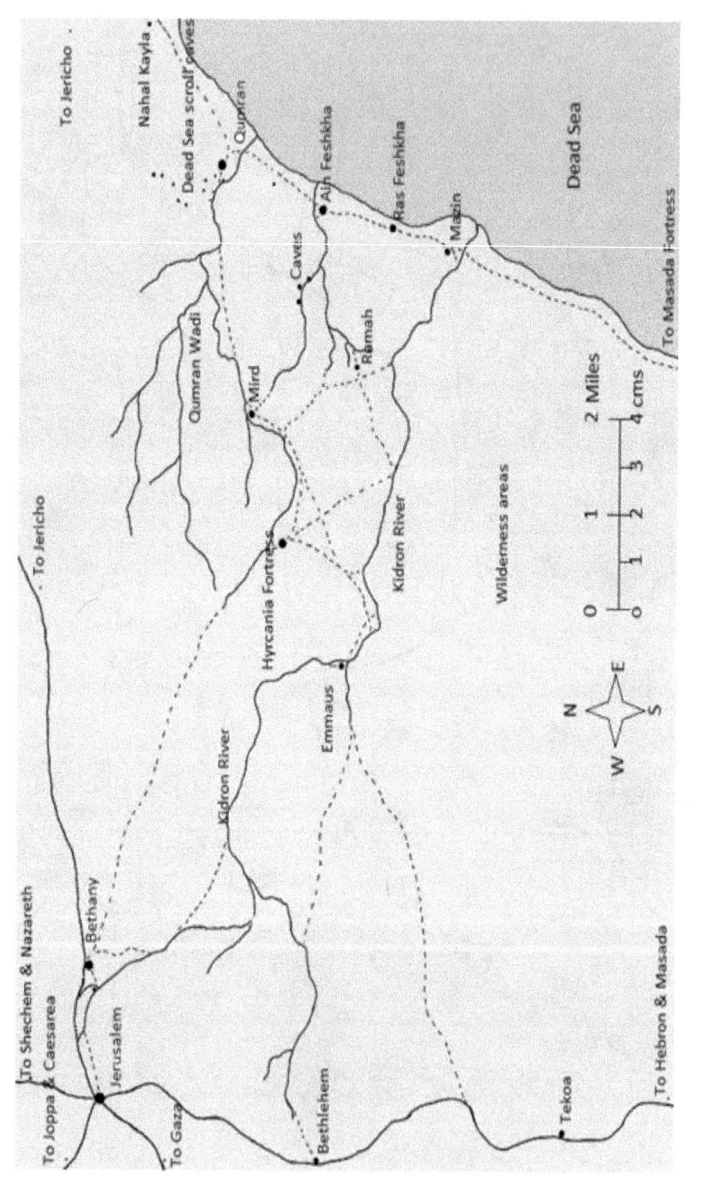

CHAPTER 1: The Holy Spirit

Qumran Monastery
Dead Sea, Palestine
745 years after the foundation of Rome

Dressed in a white robe, the bishop gazed out of the south-facing window of the monastery tower. His name was Joseph Justus, and at the age of thirty-two he was ranked second in command. The clergy addressed him as either The Holy Spirit or simply as Bishop Joseph.

From the second floor of the tower, Joseph could see the holy entourage as it passed by the outer gardens and disappeared into the early morning haze. They were heading towards the oasis town of Ain-Feshkha, a two mile walk along the shoreline between the vast salt lake and the cliffs of the Great Rift Valley. He was aware the flat sandy part of the route could easily be navigated in the moonlight, and knew that once it was daylight, the troupe would be able to turn westwards to embark on the longest, hardest stretch of the journey.

Bishop Joseph turned away from the scene and walked over to his large wooden desk. He reached over and turned up a large oil lamp for more light, then checked the small lamp that marked the hours since sunset. The oil level had dropped ten notches, indicating it was still two hours before sunrise. He slumped in the chair, placed his elbows on the table and rested his forehead in the palms of his hands as he pondered the day's events and prayed for guidance. Hours earlier he had been awakened by Samuel, his night clergyman who informed him about a messenger who had run twenty-four miles through the night with an urgent message for the Chief Priest.

The monastery guard and night deacon had ushered the runner into the refectory and given him some welcome refreshment before learning of the disturbing news the man brought. *Bad news always travelled fast*, Joseph thought as he learned how the Supreme Priest had been ill for several days with a raging fever, and was lapsing in and out of consciousness. Joseph had interviewed the messenger, blessed him for his haste in delivering the message and left him in the care of the night duty deacon.

He asked Samuel to wake Chief Priest Nebedeus to inform him of the distressing news. The Chief Priest was in charge of overseeing the functions of the monastery, and was being summoned for urgent prayers. Should the gravely ill older man's condition deteriorate further, then last rites would have to be administered.

Three hours later, the holy entourage, consisting of thirteen men, equipment, food and water was ready for the journey to Jerusalem. Joseph opened his eyes, blinked and focused on the small lamp. Fifty minutes had elapsed. He must have fallen asleep. It was still an hour before sunrise, but sleep deprivation had already taken its toll. Joseph released his palm from his forehead and reached for the four clay tablets stacked close to the base of the large oil lamp. On each tablet was the name of a priest, one of whom would be promoted to Bishop until the Chief Priest returned. After some deliberation, Joseph chose the eldest priest, a man called Daniel. Well respected among his peers, Daniel was a proven leader and capable of making smart decisions when required. He also shared the same religious belief and guidance for the isolated monastery sect.

Joseph picked up the bronze bell and rang it several times before replacing it next to the time lamp. Moments later, he heard footsteps in the corridor, followed by a knock on the partially opened door. The night clergyman entered, bowed his head and approached the Bishop's desk.

"May I be of assistance, Your Holy Spirit?" Samuel asked.

"Yes," Joseph replied. "I will be retiring to my quarters soon. Please pass this tablet to Priest Daniel. I have selected him to lead the Morning Prayer service on my behalf. Inform him of the night's events and arrange for all four priests to come to my office after they end their overnight fast. I will not require your company any further this morning so finish your duties and have a good sleep. The next few days will be busy for us all. Goodnight Samuel and God bless you."

"Thank you, Bishop Joseph," Samuel said. "Goodnight and God bless you."

Sunrise found thirteen men in sight of the tiny village at the Ain-Feshkha oasis. Twelve neophyte priests dressed in white robes representing the twelve tribes of

Israel escorted the Chief Priest on his urgent trip to Jerusalem. The eight priests carried Nebedeus in a decorated palanquin while four priests followed carrying a litter that held fruit, herbs, water, utensils and other essential items for the journey.

Several children playing near the cliffs saw the men approaching and ran home to tell their parents. The adults promptly notified the village minister who recognised the entourage and rang the synagogue bell to inform the rest of the community.

Citizens gathered near the town square, separating into two groups. Men and boys over twelve years of age lined up on the eastern side while the women and children congregated on the western side. The married Essenes had separated in respect for the strict celibate Essenes from the Qumran Monastery. A tall, well-built man dressed in a pale blue robe of a married minister, approached the incoming party that had stopped thirty yards away. After talking to the leading priests, he turned and led the entourage towards the excited crowd.

The priests followed, entering the white pebbled courtyard. Amid the cheering crowd, they carefully lowered the palanquin and litter onto twelve white stone cubes that had been especially placed by the elders. The Chief Priest rose from the palanquin chair and stepped down, greeted the village leaders and waved to the crowd.

"Welcome Your Holiness," the congregation chanted in unison three times.

On each occasion, they bowed. Much clapping and cheering followed. Nebedeus knew his mission would not allow an extended stay in the settlement, and raised his hands until the village Essenes were silent. Then he lowered his hands and commenced speaking.

"May God bless you all for your warm, gracious welcome, and for offering the fruit and water that is being prepared as I speak. Unfortunately, our time in your company will be short as we have pressing matters to attend to in Jerusalem. I regret to inform you that the Supreme Priest, King Herod, is seriously ill."

The crowd gasped, and then murmured amongst themselves. Nebedeus raised his hands, and everyone fell silent.

"I would like the elders to select three men to accompany our mission to Jerusalem. We will need two messengers and a guide who knows the way through the gorges. One runner will return after seven days to inform you of the King's health. The second man will return after a fortnight. The guide will be required for the return trip and must be prepared to wait for four weeks if necessary. Thank you and God bless you all."

The crowd became restless and began talking fervently amongst themselves.

"Let us gather under the shelter to feast on the fresh fruit and vegetables that your community has so generously harvested," Nebedeus said.

The elders and deacons walked towards the simple thatched roof shelter while the crowd chatted and followed in an orderly manner. The shelter housed three rows of wooden tables with four tables in each row. There were no chairs or benches. People could walk from one table to any other table in their designated row, thus enabling them to choose a greater variety of food dishes. The women, girls, and boys under twelve ate on the western side tables. The men ate on the eastern side tables while the clergy and honoured guests ate in the middle. This practise of eating communal meals, usually the midday meal, brought the community together on a daily basis and allowed dialogue between the laity and clergy.

A spring-fed well, three feet high and thirty feet in circumference, stood close to the shelter. Chrystal clear water bubbled over the lowest section of the wall and into a shallow creek that ran through the village before it meandered through the communal vegetable gardens. Most of the water was used for irrigation, and then became a trickle quickly absorbed into the sandy soil before it ran underground, resurfacing near the edge of the vast salt lake.

The crowd followed the Essene leaders as they walked through the sandy creek bed, allowing the cool water to soothe their tired feet. Shortly afterwards, they washed their hands and faces at the well. Those eating at the western tables washed at the left-side of the well while guests at the centre and eastern tables washed at the right-side of the well.

When everyone had found a place to eat, the village minister raised his hands for silence.

"Let us pray," he said. "Thank you God for providing a plentiful harvest this season, and for protecting our community from evil. Thank you God for safely delivering Chief Priest Nebedeus and his entourage to our village and may we be blessed by their wisdom and company. May God grant our Chief Priest a safe passage to Jerusalem so that he can administer prayers and medicine to the Supreme Priest. If it's your will God, may he recover soon. God bless our meal that we eat in your honour. Amen."

"God is great. Amen," the crowd said in unison.

They started eating, drinking, milling around and talking for the next twenty minutes. The short morning twilight period of summer had now disappeared as the sunlight shone through ashen clouds on the horizon. The village looked particularly inviting on sunny mornings when the limestone cliffs glowed white, and the dark blue lake surface shimmered after every gust of wind.

The entourage was ready to leave. The twelve priests walked over to the empty palanquin and food litter accompanied by the three villagers. Isaac was chosen as the guide, while Amos and Levi would be couriers. The priests stayed in their original groups of four, but would change positions every rest period until they reached Jerusalem. The former leading four priests would now carry the food litter while the litter bearers moved forward to carry the rear handles of the palanquin, and the remaining four priests moved to the front.

The Chief Priest said his final farewell, walked to the palanquin and sat on his chair. Nebedeus then issued instructions to the guide to choose the safest route, preferably one that avoided steep hill climbs or recent rock falls.

"Even if it adds an hour to the journey," he said. "The two couriers will act as lookouts."

Recently there had been reports of skirmishes between bandits and Roman soldiers who escorted the tax money collected from the villages and monasteries. The three men acting as scouts briefly discussed the best course to take, before deciding on the north-western route.

The twelve novice priests grabbed their assigned handles, lifted the palanquin and litter and followed the men in front. The entourage moved in a semicircle around the village square, the Chief Priest acknowledging the crowd with a slow wave.

The entourage commenced their journey to Jerusalem. As they headed towards the cliffs, Nebedeus pulled the cords that dropped the palanquin side nets to enjoy the ride without the hindrance of flying insects. As the entourage continued, the villagers watched the men cross the sand and head towards the *wadi* that led to the wilderness town of Mird.

Once the entourage disappeared out of sight, the Essene community dispersed and went about their daily duties. A group of women returned to the shelter to clean up and gather the uneaten food. Teachers organised the children between the age of four and twelve and led them to the school building for ritual prayers and lessons while men headed for the vineyard and gardens to attend to the crops. Several young children remained near the well, playing in the shallow creek, floating leaves or making sand castles while their mothers kept watch nearby. When the minister, clergymen, and councillors observed everything was running smoothly, they disbanded and headed indoors. The community at Ain-Feshkha resumed its daily routine.

The holy entourage made substantial progress over the first two miles as they trekked along the sandy bed of the Mird *wadi*. They wound their way around the hilly countryside, with the gorge walls becoming progressively higher and steeper having been carved by torrents of water rushing through during heavy rainstorms over thousands of years. For the safe passage of travellers, roughly cut steps led to natural ledges or caves that provided some protection above flood levels. As soon as travellers heard the sound of rushing water, they would have to run hard and fast to locate the nearest steps before climbing fifteen to twenty feet high to be safe from the oncoming turbulent head wave. As the cortege made its way further into the canyon, the priests were undoubtedly praying more fervently than usual for a safe journey.

Apart from natural disasters, the greatest threat came from the marauding bandits that lived in the mountains. Heavily armed with swords and daggers, these men were ruthless thieves, torturers and rapists who indiscriminately murdered men, women and children and left no witnesses. Rumours portrayed them as gladiators and slaves from foreign countries, or deserters from the occupying Roman forces in Judea. They were called Iscariots, silent assassins who frequently left their victims naked and mutilated.

The entourage rounded a long bend in the gorge where the *wadi* widened. For the first time in two hours since they entered the gorge, sunlight shone upon the cavalcade. Here the *wadi* separated into two gorges. The one on the right had a sandy bed while the left branch was narrower and had a rocky bottom that was around five feet higher. After wet weather, it would become a babbling brook with a small waterfall cascading into a shallow pond.

The Chief Priest asked the bearers to lower the palanquin and litter onto the sand.

"We will rest here for twenty minutes," Nebedeus said. "Prepare the fruit and drink while I talk to our guide and couriers."

Nebedeus spoke with the three men, enquiring if both *wadi* gorges went to Mird. With the extreme temperatures they were experiencing, he wanted to know which would be the most shaded path. After some discussion, the men agreed the sandy gorge on the right would be better, cautioning that it would prolong the journey by another mile. They were almost halfway between Ain-Feshkha and Mird, and had three more hours of comfortable, but mostly uphill walking.

The sixteen men gathered around the fruit bowls and water jugs. Malachi, one of the novice priests said grace.

"God, please join us in celebrating our meal that we eat in your honour. Amen."

The men commenced eating, drinking, chattering and laughing. Even Nebedeus dispensed with the usual formalities, and enjoyed sitting on the cool sand. It was something he couldn't do as Chief Priest at the monastery or anywhere in public.

***

Qumran Monastery
Shortly after sunrise prayers

Back at the monastery, four priests, led by Daniel, climbed the two flights of stairs on their way to the scheduled meeting with Bishop Joseph. Daniel, the eldest priest, had performed the main sermon on behalf of Joseph as instructed. Prayer services were conducted hourly at the monastery. The sunrise, noon, and sunset ceremonies included meals, and were the prayer services a bishop conducted while the priests gave hourly sermons between those hours, and the neophyte or novice priests gave services hourly during the night. It was a sin to start any sermon late or early as it was one of the priests' duties to announce the hours of the day.

The office door was open, and Bishop Joseph summoned the priests to enter, directing them to sit on the four chairs, previously arranged by Samuel for the meeting.

"Good morning, Your Holy Spirit," the senior priests said as they sat with their hands clasped together.

"Good morning brothers," Joseph replied. "I believe you are aware of the circumstances for this meeting, so I will get straight to the heart of the matter. Nebedeus will be staying in Jerusalem until further notice and I will be officially acting as Chief Priest after my anointing ceremony tomorrow. Soon afterwards, I will anoint one of you to act in my position as Bishop, the rank of Holy Spirit. Normally we would also promote a neophyte priest as a senior priest, however, twelve of them have been chosen to accompany Nebedeus. That leaves us understaffed at the novice level, and one less at your senior priest level until the holy entourage return."

"How long will the Chief Priest be absent?" Daniel asked.

"That depends entirely on the King's health and is in the lap of the Gods."

Joseph opened the cupboard door and produced a tray containing a long white feather pen, a pot of ink, a small amphora shaped vase and four small parchment pieces. He slid the tray towards the priests, asking each of them to take a piece of parchment and write the initial of the priest they wished to act as Bishop.

"I want you to place your own initial if you yourself would like to perform the duties of Bishop," Joseph said. "If you do not wish to act in the position yourself, select one of your peers or draw a cross. Are there any questions before you cast your votes?"

"Yes," Caleb said grinning. "What if we all write down our own initial? Will we all be anointed bishops?"

"I want you all to have the chance to select the best person among you to act as Bishop," he said smiling. "However, should the vote be one each or two priests with two votes each, I will cast the deciding vote. The anointing ceremonies have been arranged for tomorrow afternoon in the enclosed courtyard that separates the male and female sectors, the one with the small waist deep ceremonial bath. Ilana, the Chief Priestess, will be organising the whole event, using the women's access. The nuns will supply five white robes for us, the scented oil, towels and two ceremonial headdress mitres. Please vote now and then return to your rostered duties. God bless you all."

The priests stood up one at a time, bowed, approached the Bishop's desk and picked up the pen. They wrote on their piece of parchment and placed their vote in the vessel. As the priests stepped back, they bowed again.

"God bless you Holy Spirit," they uttered.

The priests returned to their quarters. All of them wondered who would be elected Bishop.

Joseph reached for the handles on the vase. He tipped it upside down so that the four votes fell onto the desk. The first vote was a T, for Timothy, the second, D for Daniel, the third vote, M for Micah. *Don't tell me this last one is C for Caleb*, thought Joseph as he hesitated for a moment before flipping the last piece of parchment over. Caleb was the youngest and most recently promoted priest. D for Daniel, the Priests had chosen wisely.

Joseph penned some notes for the upcoming ceremony and his Chief Priest speech. He laboured over the speech for a while and then retired to his quarters for a much needed sleep.

***

Wadi Mird

When he had satisfied his thirst and hunger, Nebedeus stood up and dusted himself off.

"Let us proceed on our journey so that we reach the Mird Abbey before the noon prayers and for the midday meal," he said.

As they prepared to leave, the twelve priests rotated their carrying positions, keeping in their corresponding groups of four, as they did on every break. Nebedeus climbed into the palanquin while the three scouts commenced walking. The party was on the move again, feeling refreshed and relaxed.

In the first hour, they made good progress, though Amos cautioned the lead priests to expect more bends and steeper climbs over the next mile. Isaac was walking one hundred yards in front of the main group. Suddenly, he turned and raised his hand, motioning to the others to stop before jogging back to Nebedeus.

"Sir, I can smell smoke, someone is cooking. I know there are caves and tunnels up ahead with steps leading to the plateau. It's a popular place for the herdsmen to gather when they graze their goat herds, but not at this time of the year, especially near the end of the dry season."

Nebedeus sensed concern in the scout's voice.

"Yes, I agree," he said softly, "it's more likely to be pilgrims and their families at this time of the year. We will remain here while you confirm who is ahead. Take one of the couriers with you."

"Sir," replied the scout, "I would rather proceed alone. Both couriers are inexperienced, and I need to proceed quietly."

Nebedeus thought for a moment.

"Take a courier, but tell him to obey your instructions at all times. When you get close to the caves, tell him to stay out of sight until you give the all clear. Once you are satisfied the route is safe, he can return with the message for us to continue our journey."

Realising he had over-reacted Isaac chose Amos and informed him of Nebedeus' instructions. The two men set off to explore the source of the smoke that was wafting towards them. As soon as they heard voices, they stopped. Isaac instructed his companion to remain behind a natural crevice in the *wadi* wall while he crouched down and quietly moved forward.

The smoke thickened. The smell of cooked meat filled the air as Isaac made his way until he was close enough to see the camp through the smoke haze. He observed at least twenty men sitting around the fire while more were in the nearby caves. He saw a metal rotisserie with an animal carcass being slowly turned by a stout, heavily bearded man. It smelt like pig, but the body was the wrong shape. It was certainly not a goat—maybe a calf with the front legs cut off.

The smoke cleared. For the first time, Isaac could see the whole camp clearly. He focused on the revolving carcass then gasped in horror. His hand flew to his mouth. The roasted animal was human. Decapitated, the body had an iron spit running through its length, the victims' legs tied together and the feet still attached.

Two more naked bodies lay nearby, one beheaded. Isaac saw a man pull a woman's body onto a rock, and sever the neck with a sword. The head was picked up by the long black hair and thrown onto the hot coals. The fire crackled fiercely as the hair burnt from the scalp, and Isaac watched as a dark plume of smoke rose in the air, as though her soul was escaping from the heat.

Isaac managed to hold back the urge to scream. He swallowed the vomit in his mouth to maintain absolute silence and scrambled back toward Amos waiting in the crevice, hoping he would remain hidden. He knew the men were the feared band of escaped gladiators. Wanted dead or alive by the Roman authorities, they all had rewards on their heads.

Isaac crawled another fifty yards before coming to an abrupt halt. A boulder had fallen within a foot of his head. Instinctively he looked up the canyon walls and swore. Several men were staring at him. They had been waiting in ambush.

More rocks fell. One hit Isaac on the shoulder. He lurched to the side in excruciating pain then leant against the cliff wall and managed to deflect the next two rocks by holding his arms above his head. He made a dash for safety, zigzagging down the gorge. The rocks rained down around him until one hit his head and knocked him unconscious. Isaac experienced a bright flash in his mind and collapsed onto the ground, a mere six yards further on. The bandits dropped a rope, and two of them scaled down the sixty foot cliff face and landed near Isaac's prostrate body. One man checked him for weapons, money and valuables. Finding nothing, he dragged his unconscious body to their camp while another bandit walked down the ravine until he reached a bend. He could see the *wadi* was clear for some distance. Satisfied the stranger was alone, he signalled to the men on the plateau above and caught up with his companion.

Hiding only a few yards away from the approaching bandit, Amos had heard his friend yell out in panic. He peered out from the crevice. He had witnessed everything that happened in what seemed like a blink of an eye. Petrified by fear, he withdrew into the crevice, unable to comprehend what had happened or what to do next. He heard Isaac scream in agony and knew he was being tortured. The poor bastard would be begging to be killed, but that would not come until he had divulged the existence of the Holy entourage. Amos knew the bandits would capture, and eventually cannibalize everyone, except for the Chief Priest, whom they would ransom. Nebedeus would be fed on the human flesh of his fellow priests until the ransom was paid.

Amos heard another scream. Unable to control his anxiety any longer he ran, occasionally looking behind. He did not stop until he fell at the feet of Nebedeus.

"We heard screaming. What happened? Where is Isaac?"

"Bandits have captured Isaac," Amos said breathlessly. "They are torturing him."

"We have to withdraw immediately," Nebedeus yelled. "Run back to the fork in the *wadi*. We'll regroup there."

For the first time on the journey, Nebedeus was on foot. Like everyone else, he was running for his life. The priests carried the empty palanquin and fruit fell off the litter as they ran. Eventually, they reached the fork in the *wadi* and dropped to the ground, gulping air into their aching lungs. Nebedeus ran with a limp and was the last to arrive. When he caught his breath, he told everyone to listen carefully.

"We must act quickly," he said. "Isaac is a good man. He will hold out as long as he can. I must complete my task peace in Judea depends on it. I will go to Mird following the other *wadi* with Levi and four volunteer priests."

"How long have we got?" Amos asked.

It was the question on everyone's mind.

"Only a few minutes," Nebedeus replied. "When we climb up onto the higher *wadi* the remaining group must sweep aside any trace of our steps. Make the remaining tracks look like we all went back to Ain-Feshkha. Report what happened to the authorities as soon as you reach the village. Tell them to contact the soldiers stationed at the Mazin compound. They can engage the bandits from the east. I will report to the commander at Hyrcania. His soldiers will ambush the bandits from the west. I want Amos and the eight priests to remain in Ain-Feshkha overnight, and then return to Qumran after the midday meal tomorrow. Now make haste and God Bless you all."

Nebedeus and his group climbed up onto the higher rocky *wadi* with the litter. They watched the remaining group clear their tracks. Satisfied with their efforts, they gave a parting wave and trekked along the steeper route to the top of the plateau. Though they saw the smoke rising from the camp fire, they managed to stay out of sight of the bandits.

They heard two more blood curdling screams from the tortured scout, followed by a deadly silence. Before them lay the desolate and arid plain that stretched to the township of Mird. It was hot and dusty, but not one of the men complained. They knew Isaac had given them the time they needed to escape.

Amos led the remaining eight priests carrying the empty palanquin back to Ain-Feshkha. The stunned villagers welcomed the exhausted men and gave them refreshments. After listening to their horrific story, they dispatched messages to the Roman soldiers, informing them the bandits were camping in the caves of the Mird *wadi*.

Feeling tired, dusty and despondent, Nebedeus, Levi and the four priests walked into Mird. Most people were already inside their houses sheltering from the heat of the day. The townsfolk in the main street didn't recognise the Chief Priest among the travellers in his soiled robe. The priests were glad to reach the quiet sanctuary of the local monastery without the normal fanfare.

Nebedeus rapped on the massive wooden door with the bronze knocker and waited for a response. A bald monk wearing a black habit opened the door. He knelt and kissed Nebedeus on his feet.

"Your Holiness, welcome, and God Bless you. We were not expecting your visit, please come in and refresh yourself. I will notify Abbot Esau of your presence."

The monk led Nebedeus into a side room where he could bathe and change into fresh robes that were stored in the cupboards. Then the monk returned and introduced himself to the others.

"Good morning," he said. "My name is Yanis. I see you have had a long hard journey. You need to rest, wash and eat. Please follow me."

The monk led the tired men out of the abbey and into an enclosed yard where vegetable gardens lined both sides of the pathway. Several monks were gardening in the shaded areas of the compound. A couple of monks looked up and waved, but no one talked.

As the novice priests passed the monks who were busy harvesting, weeding or watering, Eron introduced himself, Levi the courier and the other three priests to Yanis. He mentioned they had travelled from Qumran and were heading for Jerusalem.

"It's always a dusty trip through the Mird *wadi* in the summer months," the monk said.

He guided the men to the stone buildings that abutted the end wall of the enclosure. Yanis ushered Levi into one of the smaller buildings. He handed him clean clothing, a face cloth and a towel from the cupboard before filling the pitcher with water and placing it beside the washbasin.

"Freshen up and rest for an hour," Yanis said. "There is a bunk in the other room if you need to lie down. Meet us in the refectory building for the midday meal."

"Thank you for your kind hospitality Yanis," Levi said.

The monk shut the door on the way out and met the priests waiting outside.

"This way Brothers, your quarters are waiting for your weary bodies."

He directed the travellers to a large building at the end of the row. The monk opened the door and showed them the three large bedrooms, the kitchen and dining room.

"You have very spacious quarters," Eron said.

Yanis opened the side door. The monk had saved the best for last. The courtyard was completely private with a communal bath that was built around a small thermal pool. The whole area was paved in slate with wooden benches on three sides enabling a person to sit in the shade or the sunlight, depending on the heat of the day. The fourth priest stood in the doorway, amazed at the luxurious setting. The monk placed his hands on the young man and moved him to one side as he squeezed through the doorway.

"May I suggest you pass me your soiled robes and submit your aching bodies to the warm water? The spring reputably has healing properties," Yanis said.

Yanis still had one hand on the young priest's buttock, and helped him take off his robe before approaching the other priests and collecting their robes.

"I will wash these for you and bring them back within the hour. The robes should be dry enough to wear by then. I will also bring back towels. Now go ahead and immerse yourself. You have the best part of an hour before noon prayers begin."

The priests entered the warm thermal water of the communal bath and stayed submerged up to their necks for the whole time Yanis was absent. They thoroughly enjoyed the warmth on their aching limbs and tried to forget the horrific events that occurred earlier in the *wadi*. No words were spoken about the scout, the bandits or the mission, though all the priests silently prayed for

Isaac. Without his heroic sacrifice under torture, they would not have eluded capture.

Yanis handed the robes to a junior monk who was working near the path, and directed him to wash the garments immediately and hang them in the sun to dry. Then he went to the Abbot's office and informed Abbot Esau that Nebedeus, four Essene priests and a guide from Ain-Feshkha had arrived unexpectedly. Yanis mentioned where he housed everyone and that the Chief Priest should be dressed in clean ceremonial robes by now, having been attended to first.

"Please ask His Holiness to visit me before noon prayers," Esau said pleased with the diligence of his head monk. "Escort Nebedeus here, and when he sits, excuse yourself, close the door and leave us to talk in private."

"Yes, Abbot Esau," Yanis replied. "I will follow your instructions to the letter. I will seek the Chief Priest immediately."

Yanis left the Abbot's office with only one thing on his mind. What was that young blonde haired Essene priest's name? Yanis knocked on the door.

"Is that you Yanis?" Nebedeus asked.

"Yes sir. May I enter?"

Nebedeus opened the door. He looked refreshed and very regal in his ceremonial robe and headdress mitre.

"Your Holiness, Abbot Esau would dearly like to see you before noon prayers if you are feeling refreshed. I would be most happy to escort you to his office if you so desire."

"Yes, I need to speak with Abbot Esau about the trip to Jerusalem. Are the priests and the man acting as our guide recovering from our exhausting trip?"

"Yes, Your Holiness, although the young blonde hair priest, I can't recall his name, seemed overcome with heatstroke."

"His name is Eron," Nebedeus said. "It is his first trip away from the monastery since he enrolled three years ago."

Esau heard the men approaching and met them at his office door.

"Welcome, Your Holiness," Esau said as he kissed Nebedeus on his ring hand. "Thank you, Yanis. Please see to the other guests."

The monk bowed and shut the door as he left Esau and Nebedeus to talk in private. He collected the priest's robes and four towels from the main bedroom cupboard. In the courtyard, he talked to the priests.

"The robes are clean but still slightly damp," he said. "Hopefully they will dry from your body heat before mealtime."

The priests were still enjoying the warm water, and reluctantly stepped out of the bath and walked to Yanis for a towel. The priests wiped themselves and rifled through the robes until Yanis held one more robe, the smallest robe.

"This must be yours, Eron," he said.

"Yes it is Yanis. You remembered my name. Most people seem to forget it for some reason."

"I like your name. It is unusual, and it suits your cheerful disposition."

"Would you mind holding the robe a little longer while I dry my hair?" Eron said.

"Not at all, there's no rush."

Yanis observed the young priest appeared to be growing fond of him. The feeling was mutual. The three older priests had already walked out of the building and along the path towards the refectory where they met and talked with the monks who had finished working in the gardens.

Yanis helped Eron with the robe, which was made from one piece of cloth with a hole for the head, and two slits for the arms. The monk slowly let the robe slide down until the hem was at waist level.

"If you hold your robe, I will tie your lap-sash around your waist."

Yanis briefly touched Oren, with only the thin white cloth separating the two celibate men. Eron smiled and nervously combed his damp hair with his fingers.

"We have to go now," Yanis whispered. "But would you like to meet me back here in one hour?"

Eron stopped combing his hair.

"Yes, I want to see you again."

Yanis and Eron held hands until they reached the front door before swiftly walking towards the refectory to join the other monks and priests.

In the Abbot's office, Nebedeus talked to Esau about the day's events. Couriers would have to be dispatched to the nearby fortress of Hyrcania and Ramah homestead. As they conversed, the bells started tolling in the refectory, the final call before noon prayers which the Abbot normally conducted. The two men walked to the hall, agreeing to discuss the matters further during the midday meal. They entered the refectory archway together; the large double doors had been wedged back against the wall for maximum air flow.

The monks had moved four wooden tables together making one large table with room for the Abbot and Chief Priest to sit together at the head of the table. The four guest priests and twelve monks sat on the right side of Nebedeus, sixteen monks on the left of Esau, with the messenger and Esau's page boy at the foot of the table. There were thirty-six place settings, thirty-six chairs and thirty-six diners. The Abbot always expected the seating and table arrangements to match precisely.

When Esau was elected Abbot by his peers several years earlier, one of the first chores allocated to the carpenters was to shorten a table that could be added to the end of two abutted tables. The smaller table was used whenever the number of diners was uneven, and the Abbot's favourite table when dining at the head, with an honoured guest sitting next to him. Esau looked around the room, mentally noting that the spare tables and chairs were neatly positioned against the side walls while the monks and guests stood behind their chairs, waiting for Nebedeus and himself to arrive.

Esau and Nebedeus walked across the slate floor and stood behind their chairs. Esau waited for complete silence before speaking.

"Today's prayer is from the Hebrew book of Deuteronomy. It was written one thousand, five hundred years ago by Moses, on the plains of Moab," Esau said commencing the noon prayers. "The Lord is our God, the Lord is one. Love the Lord with all your heart and with all your strength. Amen."

"Praise the Lord our God, Amen," the gathering repeated.

"Today we are honoured to have the Chief Priest Nebedeus and four Essene priests visit us," Esau said. "I have invited our guests to stay in our company overnight before they continue onto Jerusalem tomorrow."

Everyone applauded especially Yanis and Eron, who also gently nudged each other. They had managed to be seated next to one another in the only priest-monk order of seating.

"Thank you for your kind offer, Esau, which I shall accept as we have much to discuss," Nebedeus replied. "I am sure the young priests would appreciate your hospitality and later visit your famous winery and vineyard. However, I believe there is something more important right now. Esau, please proceed with the midday meal ceremony."

Again there was generous applause before Esau raised his hands for silence.

"Let's be seated and toast the Lord our God and our honoured guests," he said.

He reached over to the small bronze bell and rang it to advise the kitchen staff to proceed with the three course meal. The first course was chicken broth or tomato soup, with bread rolls. The main course was lamb, goat or chicken with potatoes, carrots, peas and gravy. Everything had been produced on the monastery farm, including the red wine that was served with the midday and evening meals. The third course was a variety of fruit and sweet-bread rolls.

The midday meal was traditionally eaten over an hour. Today the refectory hall was abuzz with conversations, the journey through the Mird *wadi* being the most popular topic, followed by the food and wine, and life at the two monasteries. Nebedeus and Esau announced to their immediate staff that they could extend their meal break by having an extra hour before resuming normal duties.

Nebedeus and Esau were the first to leave. They strolled back to the Abbot's office to further their discussions while the courier retired to his room for a much needed sleep. The page boy went outside and played with Abby the dog. Most of the priests and monks had one more round of wine tasting before excusing themselves. Five monks and a priest took leave, among them Yanis and Eron. Yanis and Eron met in the enclosed courtyard, laid their habit and robe on the bench and leapt into the thermal bath.

"Why did you become a priest, Eron?" Yanis asked after they had frolicked in the water for half an hour.

"My father died when I was three years old, and my mother worked hard to raise me by herself. When I was thirteen, my mother knew I had different interests than other boys at the village. I liked learning and religion, and wasn't interested in girls at all, so my mother enrolled me in a class to learn to write and study priesthood. I was quite naive then. I thought celibate meant abstinence, but the older boys explained that it meant not believing in marriage rather than abstaining from sex as I once thought."

Yanis laughed.

"So you thought you joined the priesthood for a life of misery. What a brave lad."

"Well Yanis, why did you join the Abbey as a monk?"

"Not quite for your saintly reasons," Yanis answered. "I wanted security, protection, celibacy and privacy. I like communal farming and discussions with men on a higher level. I also enjoy our meals and red wine. Today, I am enjoying your company."

In the Abbott's office, Nebedeus and Esau stood by the window and continued with their conversation. They could see a red dust storm approaching from the west. It would probably reach the monastery within four or five hours.

"Esau, I need to send two messages out before the storm hits. Would you be able to provide two men that are strong runners?"

"Yes, Your Holiness," Esau replied as he reached for the bell to ring for assistance. "The monk on duty will select the men you need."

A monk appeared at the doorway.

"May I be of service, Your Holiness?"

"Yes, Ben. Please select two reliable men from the community who are strong runners and bring them back here as soon as possible. Take four loaves of bread from the kitchen and give them to the men's families with my blessing."

"Yes, Abbot Esau," Ben replied before bowing and leaving.

"Thank you, Esau," Nebedeus said. "Your help and hospitality have been most noteworthy."

Nebedeus quickly explained why he needed the couriers. Both men would travel together for one hour. One courier would go to the nearby homestead at Ramah and deliver a message to Bishop Joseph's parents informing them that Nebedeus was staying overnight at the Mird Monastery and required their presence for a period of three days. The other messenger would run another hour until he reached the fortress at Hyrcania to inform the Roman commander that the wanted bandits were camped at the Mird caves. Esau listened intently as Nebedeus talked about the ill-health of King Herod, the trek through the *wadi*, the Iscariot bandits and the torture of Isaac. Talking about the trip took its toll on Nebedeus, and he stopped from time to time to gather his thoughts. He was obviously deeply troubled.

"Esau, I need to rest before Jacob arrives. Would you accompany me to my room?"

"Yes, Your Holiness," Esau replied. "If your guests arrive while you are sleeping, shall I wake you immediately?"

"Please wake me after four hours sleep so that I can freshen up before their arrival."

"When I send the messenger to Ramah, whose surname shall I give to him?" Esau asked.

"Oh, I apologise. Didn't I mention I left Bishop Joseph in charge of the monastery in my absence," Nebedeus said.

Esau realised he should have known Joseph's parents especially as Nebedeus had referred to him earlier, and ruefully slapped himself on the leg as they walked along the hallway.

The Justus family mansion at Ramah was built on a hill overlooking a fertile valley with two natural springs forming a creek that meandered through the valley. It was one of several places for married Essenes living outside of Jerusalem. Joseph's parents, Jacob and Miriam, were descendants' of David Justus. King David appointed his son Solomon as the Pharisee sect Chief Priest, beginning the King David heir line of Jewish priests. The Essene sect was a breakaway group that ate mainly vegetarian meals though it included fish, poultry and eggs.

The men reached the room prepared earlier for His Holiness, the monks having anticipated an overnight stay. The Abbot opened the door for Nebedeus and waited in the hallway while he looked around. The room was enormous, elegantly decorated in shades of red with a massive double bed, walk-in-robe and separate bathroom. Not quite to the quality of his room on the third floor at the Qumran Monastery but certainly comfortable enough for his needs tonight.

"Is everything satisfactory, Your Holiness?" Esau asked.

"Yes Esau, the room is acceptable. I should be able to sleep comfortably, thank you."

"God bless you, Your Holiness," the Abbot said, bowing and closing the door.

Nebedeus removed his mitre and robe, placed them on the bed where he slept solidly for four hours.

Abbot Esau saw a palanquin approaching town. The courier was leading eight men carrying two people. He rang the bell and Ben appeared.

"Where is Yanis? Nevermind, tell the kitchen staff there will be an extra ten places for the evening meal. Find Yanis and tell him I want five tables placed in the U-shape formation. Set eighteen places inside and twenty-four places on the outside. Position my table one table length clear with a setting for four. Ask the four priests to help with the chairs, they will be happy to assist. Finally, tell Yanis to receive Mr and Mrs Justus and their companions, and arrange cover for their palanquin."

"Will that be all, Abbot Esau?" Ben asked with a touch of sarcasm.

"Please remind the monks and priests that the eight Essene men are married, but that doesn't mean you can't—" Esau coughed twice and cleared his throat. "—can't talk to them."

Ben clasped his hands and bowed. As he walked away, he muttered to himself about married men being allowed in the monastery.

Yanis answered the loud knock at the Abbey door and greeted the entourage as instructed. Mr and Mrs Justus were ushered into the same room Nebedeus had used when he first arrived. They were given towels and warm water to freshen up while the eight married Essene men were shown to their quarters by the page boy.

Nebedeus was advised that his guests had arrived, and he met them in private without wearing his mitre. There was no need for protocol. They had known each other for years. Jacob and Miriam knew his parents well and often visited them when they came to Jerusalem. As a young boy, he and Joseph played together.

"We came as soon as we could," Jacob said. "What is the occasion, and why the three days, are you getting married?"

"It's nothing like that. I will explain a little now, and the rest over dinner. I have left Joseph in charge of the monastery while I visit King Herod who is gravely ill. He fell ill while touring Jerusalem, and has been lapsing in and out of a coma for the past week."

Jacob and Miriam gasped at the news, acutely aware of the potential consequences should the King die. Emperor Augustus had ordered an increase in taxes, and the Jewish citizens were protesting in the streets. If the monarchy was replaced by a Roman governor, or prefect, the Jews would lose all sense of national autonomy and tradition.

"That could lead to anarchy and conflict," Jacob said.

"That is only part of it," Nebedeus continued. "Herod is being cared for in the Essene Monastery in Jerusalem, not in the ruling High Priest's care."

"Why?" Jacob asked.

"That I don't know yet. I have kept that information to myself. No one is aware of my actual destination."

"How long will you be in Jerusalem?" Miriam asked.

"That depends on God's will," Nebedeus replied. "We must speak carefully while sharing the table with Esau. The success of my mission depends on it."

"Where is your mitre?" Miriam asked.

"My ceremonial mitre is in my room, but there will be a Bishop's mitre in the cupboard I can wear to dinner."

Abbot Esau met Nebedeus and Mr and Mrs Justus in the hallway and escorted them to their table. The monks, priests and family men stood by their chairs as they waited for the honoured guests to arrive and for the Abbot to perform the prayer service.

"We are honoured to have Mr and Mrs Justus visit our humble monastery. They are from the King David lineage and are accompanied by their married male workers. After dinner, show the men around the monastery and show them our best hospitality. Now please bow your heads while I pray. Dear Lord, our one true God, thank you for the safe passage of our guests. We praise you Lord for your guidance, and we pray the dust storm will seed the clouds and bring rain for our crops. Love the Lord with all your heart and all your strength. Amen."

"Praise the Lord our God. Amen," everyone mumbled.

Esau rang the bronze bell to inform the kitchen staff to deliver the first of the three courses. The first course was one of Esau's favourite, sweetcorn soup with bread rolls which was followed by roast beef, or chicken, and vegetables. The last course was fruit salad with fresh thick cream. There were two varieties of red wine, and a white wine was served with the chicken meals. The table candles were lit, and the conversations continued long into the night.

The sand storm arrived an hour after sunset. Fortunately, the winds were lighter than expected and storm clouds developed overhead, releasing the first steady rainfall in four months.

"Our prayers have been answered," Esau declared.

"Praise the Lord," Nebedeus said. "We certainly need the rain to refill our cisterns at Qumran, and it will help settle the dust. It will also make your trip to Ain-Feshkha more comfortable Miriam."

"Pardon?" Miriam asked. "What did you say?"

"I thought you could do me a favour and pick up my palanquin in Ain-Feshkha," Nebedeus said. "I left it in the care of eight priests. You can head to Qumran and witness a good friend of mine being anointed as the Chief Priest. His name is Joseph."

"Is Joseph expecting us to be present at the ceremony?" Miriam asked.

"No," Nebedeus replied.

"Has Joseph performed any of the Chief Priest duties yet?" Jacob asked.

"Joseph follows rules and protocol to the letter. I know for a fact he wouldn't enter the third floor of the monastery before taking the oath of office. In fact, unless you pass Joseph this key he will not be able to enter into heaven at all."

"Thank you, Nebedeus. You are always like the second son with whom we were never blessed," Jacob said, "not taking anything away from our four daughters and our son-in-laws of course."

"We all have a big day ahead of us, and I strongly urge you to have a good night's sleep," Nebedeus replied. "However, there are two more salient topics we need to consider. You must take the longer southern route through Mazin to avoid the marauding bandits. Their camp is in the Mird *wadi*, and they may be occupying adjacent *wadis* to the north as well."

"We will certainly heed your advice, Nebedeus. What is the other one?" Jacob asked.

"Well, it is more a favour really. I was wondering if I could borrow your palanquin and eight bearers for the trip to Jerusalem."

"Of course," Jacob said.

"I will arrange with Esau for six monks to accompany you to Mazin and they can return the next day. My palanquin and eight priests will be available to take you to Qumran if you reach Ain-Feshkha by midday," Nebedeus said.

"Nebedeus, we will have to leave at midnight to reach Ain-Feshkha by midday," Jacob replied. "If you can arrange everything by then it is a deal. Anyway, it is mostly downhill to Mazin from here, and Miriam and I are accustomed to walking long distances."

Jacob and Miriam said goodnight to Nebedeus and Esau, and Ben escorted them to their room. Esau had been sitting at the table, motionless for some time now with both hands clasped around his empty mug of wine.

"Why don't you walk?" he said speaking in a slurred voice, knowing Nebedeus required the Abbot's six monks for two days.

"I broke my left leg when I was nine," he said. "It healed over time, but now my right leg is one inch longer. When I run or walk long distances, the pain becomes unbearable.

Nebedeus looked at Esau and thought, *this man will most likely still be asleep when the entourage leaves in the morning.* He left the Abbot in the care of two monks and asked Esau's page boy to accompany him to his room. The night was still young, and he liked the lad.

The pageboy stirred. He turned his head and looked at the dimly glowing time lamp. The oil had dropped almost five notches, indicating it was now an hour before midnight. He listened and waited for the monks on night duty to orate the hourly prayers before lighting the bedside lamps and pouring a full tumbler of lemon juice for Nebedeus. He drank some of it and spat in the remainder, stirring in his saliva with his finger as the ritual prayers echoed down the hallway. *Time to wake the R-soul* he thought.

The pageboy woke the righteous soul, and then walked down the hallway and knocked on the heavy wooden doors. After waking Mr and Mrs Justus, he went outside to the guest quarters and woke the courier. Levi woke the priests and their monk companions to help prepare breakfast. The pageboy found Yanis and Eron and woke the monks who had volunteered to accompany the aged couple to Mazin.

The twenty-two travellers ate breakfast while the monks prepared the palanquin and litter for the journey. Several monks, including Yanis, waved as the entourage left the monastery grounds. The road to Hyrcania had been reconstructed by the Roman engineers and was flat and wide, perfect for walking in the moonlight. The monks traipsed back indoors, making their way to the refectory where they cleaned the room, and readjusted the table and chairs to cater for the number of people expected for breakfast. Esau would not sound the service bell at meal times until the seating was perfect, and everyone was standing behind their chairs.

Nebedeus had insisted that Miriam and Jacob rode in the palanquin until they parted company at the fork leading to Ramah or Emmaus. To save time, one of the Essene men ran ahead to inform the household wives about the unexpected trip to Jerusalem with Nebedeus and four priests.

An hour later, the troupe arrived at the junction that lead to Emmaus, Ramah and back to Mird. The Essene messenger and the eight Essene wives were waiting on the corner with bowls of fruit and containers of drinking water. The wives sought out their respective husbands, hugging and kissing them before thrusting oranges into their hands to eat on the trip to Jerusalem. Two clay vessels were placed on the palanquin floor, containing water for the trip. Nebedeus advised Jacob and Miriam to begin their journey east to Mazin without further delay to ensure they met with the eight priests staying overnight in Ain-Feshkha. Nebedeus approached the six monks and warned them to defend Miriam and Jacob with their lives, and that they should set off immediately.

Nebedeus climbed onto the palanquin, placing his legs each side of the water vessels while Levi acting as the guide, headed south-west for Jerusalem. The eight Essene men carried Nebedeus on the palanquin, and the four priests carried the litter borrowed from the Abbey.

The eight wives headed south to the Justus family mansion in Ramah, waving a final goodbye to their husbands. When they arrived at the two storey residence, the building seemed eerily quiet without the men and owners. The women paired off and went upstairs to bed, enjoying a rare sleep in.

The track to Mazin was mostly downhill, but two miles after leaving Nebedeus at the crossroads, Jacob needed a break. He sat on a rock and talked to Miriam and the Monks.

"I may have bitten off more than I can chew," he said. "I momentarily forgot I will be turning fifty-eight this year. At the rate I'm walking, we may miss meeting up with the priests in Ain-Feshkha. Nebedeus instructed them to leave after the midday meal, and unfortunately they are not expecting us."

"Sir, I can run ahead and ask the priests to wait for your arrival," a junior monk said.

"That would help. However, I also think the sandy path between Mazin and Ain-Feshkha will slow me down, and I fear we will miss my son's anointing ceremony. I would like you and another monk to run ahead and ask the eight priests to head for Mazin with the palanquin. Tell them time is of the essence."

The two monks quickly distanced themselves from the walking party. When they reached Mazin, they rested at the synagogue for a few minutes while the elders gave the messengers watermelon to quench their thirst. Soon the monks were running on the damp sand along the shoreline of the Dead Sea. Near the Ras Feshkha oasis the monks stopped and faced towards the east where they knelt and prayed, honouring God for the gift of light.

Two hours after sunrise, they reached Ain-Feshkha feeling exhausted. The monks found the priests talking to the village minister and explained the situation. The monks stayed in the village to rest and talk to Amos and the Minister. The eight Priests jogged along the foreshore with the empty palanquin until they met the oncoming party near Mazin. Miriam and Jacob gratefully climbed aboard, and Jacob instructed the priests to head for Qumran, and to change bearers every half an hour.

Jacob and Miriam talked together until the first change when the four monks took over the four rear positions. Miriam rested her head on Jacob's shoulder, and Jacob rested his head on Miriam, the euphoria of their son being anointed the Holy Spirit and head of the Essene Monastery dancing through their minds as the proud parents drifted off to sleep.

***

Levi led the holy entourage carrying Nebedeus across the arid Buqeia Plain towards Jerusalem. The troupe had stopped several times to change the palanquin bearers, allowing four bearers a drink break and a rest from carrying. They had stopped at sunrise to pray to God, honouring the Lord for the gift of light, and to pray for a safe journey.

Five hours into the journey, with the scorching hot sun sapping their energy, Nebedeus stopped the procession and talked to the scout.

"Levi, we have been travelling parallel to the Kidron *wadi* for some time now. We need to get the men out of this heat. How much further is it before we can descend into the gorge?"

"At least another two hours walk. Then we will reach a track wide enough for two men walking abreast and carrying the palanquin," Levi replied.

"For Caesar's sake man, don't tell me we have already passed narrow tracks that lead off this God forsaken plain?"

"No, Your Holiness. The first rough track is where the gorge curves west, but it is extremely narrow and quite steep."

"Head for that track and we will evaluate the risks versus advantages when we get there," Nebedeus replied.

Sometime later, Nebedeus and Levi walked carefully towards the edge of the *wadi* and looked down at the valley floor. It was at least one hundred feet deep with almost perpendicular sides. A rough hand hewn track only three feet wide snaked down the northern wall to the sandy floor. The track looked precarious but navigable in single file. The flat, shady gorge with the creek running beside the pathway, reminded Nebedeus of the fabled Garden of Eden. One thing for certain, it was as hot as hell on the plain.

"What do you think, Levi? Can we take the palanquin down that track?" he asked.

"It will not be easy. I could carry the front section if one of the agile Essene men can carry the rear."

"The men can remove the bench seat and roof framework. That will make the palanquin lighter and easier to handle," Nebedeus suggested.

Two men untied the straps, and removed the chair and framework from the palanquin frame as instructed. The other men rested on their haunches, wearily watching proceedings and eating their oranges or drinking water from the jugs. Any remaining water was used for washing their hands and sponging their necks. The fresh, clear water from the creek would supply all their needs until they reached Jerusalem.

Levi led the group down the path, holding the front handle of the palanquin over his left shoulder. A man named Jonah held the rear handle while the other two handles dangled a few inches above the ground. Eron followed leading Nebedeus, the other three priests and two men carrying the bench seat. The leading group was followed by the remaining five men, the last two carrying the empty amphora water jugs.

The three foot path soon became a track that was barely more than two feet wide in places. Rainwater runoff from the plains above had eroded the edge of the track and some sections had collapsed leaving gaping holes. The men inched their way along, stopping and taking a deep breath whenever a rock was dislodged. The rocks that fell to the bottom of the gorge made three different distinct sounds,—splash, crack or thud, depending on whether they hit water, rock or sand. Whatever the sound, the men's reaction was the same. They would stop in their tracks and look down at the bottom of the gorge; their bodies would twitch and shiver as they felt a tingle run up and down their spines. Each man knew the dislodged rock could have made him slip and fall to a certain death.

After what seemed an eternity, they made it to the sandy bed without loss of life. Two men secured the bench seat and canopy framework back on to the palanquin. Others were content to sit on the grass and soak their aching feet in the stream while others wandered off to relieve themselves against the canyon wall. Two men found a low, shallow cave, and found themselves competing to see who could urinate highest up the wall. Unfortunately, Nebedeus caught them in the act, and the two embarrassed men returned to the main group, informing the others what had happened.

"What did Nebedeus do?" Eron asked.

"He hit the roof," one of the men said.

The men burst out in laughter.

Nebedeus was pleased the men were more relaxed, and not worrying about the bandits. He informed the young priests on their first trip that the Kidron *wadi* would lead them all the way to Jerusalem.

Nebedeus climbed onto the palanquin, and the troupe headed westerly, following the snake-like bends of the gorge.

***

Jerusalem

The entourage passed the Mount of Olives and headed towards the walled city of Jerusalem. At the gates, the troupe was stopped by the Roman guards.

"State your name and business," the guards declared.

"We are clergy from Qumran," Nebedeus replied. "We are delivering taxes to the Temple for Emperor Augustus."

"How long do you intend to remain in the city?"

"Thirty days. We are visiting the Pharisee communities and returning to Qumran during the next full moon."

"Satisfied that the men were unarmed, the soldiers allowed them entrance into the city. Once out of sight of the guards, Nebedeus directed the tired men to the Essene Monastery. Inside the monastery enclosure, the four priests and the Essene married men were welcomed and cared for with gracious hospitality, while Nebedeus was ushered to the Head Bishop's office.

Uzziah bowed and kissed the Chief Priest on his ring hand and asked the deacon to organise refreshments. The two men sat down and discussed King Herod.

"His condition is very poor," Uzziah lamented. "Herod won't recognise you even if he is conscious, but three days ago he did ask for you by name."

"What else has he talked about?" Nebedeus asked.

Uzziah thought for a moment.

"He mostly spoke gibberish with only a few discernible words spoken."

They stopped talking as the deacon approached with a tray of refreshments.

"Leave the tray on the table," Uzziah said, "Thank you that will be all."

"What were the distinct words spoken?" Nebedeus asked.

Uzziah reached for his tumbler of juice but didn't drink after observing frustration in Nebedeus' face.

"Pharisees, Priests ... Chief Priests, names of wives and ... names of sons."

"Anything else?" Nebedeus asked. "Think harder. Why did he ask for me? Why not Simeon? After all, he is the ruling High Priest."

"Th—Th—Th—There was another word spoken," Uzziah stammered, "but I didn't hear it myself. The priest on night duty thought he heard Herod say the word *poisoned.*"

Nebedeus thumped the desk making Uzziah spill his drink.

"I knew it," Nebedeus exclaimed. "That is why he asked to be brought here. Herod can't trust his family or the High Priest."

"I want to see Herod immediately, with you and the physicians that have attended him. Is that clear?" he shouted.

CHAPTER 2: Virgin Mary

Qumran Monastery
Dead Sea, Palestine

Two miles from Qumran the four monks handed over the palanquin carrying the priests. Jacob and Miriam remained fast asleep. The priests thanked the monks for their assistance and continued walking towards the monastery while the four monks remained in Ain-Feshkha to reunite with their colleagues and enjoy the town hospitality. The village minister offered the monks refreshments and overnight accommodation, but food and rest were all they required. They could still make it back to the synagogue in Mazin before dark, rest overnight, and face the uphill climb back to the Mird Monastery before the afternoon heat.

The neophyte priests walked to the outer walls of the Qumran Monastery and lowered the palanquin in the shade. Jacob stirred and opened his eyes. He realised the trip was over and gently nudged Miriam. They thanked the priests for their care and hospitality, and for not proceeding through the main gate. No one had seen their arrival, and Jacob and Miriam wanted to surprise Joseph at his anointing ceremony.

Jacob stayed with the priests while Miriam visited the nuns to enquire about the schedule. She walked beside the wall until she reached the women's sector and knocked on the Abbey door. A young nun wearing a brilliant white habit opened the door.

"Good morning, can I be of assistance?" she asked.

"Yes," Miriam replied. "I would like to speak to Ilana, the Chief Priestess. She is not expecting me. My name is Miriam."

"Please come in and sit on the bench, I will inform Mother Superior immediately."

The nun walked across the polished wooden floor, occasionally glancing back over her shoulder at Miriam before knocking on Mother Superior's door. The Chief Priestess was in a conference, discussing the anointing ceremony with Sister Mary and the senior nuns. The young nun decided the interruption was warranted, especially as it was highly unusual for a woman to be travelling alone. After all, she had asked for the Mother Superior by name.

"Yes," Ilana called. "The door is open. Come in."

"I am sorry to disturb you Mother Superior, but there is a lady asking to see you. Her name is Miriam."

Ilana and Mary stood up, looked at each other and smiled in astonishment. Ilana turned to the young nun.

"Aneh, please escort the woman here and address her as Lady Miriam."

Aneh returned with Lady Miriam and watched as Mary hugged her and called her mother. Mary saw the confused look on Aneh's face.

"I was betrothed to Bishop Joseph when I was thirteen. Lady Miriam is my mother-in-law."

"You have grown into a fine woman Mary," Miriam said. "You know Joseph probably will not recognise you without your plaits."

"I have grown a foot taller too," Mary said.

"By the way, congratulations on completing your religious study course," Miriam said. "I heard you passed with honours, and have reached the highest level, the rank of Virgin Sister."

"Yes, but it is all about Joseph today. He will be the first Chief Priest promoted internally from the monastery since King Herod constructed the third floor thirty years ago. You recall he replaced the King David heirs with priests from other sects to weaken their power."

Mary had momentarily forgotten that the Chief Priestess was also from another sect.

"Miriam, what a surprise! You have appeared out of the blue, on the day of Joseph's anointing ceremony. It is all miraculous," said Ilana.

"The only miracle is that we made it in time. Nebedeus informed us of the ceremony on his way to Jerusalem."

"I was informed by Nebedeus that his mission was to be kept strictly secret. Apparently that is not the case. Is your husband Jacob at Qumran as well?" Ilana asked.

"Yes, he is with eight novice priests. They are waiting to be let into the common courtyard to witness the anointing. We want to surprise Joseph if we can."

Mary went to her desk and pulled opened a drawer. She picked up a large iron key which she passed to Miriam.

"This will open the gate. Give it to Jacob and please come back quickly. You must have a ritual bath. I want you to wear the Chief Priestess ceremonial gown if that is alright with you, Ilana."

"Yes, that will be fine."

Miriam gave Jacob the key, and he unlocked the gate. Jacob and the priests went inside the courtyard, locked the gate and passed the key back to Miriam. She hurried back to the Abbey while Jacob and the priests went to the courtyard storeroom. The men selected two chairs and two long benches for themselves, Joseph and Miriam, the unexpected guests. In preparation of the celibate men sitting on the northern side of the ritual bath, the priests placed the two wooden benches against the wall behind the five seats already arranged by the nuns. On the southern side were chairs for Sister Mary, the Chief Priestess Ilana and two nuns. Jacob placed the two extra chairs for Miriam and himself next to the Mary's chair.

Jacob looked at the small white tents each side of the ceremonial bath and reminisced about his anointing ceremony, thirty-four years ago before he married Miriam. Jacob scooped up some water and wet his forehead. The water was lukewarm. His ceremony had been held in mid-winter when the water was cold.

Jacob suddenly realised he was standing in the courtyard by himself. The priests had disappeared through the side door to the men's change rooms to freshen up. He must do the same.

The priests were in their white robes, tying on purple ceremonial sashes and white, wide brimmed sun hats. Jacob decided to wear a Bishop's robe, with the same purple sash to match the priests and a headdress mitre. The men waited in the change room, listening for the women to arrive before they went back into the courtyard. They were expecting the noise of a gate opening. Instead, they heard the sound of drums. One of the Priests stood on a bench and looked through the window.

"Here come the four senior priests. They are chanting prayers and beating timbrel drums. Bishop Joseph is walking in the middle."

"We will wait for the women until the last moment," Jacob said. "If Joseph gets here first, someone will have to tell them to do a lap of honour before entering the courtyard."

The young priest at the window started counting down—eighty yards, sixty yards, fifty, forty, thirty... He heard the sound of a gate swinging open. The women had arrived. The men quickly filed into the courtyard, and everyone sat and watched the eastern doorway.

The door swung open, and Daniel led the Senior Priests and Joseph to their seats. The courtiers stood and applauded until the Bishop was seated. Joseph was stunned by what he saw. First he noticed the eight neophyte priests who should be in Jerusalem. Then he looked around and saw his parents sitting opposite, smiling proudly. Everyone was dressed in ceremonial clothes. The courtyard walls were decorated with gold ribbons while purple sashes, the colour of royalty, joined the two white tents. Purple waterlily petals floated on the water, and twelve white waterlily flowers floated in the waist deep section of the ritual bath. On a carved wooden bench sat a ceremonial jug filled with scented anointing oil and white towels. Joseph was overwhelmed with emotion, barely holding back tears of joy and gratitude.

The Chief Priestess walked to the ritual bath where she could see and address everyone.

"We are gathered here today to witness the anointing of the Holy Spirit," she said. "After the ceremony, Bishop Joseph will be acting as Chief Priest until Nebedeus returns. I have chosen Sister Virgin Mary to anoint Joseph while I conduct the prayer service. Later, Joseph acting as His Holiness will then anoint Senior Priest Daniel to act as Bishop and select a neophyte priest to act as the senior priest. Joseph and Mary, please go to your designated tents and change into the white robes, and then proceed to the ceremonial bath."

Mary entered the bath from the western steps, Joseph from the eastern steps. They stepped down the seven steps in a synchronised action until they reached each other in the middle of the bath, their white robes floating beneath the lily flowers like large waterlily-pads.

"You haven't changed at all in the last six years," Mary whispered. "You still look very young and handsome."

"You have changed," Joseph replied. "You are taller, even more elegant and extremely beautiful."

"Please anoint Joseph while I pray," Ilana instructed Mary.

Mary reached for the oil. Her long soft black hair touched Joseph's arm and their legs touched under the water. They looked into each other's eyes as she applied the scented oil. Mary massaged the oil over Joseph's neck and shoulders, caressing his body with soft, rhythmical strokes.

Joseph had never experienced a woman's touch, having been celibate all his life and only knowing young men. He felt the mental anxiety of the last thirty-eight hours diminish with every soothing caress and soon relaxed. He looked into Mary's beautiful brown eyes as she continued massaging. Suddenly, his pelvis reflexed forward and he ejaculated into the warm water, his erect penis rubbing against Mary's crutch.

"I felt that," Mary said smiling. "You can turn around now, and I will anoint your back."

Joseph had not listened to what Ilana had been saying, but he did hear the final prayer.

"Lord, our one true God, bless Joseph in his new position. Guide him in all his decisions for the good of our community. Amen."

"Congratulations," Ilana said to Joseph. "You are now the acting Chief Priest until Nebedeus returns. You may exit the ritual bath now and change into the Chief Priest ceremonial robe and mitre left for you in the western tent."

Mary handed Joseph a towel.

"Congratulations, Your Holiness, our most esteemed Essene Chief Priest," she said.

"Mary, your clean robe is in the eastern tent. Once you have changed please return to your chair," Ilana said.

Joseph entered the western tent and saw the pure white robe Mary had worn before the ceremony folded neatly next to his Chief Priest mitre. He could smell her perfume and sense her aura. It brought back the warm body sensation he felt earlier. Then Jacob saw the ceremonial Chief Priest's ring nestled in Mary's undergarments, like an egg in a bird's nest.

Joseph reached for the fabled ring and placed it on his finger, expecting an adrenalin rush. One came, but not from the ring, but by the touch of Mary's silk underwear. Joseph dressed in the Chief Priest Robe, placed the mitre on his head and walked out.

The onlookers had witnessed a Bishop walk into the first tent, and come out in a pauper's robe. Then they saw him enter the ritual bath where he was anointed and be prayed over, before going into the other tent and walk out a Chief Priest. Joseph held his ring hand high and slowly waved to the gathering.

"God bless you all," he said, "and thank you for witnessing my anointing ceremony. I promise to uphold the will of God and perform my duties responsibly. The Lord God is great. Amen."

"God is great. Amen," everyone said as they applauded Joseph as the Chief Priest lowered his hand.

Joseph walked over to the anointing jugs and called Daniel to come forward.

"You have been elected by your peers to be the acting Holy Spirit," he said. "Bishop Daniel, I hereby anoint you with oil and instruct you to perform your duties to God's will and testament."

"I promise to fulfil the faith shown by my peers and to uphold the will of God and perform my duties appropriately. God is great. Amen," Bishop Daniel declared.

Joseph directed Daniel to go to the western tent and dress in the Bishop ceremonial robe and mitre. Joseph looked at the row of neophyte priests.

"Malachi, please come forward," he called.

Malachi looked at the other young priests as if seeking their approval. When they applauded, he stood up and walked over to the Chief Priest where he was anointed with drops of oil and promoted to acting Senior Priest.

"Malachi, I instruct you to perform your duties to God's will and testament," Joseph said.

"I promise to fulfil my duties and to uphold the will of God. Amen," Malachi replied.

"Congratulations, Malachi. Go into the eastern tent and change into the Senior Priest Robe and wide brimmed hat."

Daniel and Malachi came out of their respective tents to a round of applause. Their first duty was to toll the bells in the court tower to signal the other members of the monastery that the new Chief Priest had been ordained.

Joseph approached Mary and his parents.

"Can anybody tell me what is going on? I was only expecting four senior priests, a nun and the Chief Priestess, not this extravaganza," he said.

"First things first," Miriam said. "Come on, give me my hug."

"Thank you for coming," Joseph said. "You have really made my day."

"I wouldn't have missed it for all of Caesar's gold. Congratulations son."

Joseph shook his father's hand.

"Thank you for being here for me, father. I know how much you have dreamt about this day happing for our family heritage."

"I am extremely proud of you, Joseph. When Nebedeus gains the High Priest position, you will become the Essene God for the Qumran community."

Joseph hugged Mary and kissed her on the cheek.

"You look absolutely beautiful," he said. "Thank you for anointing my shoulders, you relieved all my stress."

"I enjoyed every moment, including your kiss," Mary replied.

Joseph stepped back.

"Now someone tell me why eight neophyte priests out of the original twelve are milling around in the courtyard instead of being with Nebedeus in Jerusalem?"

"It's a long story," his father said.

"I can see it's going to be a long night," Joseph said. "No one is to leave this courtyard until I am fully informed, and that's an order from the Chief Priest."

The eastern gate opened, and the deacons, elders, and monastery chefs swarmed into the courtyard with trays of cooked food, fruit and wine. They went into the storeroom and brought out more benches for the extra guests, and tables for the trays of food.

Joseph heard the entire story over the next few hours. He was shocked when told about the gory incident involving Isaac the scout. Everyone prayed for Isaac's rescue and that the Roman soldiers would capture the bandits.

Mary reached for Joseph's hand and gently led him to one side.

"It will be dusk soon, and our protocol dictates we must not be in mixed company after hours. Enjoy the rest of your evening with your parents. Goodnight Joseph."

"Mary, before you go, we will probably not see each other again until we exchange our wedding vows in four years' time. I want you to know I enjoyed your company today. I am not marrying you just to produce the next line of King David heirs. I want a happy marriage like my parents enjoy."

"Oh Joseph, you have made my prayers come true. I love you and have loved you since our betrothal when I was thirteen," she said.

"I found the Chief Priest ring lying on your clothes," he whispered.

"Yes, I apologise," Mary said. "I had never seen a Chief Priest's ring close up and it looked so beautiful sitting on your mitre. I felt a powerful urge to wear something of yours. I slid it on my finger while I dressed, and I tried on your mitre too."

"Mary, I wasn't expecting you to apologise. I also wanted something of yours. I am wearing your underwear. I will wear them on this day, every third day of the week until we marry."

"I am glad. I was meant to wear those silk pants in the ritual bath," Mary said. "When I washed and changed in the tent, I forgot to put them back on. I am not used to wearing underwear. Wear them, and think of me when you do. I must go now. I love you, Joseph."

"Wait. Please take my signet ring. Wear it at night and dream of our future life together."

Ilana and two nuns were slowly walking towards the gate. The sun had already dipped below the horizon, and they were ready to leave for the abbey. Mary clutched Joseph's ring tightly in her hand and ran towards them as tears of joy welled in her eyes.

***

The Essene Monastery
Jerusalem

Nebedeus stared down at the ashen face of King Herod. The King lay on a huge bed, unconscious and barely breathing. Bishop Uzziah and two physicians were standing by the opposite side of the bed, looking glum. Nebedeus knew that King Herod had recently returned from a trip to Egypt, purportedly a secret rendezvous with Emperor Augustus at the Roman garrison in Alexandria. Both leaders returned to their respective homelands when a plague causing severe illness spread through the population.

"Could he be suffering from the Egyptian plague?" Nebedeus asked.

"I do not believe so," the older physician replied. "There are no tell-tale signs of skin turning dark or nose bleeding."

"It cannot be just a fever. This man is nearly dead," Nebedeus said. "Uzziah thinks he was poisoned. I suggest you treat him for poisoning."

"We have ruled out snake poison sir," the younger physician said. "That's my field of expertise."

"Thank you doctors, you may leave now," Nebedeus said. "Uzziah, I believe the chief Therapeut Priest and his followers are in Jerusalem for the summer fruit festival. Send a message for him to see me most urgently. His name is Theudas. Ask him to bring a stomach purgative for an unknown type of poisoning."

"Yes, Your Holiness," Uzziah replied.

Nebedeus stayed with the King, frequently checking for any signs of poisoning or puncture wounds. He took a damp cloth from the bowl at the foot of the bed and placed it on Herod's forehead. The King murmured incomprehensively, perhaps sensing someone was caring for him. Nebedeus had been told long ago by a priest that dying people could hear right up until the final moment of death, even in a coma.

Nebedeus leant over and talked in Herod's ear.

"Help is on its way, keep fighting with all your will, I am praying for your recovery."

Nebedeus sat on the side of the bed for two hours, changing the damp cloth on Herod's forehead when necessary and spooning water into his mouth, one drop at a time.

Nebedeus heard footsteps and saw Uzziah with Theudas and two female companions. The women were dressed in colourful clothes, nothing like the pure white robes of the Essenes. They were carrying bundles of herbs and several containers of medicinal products.

"We came as soon as we could," Theudas said. "It's good to see you Nebedeus. It has been far too long between drinks. Uzziah has informed me of Herod's ill health and that it may be poisoning."

Nebedeus and Theudas shook hands.

"We live in busy times, I am sorry we had to meet under these circumstances. Perhaps we can catch up during the festival."

Theudas glanced at the patient.

"He is very weak. It will be difficult to administer a purgative mixture. It will be a miracle if he survives."

Theudas opened the Kings eyelids.

"His pupils are dilated, and there are blue-green rings around his eyes. That means he has been eating too much salt and food with a high level of arsenic content, probably over a long period of time."

"He has been poisoned then," Uzziah exclaimed.

"Uzziah, could you arrange some refreshments for us?" Nebedeus wanted him out of the room.

"Yes, Your Highness, straight away," Uzziah replied.

Theudas spoke to his two nurses.

"I need you to mix the ingredients from the containers. Add an equal amount of water and stir well. Mash the aloe, rosebuds, charcoal, whole grain, onions and garlic. Then add four raw eggs, pour in the wet mix and stir again. Sieve it through cloth and let the mix stand for ten minutes."

Nebedeus waited until the nurses were out of earshot.

"Do you believe Herod was deliberately poisoned?"

Theudas looked at Herod's fingernails and shook his head.

"See the white spots throughout the length of his fingernails. That indicates small dosages of arsenic over a long period. The blue rings around his brown eyes indicate too much salt in his diet. Other members of his household would probably show similar symptoms. The cooks at his Masada palace may have used salt from the Dead Sea in his meals. That would probably explain the high content of arsenic in his body."

"If you can save the King, he will be forever grateful," Nebedeus said, "but it's imperative that he believes he was deliberately poisoned. Do you understand?"

"Yes," Theudas replied. "From what Uzziah told me Herod believes his eldest sons and the High Priest are behind the poisoning."

"We could persuade Herod that it would be in his best interest to select a new High Priest," Nebedeus said. "Simeon, son of Boethus is aligned with the monarchy but secretly opposes the Roman occupation. I am more tolerant towards Roman authority because Judea would become politically stable with fewer conflicts along our borders."

"I agree," Theudas said. "However, we are talking treason and must be careful not to overplay our hand."

"We must remain silent. No one else should be involved, not even the Essene hierarchy," Nebedeus said. "Here come the nurses with bowls of medicine. First we need to save this man."

Theudas checked the consistency of the mixture in the two bowls. He selected the thinner one, and asked the nurses to climb onto the bed to be close to the patient. He asked Rosina to hold Herod's mouth wide open and the other nurse, Shona, to pull out his tongue. Theudas slowly poured the liquid down the unconscious man's throat. He stopped at regular intervals, pushing his finger down the throat to ensure Herod swallowed. Once Theudas finished administering the concoction, he asked the nurses to clean the patient.

"Now we wait," he said. "I don't think he will vomit in his condition."

"How long before we can expect any reaction?" Nebedeus asked.

"If Herod does vomit, he will do so within an hour. I believe his stomach is empty. The mixture will most likely pass through his body, absorbing the arsenic in his system."

"When can we expect to see any signs of recovery?"

"If he lives for another week, Herod will gradually regain strength over time."

"Can you supply nurses to look after Herod, and administer the medication?" Nebedeus asked.

"Therapeutic medicine is our main source of income. I can have two nurses on duty working four hour shifts. They will administer the ingredients every four hours, cutting down on the onions and charcoal a little each day."

The two men reached an amicable agreement on fees and costs. Nebedeus paid half the fees up front, and agreed to arrange in-house accommodation for six nurses. The nurses would work for at least two weeks provided the King stayed alive.

Uzziah and a neophyte priest arrived with tumblers of juice and sweet-bread rolls.

Nebedeus asked Uzziah to arrange the nurses' accommodation and to check regularly on Herod's health. The Chief Priests enjoyed a three course meal in the monastery refectory where they continued their conservation about Judean politics, all the time swilling red wine.

Two hours later the two men parted company, promising to see each other more often and to meet at the festival if they didn't cross paths beforehand.

Theudas went back to the villa and self-sustaining farm he owned a mile outside the walled city where he grew all his food and herbs. He chose four nurses from his harem to attend to Herod and join Rosina and Shona. He selected three nurses to work in the garden, milk the goats and feed the fowls. That left three nurses. Theudas asked one to prepare dinner while the remaining two nurses smiled at each other and followed him to his bedroom.

Nebedeus was extremely tired after the long, dusty journey and the stress of seeing the King so gravely ill. He opted for a much needed sleep alone in his quarters.

***

Qumran Monastery
Dead Sea, Palestine

Dusk turned to a moonlit night. The elders poured hot coals onto the firewood. Both bonfires were soon ablaze, and cast long flickering shadows of people moving around inside the courtyard. The setting had changed from a formal ceremony to a jubilant party atmosphere. The choirboys sang harmoniously in the background while the guests ate and drank amid much talking and laughing. Joseph mingled with the crowd, making sure he frequently returned to talk with his parents. Later in the night he observed they both looked tired.

"You have been awake since the early hours. We can talk tomorrow if you would prefer to retire," he said.

"Please join us tonight in our humble abode," Miriam said.

"But mother, the rooms in the guesthouse are small. My presence would make your stay hot and uncomfortable."

"Oh ye of little faith," Jacob said. "Do you think we would let the Chief Priest sleep in the guesthouse?"

Joseph was dumbfounded. His father reached for the fine leather strap around his neck and pulled out the attached key. It was no ordinary key. It was the gold key for the Chief Priest's apartment on the third floor.

"Nebedeus gave us the key in Mird," Miriam said. "He wanted you to enjoy all the comfort and privileges of being Chief Priest before committing yourself to a lifetime of marriage. All he stipulated was for you to enjoy the position during his absence, and to keep the oath of office."

For the seventh time today, Joseph was totally surprised—his parent's unexpected visit, the unexpected return of the eight neophyte priests, the grandiose ceremony, the wonderful time with Mary, the horrible bandit incident, the fabled Chief Priest ring and now the golden key.

Joseph asked everyone in the courtyard to gather around.

"I wish to thank you all for witnessing my anointing as the Chief Priest, Daniel's anointing as Bishop and Malachi's anointing as Senior Priest. I have enjoyed the day immensely, and judging by the party atmosphere, I believe you all have too. I will be retiring soon as I wish to spend some time with my parents. The four senior priests will oversee the party and the festivities in my absence. Good night and God bless you all."

Joseph gave his key to the Bishop quarters on the second floor to Daniel, now acting in the Holy Spirit position. He waved goodbye, using the hand sporting the Chief Priest ring, for all to see one more time.

"God bless you Holy of Holies," the crowd cried out and applauded as Joseph and his parents left the courtyard, each carrying a lit oil lamp.

Mary heard the applause from her room in the abbey and looked out of the window. She watched Joseph and his parents walk towards the monastery. She rubbed the signet ring on her finger and pondered about married life. At the same instant, Joseph felt the hairs on the back of his neck tingle. He was compelled to look around, and saw Mary holding a lamp, her face glowing like an angel in the darkness, and her warm aura spread throughout his body. He waved goodbye, knowing it was not enough, but it was all he could do. Mary blew him a kiss and waved back. She felt happy, lonely, and intensely emotional. She felt comfort in wearing Joseph's ring and knew that Joseph would wear her silk underwear tonight, and every third day of the week until they married. Mary blew out her lamp and went to bed, dreaming of the new love pact and her and Joseph's secret ritual that would keep them spiritually united.

Joseph and his parents climbed the outer stairs to the third floor apartment. Joseph opened the door and lit the oil lamps on the wall. This section of the building had been built by King Herod to house the incumbent Sadducee or Pharisee Chief Priests. None of them had been here before. The task of the Chief Priests was to report on the Essene Monastery activities and provide King Herod with information about the hierarchy. Provided the Chief Priest supported the Herod monarchy and proved to be competent, he would be in line to become the next High Priest in the Temple.

Joseph and his parents stepped into a lobby where there were three other doors. They chose the door on the right, and Joseph ushered his parents through to a balcony that wrapped around the building and back to the lobby. There were four large arches on each side, all with magnificent views. Facing west were the limestone cliffs and the male quarters, facing south was the view to the gardens and Dead Sea coastline while east was the abbey and the vast lake of the Dead Sea. North were the vineyards and the animal enclosures.

They passed several doors. Five led into the rooms from the veranda, while the other two went to a north-south inner passage which led to the kitchen, dining room, the main bedroom two smaller bedrooms, a locked room and the Chief Priest's office. The latter was the only room Joseph had previously entered. Inner steps led down to the foyer near his Bishop's office on the second floor. The complex was immense and magnificently decorated throughout. Opulent, it was specifically designed for the Chief Priest to entertain visiting officials in private.

Joseph and his parents found their way through the dining room and into the kitchen where they enjoyed freshly made orange juice and reminisced for an hour before hugging each other and saying goodnight. Miriam and Jacob walked hand in hand to the guest room where they found a chamber pot built inside a chair. They vowed to get some for their house. They kissed each other goodnight. Jacob turned down the wicks of the oil lamps so that they would glow all night, and they headed for bed for a much needed sleep.

Joseph found the master bedroom which had a small separate room with a sophisticated toilet built over a hole in the floor. As he urinated down the shaft, he wondered where the waste went. When he'd finished, he threw a bucket of water down to flush the system. Joseph was surprised that the bucket refilled with water after he replaced it in the wall cavity. Tired from his day, he decided to investigate the intricacies of the building tomorrow.

He was enjoying the role of the Chief Priest, especially not being required to supervise others or undertake regimented prayer rituals day after day. Joseph took off his robe and went to bed, blowing out his oil lamp and placing it on the side table. He tossed and turned for a while, thinking whether he could give up all this for marriage. He cursed the fact he was the only male child to carry on the David Justus heir-line. Joseph turned on his side to sleep, his hand touched silk, and his thoughts turned to the beautiful Virgin Mary recalling how she looked in the thin white pauper's robe as it floated in the ritual bath. Under water, their naked bodies touched nearly every time Mary massaged him with oil. Her beautiful brown eyes looked into his while she massaged and caressed his shoulders. He had glanced down when he prematurely ejaculated into the warm water, noticing how Mary's erect nipples protruded out under the oil-wet cloth. As thoughts of Mary's massage swirled around him, Joseph drifted into a blissful sleep.

***

The Essene Monastery
Jerusalem

Nebedeus slept soundly from nightfall until one hour before sunrise. When he woke, his first thoughts were of King Herod. He feared that he may have died overnight, leaving his eldest and most ruthless son as heir to the throne. Nebedeus dressed in his robe and hurried down the hallway to find one of the relief nurses asleep. She was lying on the bed next to Herod with her arm on his chest. The nurse was only in a light sleep and instantly woke as Nebedeus entered the room.

"Good morning sir," she said. "My name is Jenah. We have had a busy night with our patient. He was fed three bowls of medicine over the past four hours, the last one just half an hour ago."

"Has he vomited yet?" Nebedeus asked.

"No," Jenah replied, "but he has wet the bed three times and had several bouts of diarrhoea overnight."

"Is that good or bad?"

"Good for the first three days. Once the poison is out of his system, we hope to see firmer stools."

"Has Herod spoken or improved in any way?" Nebedeus asked.

"No, he has remained unconscious with just a few moans, but there is some encouraging news."

"What do you mean?"

"Among his waste were small traces of crab shell."

Jenah observed no change in Nebedeus' expression.

"I believe he is suffering from a bad bout of food poisoning, made worse by traces of arsenic in his every day food consumption."

"I see," Nebedeus said. "Did anyone else see the crab shell?"

"No. Mira, the other nurse, went to fetch more sheets and pillows."

"Where is Mira now? Shouldn't she be here helping you?" Nebedeus said.

"We had a tough shift. As I am the most experienced nurse, I let her leave an hour early."

"Fair enough," Nebedeus said. "Do you think Herod would be all right on his own until the next shift if you were not in here to look after him?"

"Quite sure," Jenah replied looking forward to some sleep.

In one swift movement, Nebedeus lurched for her head with both hands and savagely twisted her neck. Jenah's body fell to the floor. She died immediately from a broken neck. Nebedeus looked down the passageway and observed it was empty. Then he carried the dead nurse to the stairs and threw her down the steps. Nebedeus made the nurse look dishevelled with one sandal off and her robe up around her waist. He noticed she wasn't wearing underwear. He hurriedly made her look decent and prayed her sins would be forgiven by God.

He walked back up the stairs, looked both ways, and then dropped one of her sandals on the top step. Nebedeus returned to his bed and waited for the next shift to start. Today a woman had been sacrificed for her country so he could prevail over the current High Priest. No one must know the King wasn't deliberately poisoned. No one. Nebedeus felt vindicated over his actions.

Two long, high pitched screams came from the relief nurses who were beginning their shifts. Nebedeus wrapped a towel around his waist, and ran barefoot towards the direction of the screams to discover the two nurses bent over Jenah. Their training had taken over as they searched for some sign of life. Nebedeus was the third on the scene.

"I thought the King had died. What happened? Has she fainted?" he said.

"Jenah must have slipped and fallen down the steps. Her neck is broken. I fear she is dead," one of the nurses cried.

"Where is the other nurse she was working with?" Nebedeus asked. "She must know what happened."

The three relief nurses and two Essene priests arrived on the scene with the sound of more footsteps behind them.

"I was working on the same shift as Jenah, but she told me to finish early," Mira said shocked.

"That means you were the last to see her alive. Did you argue during your shift?" Nebedeus asked.

"No. We are— we were best friends. We worked hard. We changed the bed sheets three times during the shift," Mira cried. "We were both extremely tired and exhausted. She must have misjudged the step and fell."

Uzziah arrived on the scene. Nebedeus quickly informed him what had happened.

"I will need to hear from all the nurses in my office," Uzziah said. "I will interview Mira first, followed by the nurses who found the body, and then the other two nurses."

"Uzziah, we had better move the body to the basement where it is cooler," Nebedeus said.

"I will also have to notify the authorities," Uzziah said.

"No, let me talk to Theudas first," Nebedeus said. "We may have to move the body outside of the monastery, otherwise word will spread that Herod is in our care. We must maintain secrecy at all cost."

Uzziah didn't like the idea. He always did things by the book, but he knew this was not a time to provoke the Chief Priest.

"Send a messenger to advise Theudas of this tragedy," he said.

"I need two nurses to watch over King Herod now," Nebedeus said. "The nurses must work in pairs at all times. No one is to leave the shift early. Is that understood?"

The nurses nodded, glancing in disbelief at their lifeless colleague. Nebedeus told Uzziah he would leave everything in his capable hands. He returned to his room to change into his robe, deciding he would definitely have to stay in Jerusalem for thirty days and return to Qumran during the next full moon. Nebedeus could not risk leaving Herod until he fully recovered and could communicate. He had to remind the King that he had been poisoned. Nebedeus sent a messenger to inform Levi that he was required immediately.

Levi knocked on the door.

"Sir, may I enter?"

"Yes, come in," Nebedeus said.

"How can I be of assistance, Your Holiness?"

"Tomorrow morning, you are to take the eight married men back to Ramah and thank Mr and Mrs Justus for their help. You can stay at their mansion overnight if they offer accommodation, otherwise stay overnight at the Mazin Synagogue. You must report to the minister at Ain-Feshkha and inform him the King is seriously ill but in a stable condition. You can remain there if you wish, but a reliable person must deliver the same message to the Qumran Monastery. He must also report to Bishop Daniel that I will return with the four novice priests during the next full moon cycle."

Nebedeus dismissed Levi and waited for Theudas to arrive. He contemplated what to say and do to keep Theudas on side especially as he still required the nurses. They were vital for administering the King's medicine and attending to his personal hygiene. He needed to relax. Killing the nurse was affecting his nervous system. He rang the service bell, and a deacon promptly responded.

"Yes, Your Holiness. May I help you?"

"I would like an experienced pageboy sent to my room," Nebedeus said. "I will require his services for two hours."

The deacon bowed and went to the boys' quarters in the basement. Nebedeus started shaking, unable to control his emotions. He ate the two sweetbreads on the table, but left the juice untouched knowing it may have an adverse effect.

A handsome young boy appeared at the door.

"Come in lad and lock the door," Nebedeus said. "What is your name?"

"Rafael."

"Do you know who I am?"

"Yes sir. You can save my soul from burning in Hell."

"That I can, but first I want you to wash," Nebedeus said, beginning to feel on fire himself.

Rafael went to the bowl, poured water from the jug, removed his clothes and bathed while Nebedeus watched.

"That is fine. Now bring the scented oil over here and massage my back and shoulders"

The boy massaged Nebedeus from head to foot for half an hour. Then Nebedeus turned over and Rafael began massaging his chest, arms and legs.

"Before you oil the rest of my body I want to be aroused," Nebedeus said.

Rafael started to use his hands, but Nebedeus rebuked him.

"I asked for an experienced boy. Use your mouth and perform at your best."

The young boy was shaken, but he regained his composure and aroused Nebedeus fully, using his tongue and performing fellatio.

Nebedeus enjoyed the pleasure of oral sex for as long as he could. He stopped the boy, moved off the bed and pushed the boy face down on the bed with his legs straddled on the floor. He looked at the boy's beautiful olive body and then sodomised him.

Rafael was pleasantly surprised by Nebedeus' gentleness and quickly became aroused himself. While Nebedeus was satisfied with anal intercourse, Rafael pushed back off the bed a little and masturbated. Rafael and Nebedeus enjoyed mutual satisfaction, ejaculating simultaneously.

Rafael went to the table and brought back a bowl of fresh water to Nebedeus and wiped his body with a damp cloth. When Nebedeus dipped the cloth in the water and washed him, even his feet, Rafael was pleasantly surprised.

"From this day forth, you will always be by my side," Nebedeus said. "Now dress. I am expecting a man called Theudas."

Uzziah visited Nebedeus and informed him that he had interviewed all the nurses.

"They all said Jenah was kind, helpful, friendly and talented. I have come to the conclusion that she slipped at the top of the steps, fell and broke her neck. She must have died instantly."

"That will be a relief to Mira," Nebedeus replied. "She should have been working with Jenah at the time of the accident."

"Theudas is in the basement looking at the corpse," Uzziah said. "Apparently Jenah was his most experienced nurse and favourite partner."

"I will check on King Herod and then see Theudas. We need Herod to regain his health as soon as possible, before his family or the High Priest realise that he is not in either of their company."

Nebedeus checked on the King and asked the nurses whether his condition had improved. He was relieved when they mentioning how the colour in King Herod's cheeks had improved and that he was swallowing the medication easier.

"We are still changing his sheets twice a shift," a nurse said, "and because he is heavy, we are folding the sheets in half. Then rolling him onto his side and placing the sheet under him. We do the same thing on the other side. That saves us from having to lift him off the bed, and it is less of a disturbance for him."

"I am extremely pleased with your work nurses. I will tell Theudas and the King how impressed I am."

Nebedeus went to the basement and saw the blank look on Theudas' face. He was sitting near the corpse staring at Jenah's face as if he expected her to open her eyes and say *why are you troubled, I was just sleeping.*

"Theudas, please accept my deepest sympathy," Nebedeus said. "No one could have foreseen this terrible event."

Theudas shifted his gaze towards Nebedeus and then back to Jenah. He didn't say a word. Nebedeus placed his hand on Theudas' shoulder.

"I know how much this woman meant to you. I was third on the scene when the nurses found her. I prayed for her soul before she was cold. I am sure she has ascended to Heaven."

"Save that crap for the weak minded who are scared of dying. This woman knew how to live and how to save lives."

Nebedeus was caught off guard. Theudas had always believed in God.

"You are in shock, Theudas. You must understand Jenah did not die in vain. Jenah has sacrificed herself for the health of Herod and the benefit of the whole of Judea."

Theudas broke down and cried. Nebedeus let him release his pent up emotions before he spoke again.

"We need to talk about Jenah," Nebedeus said handing Theudas a cup of water.

"What about Jenah?" Theudas asked. "You mean her burial?"

"Yes, but before that, we must move her body."

"What? Why would we do that?"

"I know this is difficult and painful, but you must be strong. Jenah must be moved away from the monastery and placed somewhere near a cliff. We must do it soon so that she can be found by strangers. Jenah can still be buried before sunset, honouring her Jewish burial tradition. If the Sadducees or Pharisees find out she died in an Essene Monastery, they will question why she was here. They may find out she nursed the King, and discover Herod is here."

"I understand," Theudas said. "For the good of the country, I understand. I know a place where she walked on a narrow path, when she visited her parent's grave."

"Well done, Theudas. I will repay you back one hundredfold one day," Nebedeus said. "I will arrange for a donkey and some rugs to wrap around her body. You and I will have to dress like local merchants going to the market place."

Nebedeus and Theudas walked along a cliff track in single file. Nebedeus walked in front, with Theudas leading the donkey laden with rugs and mats. Inside the largest rug was the body of nurse Jenah. The men stopped at a section of the track where they could turn the donkey around. Theudas tied the donkey's lead to a protruding rock and then helped Nebedeus lift the rug before they walked along the track to a narrow section. The men checked that the track and cliff base were clear of any potential witnesses. Satisfied that the area was deserted, they placed the rug on the ground.

As they stood on the bottom layer, they rolled the rug over the edge. The rug unwound and the body dropped to the rocks below with a sickening thud. Nebedeus helped Theudas pull up the rug and roll it back into a bundle where they secured it on the donkey and headed for Theudas' villa. As they passed the narrow section of the track, both looked down at the body sprawled on the rocks below. Theudas felt distraught. He couldn't comprehend the death of Jenah, his best nurse and faithful companion.

He remembered back three days ago when she wanted an afternoon romp. Jenah had suggested her preferred intercourse, which she called the *movaan*. Jenah would sit on the side of the bed with her robe high up around her waist. Her legs straddled and her feet on the floor, usually with her sandals on. Theudas, the strong, robust, young Therapeut Priest, would stand in front her, between her lovely long legs. Jenah would start the *movaan* by placing her hands on Theudas' buttocks and pulling his body towards her. She would perform fellatio to arouse him, and then lie on her back. Theudas would spend an equal amount of time on foreplay. Jenah would arch her back and watch Theudas' facial expressions as he penetrated her and they became one. Jenah enjoyed the *movaan* sex because it lasted longer than other positions. I love it like this, Jenah would whisper, and Theudas would smack her bottom to let her know when he was about to ejaculate. She would prevent an unwanted pregnancy by asking Theudas to finish anally, or in her mouth, whichever she preferred on the day.

While Theudas was reminiscing, Nebedeus dropped one of Jenah's sandals on the path for someone to find. He kicked the edge of the path, causing a small avalanche of rocks to cover part of the body. Nebedeus felt sorry for Theudas, but the nurse had to die, she knew too much. Theudas would never forget Jenah. When someone found her body he would give her a grand funeral. He would miss her terribly. He would have to teach another nurse the *movaan* method. That way he would always remember Jenah, or at least what she loved doing best.

Two hours before sunset, a messenger came to Theudas.

"Sir, we have found a dead woman. She may be one of your nurses."

"What happened?"

"The nurse must have slipped on the edge of a track and fell on rocks. She would have died instantly. The doctors have already examined her, and there are no signs of foul play or recent sexual assault."

"What do you mean by recent sexual assault?" Theudas asked.

"Well sir, apparently she had anal bruising from a few days earlier."

"I see," Theudas said. "Where is her body now?"

"I will accompany you to the doctor's surgery, and you can verify the woman's identity. If she is one of your nurses, we can release her for burial. She is being washed and dressed in white linen garments for burial."

Theudas, Nebedeus and the six nurses at the villa went with the messenger. They reached the doctor's house in half an hour. Theudas went in alone and verified the nurse as one of his staff.

"Her name is Jenah," he said. "She went to visit her parent's grave earlier today and did not return. I thought she may have visited friends as it was her day off from work."

Theudas signed for the body and arranged for a litter for Jenah's funeral procession.

"Nebedeus, would you advise the five nurses at the monastery about the funeral, and escort them back here?" he said.

Theudas and the six nurses anointed Jenah with oils and spices in the Jewish tradition, and Jenah was buried next to her parents before sunset. Nebedeus prayed for her soul to ascend to heaven and Theudas delivered a eulogy. The eleven nurses wept and mourned loudly, as did Theudas. Nebedeus showed little emotion; after all he didn't know the woman.

Three days later, Theudas laid a granite marker on Jenah's grave with her name, age and occupation. He had carved the stone himself. Next year, he would exhume her bones and those of her parents, place them in the ossuary and entomb the boxes in his family crypt.

CHAPTER 3: Heaven and Hell

The Tower Apartment
Qumran Monastery
Dead Sea, Palestine

Miriam woke first. She lit the kitchen stove that had already been stoked with sticks, and made three cups of hot lemon and sliced several pieces of bread roll to toast. As she was setting the table in the dining room Jacob woke. He loved the smell of freshly cooked bread.

"Are you awake, son?" he said as he knocked on Joseph's door.

"I am now," the reply came.

Jacob opened the bedroom door and went in.

"Miriam has tested her cooking skills. She has cooked toast for breakfast."

"I'll be right there, but I want to show you something first."

Joseph showed his father the toilet.

"Have you ever seen anything like this before?"

"No, I haven't. It's a highly sophisticated system. I want to try it out. Where does the waste go?"

"That I haven't worked out yet, but I know it doesn't flow down the outside wall."

"Shall we have breakfast and look at the view from the balcony later?"

Miriam smiled at her two men.

"We didn't bring the cooks with us. I hope you will enjoy fig jam on toast."

They all enjoyed the breakfast and talked about what was happening within the family. Inevitably, the subject came up about Joseph being the last surnamed Justus, all their daughters having taken their husbands names.

"Tell me the story again about how we inherited our name from our descendants," Joseph asked his mother. "I loved hearing the story when I was young."

"Well," Miriam said, "as you know we are direct descendants of King David and his son, King Solomon. That was their given names, or if you prefer, their first names. Their surnames were Justus like ours."

"Where did they get the name from mother?" Joseph ribbed. "I need to know so that I can tell your grandsons."

"Who would want to marry you son?" Jacob said in a mock serious tone.

"King David Justus was a direct descendant of Adam and Eve," Miriam continued. "They were the first and second people made by God when he visited the Earth. He told Adam to make love with Eve and multiply. Adam said she wasn't his type, and she talked too much. God was cross with Adam and told him he didn't have a choice, for they were the only two humans on earth."

"What did the poor fellow do?" Joseph asked.

"Adam replied, *just us*," Miriam said. "God decreed that because he dared to challenge him, his first male descendent, and his first male born would be surnamed Justus. That would continue on from father to the first born son forever so he could trace the spirited ones. Furthermore, he decreed that the Justus surname would produce famous kings, prophets and religious leaders provided the surname line was never broken."

Joseph laughed. Soon all three of them were in stitches.

"Don't laugh son, I'm being serious," Miriam said. "You need to marry and soon."

"The Justus line is doomed," Jacob chirped. "Who would want to marry this man?"

"I am still looking. I only want the best looker to bear your grandchildren," Joseph laughed.

The three of them laughed until they all had tears in their eyes.

"Which one of you men is going to volunteer to do these dishes," Miriam said.

"That is my job, Mrs Justus," a boy's voice said from the kitchen. "Please leave the plates, and I will collect them."

"How did you enter? Joseph said. The exterior doors are locked."

"There is a tunnel built inside the outer stairway with a small doorway into the walk-in pantry," the boy said. "I stock the pantry with food, clean the wood stove, cook, wash dishes and other small jobs as directed."

"Do you know your way around the rest of the third floor?" Jacob asked.

"Yes sir, but I have been warned not to go past the dining room without Nebedeus' permission—otherwise I will end up in Hell."

"What is your name, boy, and how long have you been doing this work?" Miriam asked.

"My name is Stefan. I have worked here for three years. I like the job, but I am growing too tall for the tunnel and will be replaced when the Chief Priest returns from Jerusalem."

"Well Stefan, finish your duties," Joseph said. "You can prepare roast chicken for our dinner tonight and a plate for yourself."

"Yes sir. I will order a fowl after I have washed the dishes."

Joseph and his parents went to their rooms to change and wash, agreeing to meet in the enclosed veranda on the western side arch in fifteen minutes. Joseph arrived first and looked out at the white limestone cliffs. He could see men sitting around open fires in front of their dug out caves, cooking or eating breakfast. Miriam and Jacob joined him.

"The view from up here is incredible," Jacob said. "You can see the men in their caves and the tracks leading to the vineyards."

"There is another track leading to the caves from the top of the hills," Miriam said.

"You can see where the white limestone ends and the clay layer above begins," Joseph said. "That is where they dig the fine clay for pottery production."

They watched the men working for twenty minutes, and then walked to the southern arch where they could see for miles along the shoreline. The cliffs were on the western side of the vast dark blue lake. The white sand between the two narrowed to a small strip in the distance.

"I think I like this view better," Miriam said.

"I'm sure you do," Jacob said. "You can see the men working in the vegetable gardens. They look quite close."

"We had better move on before grumpy gets too jealous," Miriam laughed as she reached out for Jacob's hand and pulled him along the balcony to the next arch.

"This is my favourite view," Jacob said. "I can look out across the lake and feel as free as those birds."

"The only birds I can see are those white ones," Miriam chirped. "They are the young nuns washing their robes by the edge of the cistern in the Abbey enclosure."

"Who is jealous now," Jacob replied reaching for Miriam's hand.

"I wanted to stay longer at that last view to look for Mary," Joseph said.

"Mary works inside the Abbey. You are as bad as your father, trying to check out the younger girls."

They reached the northern arch where they could see the men working in the vineyards and in the animal enclosures. Jacob looked at the outer stairway.

"That is a design flaw in security. Someone could easily climb onto the balcony from that rest point."

Joseph leant on the window ledge to see where the steps led.

"You can walk right to the flat roof area. I hadn't noticed that from ground level before."

Joseph felt a small iron rod under the lip of the ledge. It felt loose, and he tried to remove it, but could only move it down and up again. After two attempts, he replaced it.

"I like this view too," Miriam said, "but when I get bored of watching those strong men harvesting grapes, I will make us some fresh juice."

"I have waved to Nebedeus from the vineyards many times," Joseph said.

He often looked out from this arch, probably because he could rest on this ledge. He was about to ask his father if he would prefer a *mulsum,* a mixture of wine and honey with water, but froze as he realised he had rung a bell when he moved the iron rod.

The pageboy had answered the call and quietly slid open a wooden hatch. Stefan put his head through the opening and up Joseph's robe. He placed his hands firmly on Joseph's buttocks and pulled him closer.

Miriam and Jacob were standing each side of him, chatting away and pointing out what interested them.

Joseph couldn't move. Stefan had begun fellatio on the surprised priest.

"I will make the juice now. Are you both ready?" Miriam said.

"I am," Jacob replied.

"I will be there soon," Joseph said.

Joseph stayed and looked at the view a while longer knowing he had lost control. He dug his fingers hard into the ledge, breaking his nails. He found himself wondering if Mary would perform oral sex with her soft tongue, her mouth and her beautiful full lips.

"It's ready Joseph," Miriam called.

Stefan heard the call, released his hold on Joseph's buttocks and withdrew from under the robe. He shut the wooden door and disappeared inside the tunnel.

Joseph walked inside.

"I will join you soon. I need to go to the bathroom first."

He washed, changed his wet robe and joined his parents.

"Joseph, what happened to your fingers? Your nails are cracked and bleeding," Miriam said.

"I scraped them on the ledge without realising. They don't hurt."

Jacob finished his drink. He was still feeling tired from the trip, even though he had slept well last night. Miriam felt the same and agreed an hour's nap would be agreeable. Joseph remained at the table. He wanted to sketch the upper floor rooms to scale. He used a two foot square piece of parchment nailed to a frame and some charcoal he found in the pantry. The tower was also square, but the outside stairs were built on the west and north walls, and he wanted to include them on the plan. Joseph pondered if that made it a rectangle, then realised it would still be square. He ruled in the seven foot wide steps first, making sure they matched the building scale.

Joseph heard a noise in the kitchen.

"Is that you, Stefan?"

"Yes sir. I have come to wash the dishes, prepare the wood stove and pluck the fowl for dinner."

"I wasn't aware that I was ringing a bell on the balcony earlier. I thought it was a loose iron rod, and I was trying to pull it out of the wall."

"I wondered that, especially as your parents were standing next to you," Stefan said. "I was careful not to make a noise. I have been feeling low in spirits with Nebedeus telling me I was too tall to continue working in the tunnel. The semen has many mood enhancing qualities, and I feel warm and relaxed now, thanks to you, sir. There is another bell in the dining room. Would you like me to show you where it is?"

"Yes, I looked for a kitchen bell but could not find it."

Stefan walked up to a small statue of Caesar on a marble pillar and lifted it up. Joseph saw a wire attached underneath the statue and running down through the marble stand.

"I can't believe it. Everything is a mystery," Joseph exclaimed. "I want you to show me the tunnel, where it goes, and how it works."

"Yes sir. I can show you, but it is extremely narrow and confined," Stefan warned. "Follow me, sir."

Joseph took off his robe, leaving on only his lap-sash, and followed Stefan through a small sliding panel in the walk-in pantry.

"I will show you my quarters down stairs first, sir."

Stefan could walk along the hidden passage with his head bent forward while Joseph followed with his hands on his knees in a crouched position. Light entered the tunnel through one inch slits left open between some of the huge blocks of stone. Stefan's tiny room was on the ground floor and was connected to a store room by a barred window. The bars were horizontal so that food could be passed to him by the cooks. Stefan was a prisoner in the tunnel and had been for the past three years.

Joseph was dismayed by what he saw.

"I will get you out of here as soon as I can," he said. "What did you do to be confined in such conditions?"

"I was caught eating bread leftovers from the refectory tables instead of cleaning."

"You could have escaped through that hatch on the balcony and run away to another town," Joseph said.

"The hatch locks when it is closed and unlocks when you move the rod that rings the bell," Stefan explained. "If I do anything wrong, I would be sent through a one way door to Hell."

"What Hell are you talking about?" Joseph asked. "Hell is for dead people whom God won't forgive."

"I will show you, sir. But you will have to unlock the door from the end room."

"That would be the main bedroom, but what am I looking for, an iron rod or lever perhaps?" Joseph said.

Stefan led Joseph back to the third floor and opened the sliding panel to the pantry.

Joseph checked that his parents were still asleep and went to the master bedroom. He looked all along the northern wall, but found nothing that would unlock a door at least six feet away. He realised the rod would have to be lower than the balcony floor. He walked into the small room with the toilet and looked down the hole. Joseph felt the inside of the toilet and reached into the cavity with his outstretched hands until he touched cold iron. He grabbed an iron ring and pulled. He felt the bar move and heard a door release. He walked back to the kitchen where Stefan was cleaning the ashes from the stove.

Joseph told him he had unlocked the door. Stefan took the ashes with him in a container and led the way to Hell. He stopped just before the door and threw the ashes down a hole that went straight down to the ground floor. Joseph knew it was the same hole into which his toilet flushed, but didn't mention it to Stefan. Joseph made a mental note to check the opening next time he was in the vineyard. Stefan pushed against the heavy wooden door. It was built on a slight angle that made the door shut as soon as it was released.

Joseph squeezed passed Stefan and asked him to hold the door open in case it locked them in this section of the tunnel. There wasn't any natural light in this section, only a red glow at the end. Joseph crept forward with his hands on his knees as a warm breeze wafted past him and flowed through the open door. He stubbed his toe on something hard. When he realised what it was, he threw it forward in shock. It was a human skull. Someone had died in this section from starvation. Joseph went to the end of the tunnel and looked down. He could see coals glowing red hot and could hear men's voices. Someone was screaming.

Joseph looked up and saw the chimney was barred with no escape. There was a long iron pole to climb down to what would be Hell. It stopped at least ten feet from the bottom. Anybody wanting to live in Hell would have to fall the last ten feet into hot coals and then jump to safety. Joseph never knew anything like this existed, but Nebedeus and King Herod obviously did. Joseph had heard the top floor was called Heaven, the second floor was Earth and the basement was Hell, but until now had not taken it literally.

Joseph decided he would confront Nebedeus about Hell and the tunnel conditions when he returned from Jerusalem. He didn't have the authority to change anything on his own, but he could pressure Nebedeus or Herod. If that failed, he would seek justice through the Roman proconsul. Joseph made his way back to Stefan and told him to head back to the kitchen. He had seen more than he anticipated.

Joseph let the door go. It swung back and clicked. When he tried to open the door, he discovered it had locked behind him.

"You were right, Stefan. The tunnel does lead to Hell. There is no way out. You were right to fear for your life and not try to escape. Had you tried and failed, your life would have been worse than death itself."

They reached the kitchen and were confronted by Jacob and Miriam. Joseph wore just a lap-sash, and he and the boy emerged together. Joseph saw the look on his mother's face, and briefly explained what he was doing and what he had seen.

"I don't want Stefan to sleep in his cramped straw bed one more night," he said. "I will also confront Nebedeus about the man-made Hell in the basement."

"I can't believe Nebedeus would treat people like that," Miriam said.

"I have seen it before," Jacob said. "Power can make men very callous and cruel."

Joseph took his robe and led Stefan to the master bedroom where they could bathe and dress.

"Wash quickly. My parents will be waiting for us in the dining room. Later, you can prepare a bed for yourself in the corner. There is plenty of room."

Stefan prepared lunch and served the meal, after which he went about his daily duties while Joseph sat with his parents.

"After we have eaten, I would like to talk to the poor souls in the basement dungeon."

"I will accompany you," Jacob said.

"I would like to visit Mary and Ilana before we leave tomorrow," Miriam said.

"You are welcome to stay longer, you know that," Joseph said.

"We would love to, but this was an unplanned visit and we have other commitments," Miriam replied.

"It certainly was unexpected," Jacob said. "We haven't much time left. We had better make hay while the sun shines."

Jacob escorted Miriam to the Abbey and returned to find Joseph.

"We need to find a door to a room we never knew existed," Jacob said.

"I am sure it is not an internal door as I know the interior of the monastery like the back of my hand," Joseph said.

"I suggest we begin our search in the vineyard," Jacob said.

They tasted different varieties of grapes. Both preferred the larger red grapes which were sweet, juicy and had fewer pips. Joseph looked up at the archway and thought of Stefan.

He had waved to Nebedeus many times from this position while the Chief Priest was standing on his private balcony enjoying fellatio.

"Father, we were standing up there earlier."

"Yes we were. It is a different world down here amongst the vines."

"What I was going to say was, I saw a curve in the outer wall. I think we should investigate near the wall first. "

"You are right. It would be hard to find a secret tunnel entrance out here."

They found a small dome that was large enough to hide a doorway. Joseph stepped over what appeared to be garden soil. He peered up the hole to see if there was a ladder but couldn't see anything. He heard a sound of some kind. Joseph turned to his father, but before he could utter a word, he was hit by a bucketful of vegetable scraps. Joseph laughed.

"I think I know what we are having for dinner."

"At least you have found where the waste goes. How lucky are you that I decided to come with you? You may have been hit by something a lot worse."

"Okay, where to now?"

"We have eliminated the northern wall. We might as well explore the eastern side while we are here."

"That side has a ten foot high wall that extends from the tower to the Abbey enclosure where the ceremony was held. We can check that from the other side."

"Maybe, but first I want to see why someone went to the trouble of laying a wide cobblestone pathway along the wall. It leads towards the lake but abruptly ends twenty yards after the tower."

"It was probably used at one time but is now overgrown from lack of traffic."

"You are probably right, Joseph, but we need to eliminate it."

They walked to the end of the tower. Jacob continued to the end of the path. Joseph leant against the building wall, knowing that his father would have to turn back soon. *I know where I get my stubborn streak from*, thought Joseph. He watched the men picking grapes and then glanced back towards his father, but he had disappeared.

Joseph ran towards the end of the path with the disconcerting feeling of his heart in his mouth.

Jacob had found a door and entered into a narrow building. Joseph found the door open and watched as his father pounded on another door.

"This must be attached to the larger building on the other side of the wall. It is used for storage," said Joseph.

"No one has answered yet," Jacob said.

Joseph knocked using a piece of wood from the stack nearby.

"State your business," a gruff voice from behind the door said.

"I am the Chief Priest, unlock this door at once."

"I require the password."

"Nebedeus has gone to Jerusalem on an urgent mission. In his haste, he did not tell me the password."

"I have orders not to open the door to anyone without the password or written papers. If you have a document, slide it under the door. If not, you must leave. This area is off limits."

"I am ordering you to open this door immediately," Joseph said.

There was no reply. Joseph knocked again.

"Open this door at once. That is an order."

"We have found what we were looking for," Jacob said. "There is little you can do unless you are permanently appointed to the position. That will not happen if you cause waves at this time. You must remain silent for now and release these poor wretches later."

Joseph agreed. Elated they had found the secret entrance, but frustrated they were denied entry. He could order the guards to break down the door, but he knew he didn't have the full authority and any action now could be reversed.

"Let's go back upstairs and enjoy a freshly made *mulsum*. Stefan makes it with half wine, part honey and water. It's delicious."

"That sounds good. At my age, I need to dress often." Jacob said.

"Why do you have to dress often?"

"Dress stands for *Drink, rest, eat and short sleeps.*"

Joseph laughed.

"What has age got to do with it? I could easily do the same."

Joseph had the uneasy feeling they were being watched. He looked around and up towards the cliff tracks but could not see anyone watching. A thought flashed through his mind. Stefan could see the cliffs and the vineyard through the one inch slits in the tunnel. He must be more careful. What if Stefan was still loyal to Nebedeus and spying on his behalf? As they climbed up the steps, Joseph realised Stefan would hear their footsteps and probably follow them inside the tunnel. He could probably hear their conversations. Joseph tapped his father on the shoulder and indicated to him to be quiet. He pointed down, and Jacob nodded, acknowledging he understood.

"Did you enjoy your walk to the vineyard, father?"

"I certainly did. I am impressed with the new variety of grapevines. I must ask Nebedeus if I can have some cuttings when they prune the vines."

"Look, mother has returned from her stroll along the lake, and she is carrying fruit from the garden. Wait here while I help her."

Miriam stopped as she saw Joseph.

"Thank you for helping. I was given more fruit than I could carry."

"I can see that. We think Stefan can see and hear us from inside the tunnel," Joseph whispered. "Keep your conversation general until we get inside. We have found the doorway to the basement."

"Where did you find it?"

"Father found it in a narrow building in the vineyard. We will tell you about it upstairs, away from the kitchen and dining room."

Jacob kissed Miriam.

"Did you enjoy your walk along the foreshore, dear?"

"Yes darling, I loved the refreshing sea breeze. We never get that in Ramah during the summer months, though we get plenty of cold winds in winter."

"That may be so, but we have the thermal springs in Ramah."

Joseph picked up the statue of Caesar and rang the bell. Stefan appeared on cue, albeit a little too quickly for Joseph's liking.

"Prepare a pitcher of *mulsum* and bring three tumblers. Wash and cut up some of this fruit and prepare some for yourself."

"Yes sir. I will serve your drinks first. You must be thirsty after your walk."

Joseph was enjoying his beverage when the bell in the office rang.

"Excuse me. Daniel must need my attention."

Joseph went to his office and spoke into a tube running down to the Bishop's office. He hated using it, but spoke loudly and clearly.

"Yes, Daniel?"

"There is a messenger from Jerusalem with news from Nebedeus," Daniel said.

"I will come down."

Daniel introduced Levi to Joseph.

"Good morning sir," Levi said. "I have two messages, one from Jerusalem and another from Mazin."

"What is the message from Jerusalem?"

"Nebedeus said the King is seriously ill, but stabilised. He has sent the eight male staff back to Ramah, and he will be detained in Jerusalem until the next full moon."

"What is the message from Mazin?"

"The Roman soldiers ambushed the bandits from two directions. They killed fourteen bandits and captured nine. The fighting was intense and limited to arm to arm combat in the narrow gorge. The soldiers outnumbered the bandits ten to one, but because only three soldiers could attack from each side, many bandits in the middle escaped using rope ladders."

"That is excellent news."

"There is one other thing. They found Isaac alive."

"Our prayers have been answered," Daniel said.

"Isaac was found tied to a stake. He had his tongue cut off because he refused to talk."

"Is Isaac married?" Joseph asked.

"No, he is only nineteen."

"When he recuperates, ask him to visit the monastery. We can teach him to write and offer him a position as a scribe. Give Isaac our thanks and wishes for a speedy recovery."

"Thank you, sir. I will gladly deliver your message."

"Do you know if the captured bandits are being held at Hyrcania, or will they be escorted to Jerusalem for a public trial?"

"The nine prisoners all pleaded guilty to murder, theft and cannibalism, and one died during torture. The commander has publically whipped the other bandits and crucified them on crosses erected outside the fortress."

Daniel went pale at the idea of men dying on crosses.

"I think beheading should be mandatory as a death penalty. Crucifixion is so inhumane."

"The commander wants the bandits to suffer over three or four days," Levi said. "That is the penalty for crimes against the Roman Empire. It gives the culprits time to reflect on their crime before dying and sends a stern warning to others not to disobey the law.

Personally, I think it is justice for what they did to Isaac and those innocent pilgrims."

"The Holy Book supports your belief, an eye for an eye, a tooth for a tooth. Thank you for delivering the messages Levi. Daniel will arrange overnight accommodation and dinner in the refectory for you."

Joseph left the two men and walked up the stairway. A myriad of thoughts flashed through his mind. He would keep the Chief Priest position for thirty days, long enough time to decide whether he would remain celibate or marry Mary. On the other hand, it was still not enough time to alter the conditions in the basement for the entombed men. That would have to wait until he replaced Nebedeus permanently. In the meantime, he would gain the trust of Stefan and enjoy his time in Heaven.

Jacob and Miriam waited in the dining room for Joseph to return.

"I feel the need for another walk. Would you like to observe the view from the roof?"

On the roof, they found a marble table and two matching benches. They were dusty and covered with cobwebs, obviously not one of Nebedeus' normal viewing platforms. Joseph marvelled at the three hundred and sixty degree view and envisaged having an outdoor massage with the sun warming his oiled body. He dusted the benches with his hands.

"Please sit down. The messenger brought excellent news."

Next morning, Joseph arranged for a donkey pulled wagon to take his parents' home and rang for Stefan.

"Good morning, sir."

"Stefan, I would like you to become my page if Nebedeus does dismiss you. I need to know if I have your complete trust and loyalty before I give you that position."

"I give you my word, sir. I would be honoured to be your page and companion."

"I have a driver's uniform here. If I grant you outside leave, would you promise to take my parents' home today and return tomorrow?"

"Yes sir. If I failed to return, I would spend the rest of my life in Hell. I know that."

"Change into the uniform, and I will write you out a two day pass."

Joseph hugged his parents and waved goodbye as Stefan proudly drove the wagon out of the monastery compound and along the foreshore towards Mazin.

Over the next thirty days, Joseph performed the Chief Priest duties diligently. He actually found the work load less demanding than being Bishop. Over the four weeks, he was required to receive travelling dignities on three occasions and send the monthly report to Herod's palace at Masada. He found a copy of one of Nebedeus' early reports with a description of the monastery hierarchy and doctrine.

Nebedeus report stated the monastery was divided into two groups, celibate males and celibate females. The men openly practised homosexual acts, the Qumran Monastery was known as Sodom. The women were strictly homosexual, only performing oral sexual acts and remained virgins. The Abbey was known as Gomorrah. They ate poultry, fish, and vegetables and drank wine. Everyone considered red meat to be unclean. They believed in an eternal spiritual life in heaven after a physical death on earth. They believed God almighty lived and travelled in the universe and was the creator of all things. The Chief Priest was regarded as his worldly representative, an earthly God that communicated with the priests. The monastery itself was divided into three zones- the third floor represented Heaven, the second and ground floors as Earth and the basement as Hell. Outside the compound was called *the world.*

Joseph was concerned, but not shocked, that such information was being leaked to Herod. The information would be passed to Roman authorities, who in turn would inform the Senate and Caesar. Joseph kept his report minimal. He stated Nebedeus had travelled to Jerusalem during the month of Tammuz to attend matters concerning the state, and he had been anointed acting Chief Priest for a period of one month, Daniel appointed Bishop, and Malachi appointed Priest for the same period. The monastery and Abbey were operating efficiently and at full capacity.

***

August, 9 B.C.
(Roman year 745 A.U.C.)

Nebedeus and his entourage returned to Qumran on the second day of the of the full moon cycle, accompanied by his new pageboy Rafael. He dismissed the neophyte priests, allowing them the rest of the day free of duties. Their daily rostered duties would recommence after sunrise tomorrow, exempting the priests from the early morning hourly prayers. Rafael was dispatched with a message for Bishop Daniel. He knocked on the Bishop's door.

"Who is it?" Daniel said.

"Rafael, I am the new page for His Holiness."

"Come in Rafael, the door is unlocked."

Daniel looked at the young man. He was slightly built with black hair, brown eyes and beautiful olive skin. Considering his small frame, the boy had an excellent physique.

"Good afternoon Holy Spirit. Nebedeus has instructed me to inform you of his arrival. He wishes to have a meeting with the three acting clergymen in his office."

Daniel asked the youth, whom he judged to be twelve years old, to find Priest Malachi and advise him to proceed to the Chief Priest office. Daniel tapped on the tube and Joseph responded.

"Yes Daniel."

"Joseph, I have been informed of the arrival of Nebedeus. Malachi will join us for a meeting in ten minutes."

The three clergymen talked about their recent higher duty experiences until they heard Nebedeus approach.

"Good afternoon brothers, I trust all went well in my absence," Nebedeus said.

"Yes, Your Holiness," Joseph said. "The anointing ceremonies were well received and all the higher duties were performed efficiently under the short notice given."

"I had a very hectic schedule with some dramas as you are aware. I would appreciate everyone resume their previous positions and accommodation within two hours. Malachi, I congratulate you on performing the duties of a priest for the first time. You are now dismissed."

"Thank you, Your Holiness and welcome back sir." Malachi bowed and departed.

"Joseph and Daniel, you may inform the monastery clergy that King Herod's health has improved and he has returned to his palace at Masada. Daniel, congratulations on performing the higher duties as Bishop, you may return to your Head Priest duties now."

"Thank you Nebedeus, and welcome back," Daniel said.

Nebedeus refrained from speaking until Daniel bowed and left the office.

"Joseph, what we discuss must remain confidential."

"Yes sir, of course."

"Herod was close to death when I arrived in Jerusalem. Without my intervention, he would have died. I summoned Theudas for his medical knowledge of poisons. His nurses administered a special herbal concoction every four hours for the first two weeks. The aloe in the mixture purged his stomach and bowels. The herbs and other ingredients absorbed most of the toxins in his body. Herod lost a considerable amount of weight, but by the third week his body accepted soups and stews. Herod was eating chicken and vegetables when I left."

"You mentioned poisoning. Was it accidental?" Joseph asked.

"Herod had arsenic poisoning," Nebedeus said. "He believes his two oldest sons and the High Priest conspired to assassinate him. The king is very grateful to Theudas and me for saving his life. He has invited me to stay in his palace in Jerusalem for two weeks in October. He wants the conspirators arrested, a quick trial conducted for public transparency, and seek Caesar's consent to apply capital punishment to the ones found guilty."

"Simeon Boethus has been a loyal High Priest to Herod for fourteen years, and his daughter, Mariamne is one of the king's wives. It seems out of character for him to be involved in a plot to kill Herod." Joseph said.

Nebedeus squirmed in his chair.

"Herod has been acting irrationally in recent months, mainly due to chronic pain from a long term illness. Perhaps his sons convinced Simeon it would be a mercy killing."

"Simeon is a Pharisee and supports the monarchy. It would cause political upheaval if a Sadducee Priest is appointed as they favour Roman rule."

"That is for Herod and his advisers to decide. Do you have you any more questions before you vacate my apartment?"

"I do have some concerns," Joseph replied, "mainly concerning the workers in the basement and staff being kept in the tunnel."

"That is my affair Joseph," Nebedeus snapped. "You can alter the system to suit your needs when you are permanently appointed. I have a new pageboy called Rafael. Stefan can teach him his duties over the next seven days. On the eighth day he will be escorted to the ground floor lockup, he knows too much about my security system to be allowed in public."

Joseph stood up. "I have promised the lad a position as my pageboy. I understand you require him for another week, but then Stefan can work for me. He knows he must keep his silence."

"I do not appreciate your tone of voice Joseph. However, I realise you have bonded with the boy and will keep him on a tight leash. If he blasphemes, he will definitely be sent straight to hell. Thank you Joseph, you are dismissed."

"Your Holiness."

Joseph bowed his head and walked upstairs to the luxurious apartment for his final hour as Chief Priest. He rang the bell and Stefan appeared immediately, he had sensed Joseph would need him.

"Remove your bedding from the main bedroom and pack my personal belongings."

Stefan fell to Joseph's feet.

"Sir, please remember me. I will be locked in the dungeon soon."

"Stefan, do as you have been told. Have faith, pray to God Almighty for a just outcome and do your utmost to obey Nebedeus right up until the time of your dismissal." Joseph held the gold key for one more time and reluctantly placed it on the bedside table. "Stefan, bring my personal belongings to my quarters next to the Bishop office."

Nebedeus was nowhere to be seen, which was a small blessing for Joseph. The last thirty days had passed so quickly that it already felt just like a dream. He had been the Essene God, worshipped and revered by the monastery clergy, and waited on by hand and foot by Stefan. Joseph sat on his bed, his head bowed, his eyes shut. Stefan placed the personal items on the table and quietly left the room.

Stefan showed Rafael the tunnel passageway between the kitchen and his straw bed. The twelve year old boy was horrified. It was not at all what he had envisaged.

"I thought I would sleep in the bedroom next to the master, not on this pile of hay."

"If you please the Chief Priest at night, he usually falls asleep afterwards. You can sleep in his comfortable bed all night and sneak out in the morning before he wakes."

"What if he wakes up and finds me in his bed?"

"Provided he didn't tell you to leave, he won't scold you, besides he is a late riser. I must warn you, we are forbidden to go past the dining room without prior permission."

The two boys walked up the enclosed stairwell. Stefan noted how Rafael could walk upright, just as he could when he began work three years earlier.

"Where do you rest during the day, between your chores?" Rafael asked.

"There is a hammock behind the pantry where you can lay down. I prefer to remain in the kitchen for as long as possible."

The service bell rang. Stefan slid the door open and ushered Rafael into the large pantry. Nebedeus was sitting at the dining room table.

"Yes, Your Highness," Stefan said. "May we be of service?"

"Raise the flag with the Chief Priest emblem, and fill the oil lamps. I will be eating alone tonight, prepare chicken and vegetables for dinner."

Stefan attached the flag to the cord and raised it to full mast.

"That indicates the Chief Priest has returned and is residing in the tower apartment."

A live cockerel was handed to the boys through the barred window. It vigorously flapped its wings until Stefan held it by the legs and dangled it head down. The rooster's legs were tied, its head decapitated and its body hung over the tunnel hole to bleed.

The Abbey raised a yellow flag to indicate the priestess wanted to meet Nebedeus in the neutral courtyard.

Gabriel, a male eunuch, pinned a written message on the notice board: *The Chief Priest will attend the court one hour before sunset.*

Two nuns arranged the chairs for the meeting and placed tumblers of water on the table.

Both parties arrived as the monastery bells tolled eleven times, announcing the final afternoon hour of daylight. Gabriel and Sister Naomi stood in the shade by their respective gates.

Nebedeus surmised Ilana wanted to hear firsthand about his trip. He told her about the horrifying incident with the bandits and how he saved the king from certain death. He glorified the events to impress Ilana, but she seemed unmindful of his story.

"You had a successful trip, but unfortunately I have some bad news," Ilana said.

Nebedeus looked surprised.

"What haven't I been told?"

"Joseph was anointed Chief Priest by Sister Mary while I performed the prayer service."

"I know that, he had my blessing. Joseph should have anointed Daniel as bishop, and Malachi as senior priest, in shorter ceremonies."

"Yes, that is what happened. However, Mary has had morning sickness every day since the event and she informed me that she missed her monthly period."

"Has she seen a doctor?"

"Our physician has confirmed Mary is pregnant, but she hasn't had coital intercourse."

"That is impossible," Nebedeus declared.

"I believe I know what happened, but I haven't got proof yet. Mary admitted that she forgot to wear the protective underwear in the ritual bath."

"I don't understand. You said she didn't have intercourse."

"The physicians believe Joseph may have ejaculated in the warm water while Mary was anointing him. The semen survived and fertilised Mary, similar to how some fish fertilise their mate's eggs in the river."

"I have never heard anything like this before, but I will interview Joseph in the morning."

"The sun will set soon, we can conclude this tomorrow," Ilana said.

"I will meet you here after noon prayers, after I talk with Joseph."

Nebedeus returned to his apartment, he felt overwhelmed and bewildered. He ate his

dinner in gulps, while he fathomed out the latest problem to solve on his road to glory.

"Stefan, clear the table and have an early night. Do not light the lamps."

"Yes, Your Holiness."

"Rafael, come with me."

Nebedeus took his frustration out on the pageboy. Rafael lay motionless beside Nebedeus, and waited until his master fell asleep. He gathered his robe and in the darkness felt his way back to the kitchen. Stefan anticipated the boy's return and led the twelve year old to his bedroom. Stefan's intimate knowledge of Nebedeus' bad behaviour prepared him for the consolation of the frightened and distressed lad. Rafael sobbed uncontrollably until he fell asleep in Stefan's arms.

Early the next morning Nebedeus summoned Joseph to his office.

"I have been informed that Sister Mary is four weeks pregnant."

"I have been betrothed to Mary since she was thirteen, but now that she has betrayed me I will divorce her," Joseph said. "I will delay any future marriage plans until later in life."

"I wish it was that easy Joseph, for all our sakes," Nebedeus said. "Virgin Mary is of royal blood, we cannot afford a scandal that will damage the monastery reputation."

"She is hardly the virgin now, becoming pregnant to an unknown man."

"You know Virgin refers to Sister Mary's rank, not her sexual status," Nebedeus said. "I have one question you must answer either yes, or no."

Joseph drank some water to moisten his parched throat.

"Did you ejaculate in the ritual bath?" Nebedeus said.

Joseph spluttered, spraying water over the desk.

"I take that as a yes," Nebedeus said. "Your semen survived in the water and fertilised Mary."

"I have never heard of anyone becoming pregnant without intercourse. I admit I prematurely ejaculated as

Mary anointed me with oil. Her hands were so gentle and soft that I couldn't prevent my feelings controlling my reactions."

"You must declare the child as yours and marry Mary."

"I will marry Mary, but not until I discuss the matter with my parents."

"I will convey your proposal to Ilana. You may go now."

Joseph bowed his head.

"Thank you, Your Highness," he said.

Nebedeus rang his service bell and Stefan presented.

"Where is Rafael?" Nebedeus asked.

"He is not well sir. He is still asleep."

"Bring me a cold lemon juice and honey."

Nebedeus thought about his options. He had to keep the nun's pregnancy quiet until he was promoted. It would be better if Joseph didn't marry before the baby's birth. That would make the child illegitimate and unworthy for priesthood later in life. The Pharisee sect had worked hard to dislodge the Justus heirs from regaining religious supremacy, and he wasn't going to let it happen on his watch. He would need to marry and have a son before Joseph had a legitimate child, so that the dynasty heritage would favour his family chronologically.

Nebedeus met Ilana for the second meeting as arranged.

"I have interviewed Joseph and he confirmed your theory," Nebedeus said

"Will he marry Mary?"

"Yes, once he has discussed the marriage arrangements with his family. Tell Mary that Joseph sends his love. He will inform her parents, arrange the wedding venue, and list his family guests."

"Mary will want to know the wedding date," Ilana said.

"I want their wedding delayed for at least another ninety days."

"Why ninety days?" Ilana asked.

Nebedeus hesitated, leaned closer to Ilana and whispered.

"That will ensure their child is born illegitimate and unworthy for priesthood. I will need to produce an heir before their second child is born."

"I suggest you marry as soon as possible," Ilana said.

"I haven't chosen a bride yet. I could marry my cousin Hannah just to produce heirs."

"I will ensure this matter is contained within the Abbey," Ilana said. "Mary will be sworn to silence, and her robe will hide the pregnancy for months."

"I will inform Joseph that Mary would prefer to marry after the birth of the baby."

"I will comfort Mary and let her know Joseph's wishes."

Nebedeus and Ilana stood up, bowed to each other and departed with their aides.

Joseph watched the meeting from his office window and pondered what had been said. He realised too late that he should have requested permission to attend. Nebedeus walked towards the tower stairway and disappeared around the corner. Joseph paced back and forth, unable to concentrate. He looked at the bell on the wall, willing it to ring. He looked towards the Abbey, and wondered how Mary was coping.

Mary sat on her bed. She was disappointed that Joseph had not arranged a meeting with her, but accepted Ilana's explanation that her conception must remain strictly confidential. Joseph had sent his love and pledged to marry her. She slid Joseph's ring on her finger. She would have to remain strong in her faith and place her trust in Joseph.

The bell in the bishop office rang, and Joseph talked into the tube.

"Yes Your Highness."

"Joseph, report to my office."

Nebedeus gestured to Joseph to sit.

"I have discussed your situation with Ilana. Mary will write out her family guest list and has agreed to your wishes. However, Mary doesn't want to show in her wedding robe, and would prefer to marry after the baby is born."

"I agree to her request, but I would like to have a meeting with Mary face to face."

"Ilana has ruled that out. The Abbey cannot risk rumours of a heterosexual affair, or even worse, a nun becoming pregnant."

Joseph slumped back in the chair, feeling disheartened by the lack of personal contact with Mary. Nebedeus reacted instinctively.

"Joseph, I have decided to take leave. I wish to visit Herod, but I am not sure you are in the right frame of mind to perform the Chief Priest duties."

Joseph sat upright.

"When would you take leave?"

"In two weeks, on Monday 12th August."

"I can assure you I will be fully prepared," Joseph said.

The meeting ended. Nebedeus had averted a possible complication by manipulating Joseph's thoughts away from Mary's predicament.

Nebedeus wrote to Hannah, asking for her hand in marriage. The betrothal ceremony would take place in the Masada palatial gardens on Sunday 18th August. He rolled the scroll and tied it with red string. He also wrote to King Herod, requesting permission to visit with Hannah and his entourage in mid-August. He tied the scroll with gold string. He melted wax over both scroll strings and pressed in his official seal.

Nebedeus rang the bishop's bell.

"Yes, Your Highness," Joseph said.

"I will drop two addressed scrolls down the tube. Despatch two reliable couriers to those addresses, and instruct them to wait for a reply."

Joseph noticed one was for Herod.

"Sir, I sent the monthly report to King Herod's palace, even though I wasn't sure if he had returned from Jerusalem."

"Thank you Joseph. Despatch mine as well, I want to know if the king's health has continued to improve."

Joseph sent a messenger to his parents in Ramah. He invited them to stay and for dinner on the 12th August, in the upper apartment.

Within a week, all the messages had been answered. Joseph's parents accepted the dinner invitation. Joseph personally delivered the two scrolls addressed to Nebedeus, hoping to gain some favourable information. Nebedeus opened the scroll from Jerusalem first, which surprised Joseph. Nebedeus read the scroll.

"Thank you Joseph, you are dismissed."

Joseph shut the door and lingered in the corridor until Nebedeus opened the second scroll. He heard a fist pound the table, followed by a loud yes. Joseph walked away quietly, scratching his head as he pondered what news the messages contained. He knew the first scroll was from Hannah, a close relative of Nebedeus. The other one was from Herod. His health must have improved. Joseph heard the bell ring in his office and ran to the tube.

"Yes, Your Holiness."

"The king has invited me to his palace; he has fully regained his wellbeing. I will be his guest at Masada for several days, before travelling to Jerusalem."

"That is excellent news, Your Holiness."

"Herod has indicated that he favours me for promotion as the next High Priest, it is only a matter of protocol and for the position to become vacant."

Joseph could hardly control himself. He gritted his teeth and clenched his hands.

"Congratulations Nebedeus, I am honoured to be the first to hear of your success. You will be an excellent replacement for Simeon and a good political adviser for Herod. I believe it is imperative that Palestine remains under the influence of Pharisee adhortation."

"The position of Chief Priest will become available after my departure. This conversation is to remain strictly confidential between us until I depart."

"Yes sir, I know there are loose ends to be tied before you can be appointed High Priest."

Nebedeus leant back in his chair and relaxed. *What loose ends? As far as he was concerned, everything had gone to plan. King Herod had survived the poisoning and had accepted Hannah and himself as guests. Hannah had agreed to his marriage proposal. Simeon would be beheaded, or at the very least, defrocked and dismissed. Joseph's wedding would be delayed, making his upcoming child illegitimate, and illegible for priesthood. The position of High Priest was almost in his grasp. He would become the most powerful man in Jerusalem. He would be the Temple head priest, be chairman of the Sanhedrin, the highest court in the land, and personal adviser to King Herod.*

CHAPTER 4: The Quest

Qumran Monastery
12th August

Joseph gazed out of the south-facing window of the monastery tower. He watched Nebedeus and his pageboy Rafael depart. They had arranged safe passage to Masada on a passing camel train. The camels passed by the outer gardens and disappeared into the early morning haze.

Unbeknown to Joseph, Nebedeus had secretly arranged to take Mary with him to Jerusalem where he would meet with Hannah. They would stay overnight and then travel to Masada, stopping briefly at Bethlehem to allow Mary to stay with her Auntie and Uncle. Joseph turned away from the scene and walked towards his large wooden desk. A strange sensation ran through Joseph's mind as he realised today's events emulated those of two months ago. The only difference was this time the changes would be of a more permanent basis.

Joseph summoned Daniel and Malachi to his office.

"Good morning Brothers. I have an important announcement that concerns both of you."

The two priests glanced at each other, frowned inquisitively and turned to face Joseph.

"This morning, Nebedeus resigned for personal reasons. Before he departed, he appointed me as Chief Priest."

"Congratulations, Your Holiness," Daniel said. "The monastery will benefit greatly from your leadership and integrity."

"Malachi, I hereby appoint you as a senior priest, in the presence of Daniel."

"Thank you, Your Holiness, I am honoured to be chosen to serve the monastery on a higher level."

"Daniel, I hereby pass on my holy spirit to you. I appoint you as bishop in the presence of priest Malachi."

"Thank you, Your Holiness. I promise to uphold the monastery traditions and the will of God."

Joseph asked Daniel to announce the day's proceedings at the noon prayer service, which included the main communal meal. The appointments would not be sanctified with an official anointing ceremony on this occasion because there had not been a ninety day break between the acting and permanent appointments. However, Daniel could arrange an anointing of heads at the noon prayer service. Joseph handed Daniel the keys to the bishop's office.

"I will leave the daily running of the monastery in your capable hands. I have changes to implement, relating to the Chief Priest office, that needs urgent attention."

Joseph bowed and walked to his new office. He thanked God in prayer for delivering the Chief Priest position to him. Joseph had thoughts materialise while he was praying to God.

"Thank you Lord God. I will implement your suggestions today. Amen."

Joseph wrote down God's instructions:

Release the poor souls in hell.

Free the men enclosed on the ground floor.

Change the naming of the hierarchy and add one more position.

Investigate the contents in the locked room on the upper floor.

Joseph talked on the tube.

"Daniel, I require your assistance for one hour before noon prayers."

"I am available now, Your Holiness."

"Good, meet me in the vineyard, and bring six workers from the mines with picks and

sledge hammers."

Joseph led the men to the ground floor building that his father had discovered. He knocked on the door and spoke to the man that answered from inside.

"Unlock the door. I have the document you require."

"Slide the document under the door."

The doorman read the article and opened the door. Joseph shook the man's hand.

"I am the new Chief Priest. What is your name and rank?"

"My name is Ike. I am the overseer."

"We are here to free you men. I want you to guide us to the room called Hell."

"That room is sealed, Your Holiness, except for the two small chutes for the prisoner's food and supplies. Anyone sent to Hell stays there forever."

"Take me to the chutes," Joseph said.

The group moved along a dimly lit passageway that sloped down to a storage room stockpiled with wood. Ike's crew would slide the wood down the chute for the prisoners to fire the inbuilt kilns. Joseph yelled down the chute.

"Can anyone hear me? I have come to release you."

A wretched soul peered up the steep shaft at Joseph.

"I am the Chief Priest. I am here to grant you your freedom."

Joseph could barely stand the heat rising up through the shaft. How the poor men survived down there was beyond him.

"Stand away from the wall. The miners will break through."

Joseph lined the miners in three pairs. He offered to pay a silver shekel to the two men who broke through the wall first—a week's wages. The other four miners would each receive a denarius coin, a day's wage. The miners toiled for an hour before the large stone they targeted split in two and smaller cracks radiated towards the edges. After another half an hour of hard slogging, a section of the stone collapsed. The men inside rushed to the hole and cleared the rubble with their bare hands. A teenage boy dived through the opening, hugging the first rescuer he saw, bringing the miner to tears. Five more men crawled through the gap, each finding a miner to shake hands or to hug.

"Bishop Daniel, please escort the six men from the dungeon and the four men from the lock-up section to the communal cistern and let them bathe."

The men filed past Joseph. Each man thanked him profusely and bent down to kiss him on his sandals, before following the bishop up the passageway. The men had not seen the sunlight for years and were blinded by the brightness as they approached the open door. Daniel picked up a branch for the leading man to hold. The other men followed in line. They held one hand over their eyes and the other hand on the shoulder of the man in front as they walked through the vineyards. The men felt the warmth of the sun on their skin, the wind in their hair and the damp ground of the vineyard soil on their bare feet.

They heard the birds chirping and smelt the fragrance of ripe grapes as they brushed against the leaves on the vines. A group of men harvesting grapes clapped and cheered when they realised the men had been freed. Daniel led the men across the sandy courtyard to the lowest cistern, used for communal bathing. The men removed their soiled robes, entered the water, splashed each other and laughed like children. For the first time in years their weary faces bore smiles.

"Remain here until the deacons arrive," Daniel said. "They will issue you with clean robes and towels, and then escort you to the refectory for a meal. One hour later, ask one of the deacons to escort you to my office on the second floor. You must attend."

Joseph rang his desk bell and Stefan arrived with a tray containing a jug of *mulsum* and a roll filled with cheese, chicken, sliced carrot and lettuce.

"That is exactly what I wanted," Joseph said. "I will be in the office for a few hours, bring me another serve at noon."

Joseph crossed off the first and second revelation on his list and pondered about the new hierarchy for the monastery. The answer came to him almost immediately.

"Thank you God. Amen."

Joseph would still be called His/Your Highness, but instead of Chief Priest, he would be called Most High. The Essene God living in Heaven. Bishop Daniel would be the Chief Priest, managing the monastery procedures and the go between himself and the Bishop. Priest Timothy would be the Bishop, orate the main prayer services at sunrise, noon and sunset, and be in charge of four priests. All other clergy duties would remain the same. He decided to discuss the changes with Daniel before the ten men were interviewed.

Stefan knocked on the door and entered with the second tray of food and beverages.

"Do you know where Nebedeus kept the key to the room next door?" Joseph asked.

"Not really sir," Stefan replied, "but I know he always came to this room before he unlocked the spare room."

"I will check this desk while you search behind the paintings and chairs."

Joseph found a hidden compartment, but it was empty. Stefan searched, but also came up empty handed. He climbed on one of the chairs and felt along the top of the walls. Joseph ate his roll, and watched Stefan reach and stretch as he searched. His robe rose and fell, framing his slim buttocks and showing his olive thighs.

"I can't find any cavities," Stefan said feeling dejected.

"Check the door jamb, it may be hollow," Joseph said.

Stefan tapped the wooden jamb, but it sounded solid.

"I will not give up, sir. The key is here somewhere, although I fear it will probably be in the last place I look."

Joseph laughed.

"It is always in the last place you look. Why would you keep looking after you found what you were looking for?"

Stefan stood on a chair to tap the bearer and held the door for support. His hand touched cold metal. The key was hidden in a slot carved in the top of the wooden door.

Joseph grabbed the key from Stefan, slid it into the lock and turned it. The door creaked open. Joseph was amazed at what he saw. On the floor lay a large clay model of the Palestine terrain. Two murals on opposite walls showed the Dead Sea Lake at different levels. One mural showed the lake above sea level and was labelled as fresh water with an abundance of fish. The other mural showed the lake well below sea level, with salt water and no fish, as the Dead Sea stood today.

The lake basin was made from copper and built on a board that could be raised or lowered to match either one of the murals. At the high position, the mural clearly showed the fresh water lake was the head of two major rivers that split into two more rivers. The rivers flowed both north and south of the lake and were much higher than the present Dead Sea level. The names of the rivers were labelled the Euphrates, Pishon, Gihon and the Tigris. The land was covered with forests and had two human figures named Adam and Eve.

It was obvious to Joseph that Nebedeus believed this area was once the fabled Garden of Eden. Joseph raised the board so that the lake would be above sea level.

"Stefan, fill two large jugs with water and bring them here."

Joseph poured water into the lake basin. One jug filled the lake to full capacity. The second Jug made the rivers flow north and south, draining the lake of similar volumes of water from two directions.

"Stefan, fetch two more jugs of water," Joseph said.

Joseph lowered the board so that the lake would be below sea level and placed a boat in the Qumran *Wadi*. Stefan and Joseph poured water over the Palestine landscape. The water rushed through the creeks and wadis, and flooded the entire valley.

"I can't believe it," Joseph said, "this model was built to demonstrate the biblical story of Noah's flood."

"Adam and Eve are standing under an apple tree," Stefan said, "near the town of Mird."

"This part of the world was very different four thousand years ago," Joseph said. "Before mankind, this area was high above sea level and the lake was filled with fresh water, supporting animal life. God created Adam and Eve. He decreed they could live in paradise, but not eat the fruit of the apple. They disobeyed his command and God destroyed the Garden of Eden with a massive earthquake."

"Did Adam and Eve survive the earthquake?" Stefan asked.

"Yes, their descendants occupied the area around the lake shoreline, even though the lake had fallen below sea level. Unfortunately, most of the population drowned when the whole valley flooded after a prolonged storm. Noah and his family lived on a large boat, they were the only survivors, together with the animals he had on board."

"What happened to Noah and the boat?" Stefan asked.

"The lake overflowed and the boat, described in the Bible as an Ark, was swept into the Red Sea. According to the Holy Book of Genesis, it rained for forty days and forty nights, and the whole Earth flooded. The Ark came to rest in the mountainous region of Ararat."

"When was the great flood?" Stefan asked."

"Two thousand, three hundred and forty years ago," Joseph said. "However, if Nebedeus is correct with his model, the event was horrific, but only flooded the valley and desert regions. No doubt, over hundreds of generations, without a written account, the story grew to be a worldwide flood."

The bishop bell rang. Joseph dismissed Stefan, locked the door, and returned to his office.

"Yes, Daniel."

"I have interviewed the prisoners and arranged their temporary accommodation."

"Good," Joseph said, "please come up."

Joseph and Daniel discussed the day's events and the changes to the monastery procedures. The prisoners were pardoned and would work for wages. The ground floor would be renovated and used for accommodation. Hell would be a lock up, but only for holding prisoners on a short term basis. New pottery kilns would be built outside, near the cliffs. There would be greater liaison among the new hierarchy, especially between Most High and the Chief Priest.

"Well, I believe we have processed enough for one day. I need to rest before my parents arrive," Joseph said.

"I will conduct a ballot for the new priest position," Daniel said. "I need to come to terms with the idea of waking up as head priest, acting as bishop for one day, and being anointed Chief Priest tomorrow."

Over dinner, Joseph had his parent's full attention. They discussed Nebedeus, Joseph's appointment as Chief Priest, tomorrows anointing as Most High, the release of the prisoners and the renovation project. The conversation turned to idle chat and Jacob topped up the tumblers with wine. Joseph used the pause in conversation to announce one more unexpected piece of news.

"I am not sure how to tell you what I am about to say, but you need to know."

"You have never been short on words before, just tell us what it is," Jacob said.

"You know I am celibate, so it might come as a surprise that Mary has fallen pregnant with my child."

"That is good news," Miriam said, "but when did this happen?"

"When I was in the ritual bath I accidentally ejaculated into the water. The conditions were favourable for the semen to fertilise Mary and she conceived."

Miriam hugged Joseph.

"I have dreamt about Mary becoming pregnant. She will give birth to a boy, and he will become a spiritual leader of our people."

"I agree," Jacob said. "It will be written. The Virgin Mary conceived by the Holy Spirit, and the son of Most High, the son of God."

"How is Mary?" Miriam asked.

"Ilana has forbidden us to meet because she doesn't want a scandal," Joseph said. "I was informed by Nebedeus that Mary is coping well, she is experiencing morning sickness, she loves me, wants to marry but not until she has had the baby."

"I wonder why Mary said that. I will visit her tomorrow and ask her why she prefers to delay the wedding," Miriam said.

"I believe it is because she doesn't want to show in her wedding robe," Joseph said.

"Mary wouldn't show for months, and besides, she would know that for dynasty marriages, you are betrothed and marry only after she becomes pregnant," Miriam said. "That is the only way succession is assured."

That night Miriam tossed and turned in her sleep, what Joseph had said about Mary did not sit right. The next day, after sunrise prayers, Miriam visited the Abbey. A short time later, to the surprise of Jacob and Joseph, she returned to the apartment.

"Mary is not in the Abbey," Miriam said. "Nebedeus has requested she act as a midwife for a woman that is seven months pregnant."

"Who is the woman and where does the live?" Joseph asked.

"Ilana does not know the woman's name, only that she lives in a village situated somewhere in the countryside of Judea. Mary has pledged her assistance for three months, including a month after the baby's birth."

"I will send a messenger to Masada, requesting Mary's whereabouts," Joseph said.

***

King Herod's palace
Masada
16 August

Nebedeus, Hannah and their entourage arrived at Masada a day later than expected. They had escorted Mary to a Pharisee Chief Priest's house in Bethlehem, a small town in the hill country. Zechariah's wife Elizabeth, who was a younger sister of Heli was middle-aged and seven months pregnant. She would need Mary to assist her in the house chores and act as a midwife. Zechariah paid Nebedeus for Mary's assistance, the money to be donated to the Abbey on Elizabeth's behalf. Nebedeus accepted the donation, though he had arranged the service for his own benefit and had no intention of returning to Qumran. King Herod greeted his guests and invited them to a royal banquet to be held after sunset on Sunday. It would be held in his lower courthouse, which included a Roman style heated bath-house. The guests were shown their quarters by the courtiers. Herod hugged Nebedeus and slapped him on the back.

"Come with me my friend, we have much to talk over," he said as he led the way to his private semi-circular portico on the upper floor of his grand palace.

The king had three palaces at the Masada fortress, this one the most opulent. He housed three of his nine wives at Masada, one wife and their children in each palace. Herod also kept wives at Jerusalem and his other palaces. Nebedeus walked to the marble balustrade and marvelled at the view. He was standing 1500 feet above the Dead Sea situated to the west. The cliff from the *wadi* below to the palace was 800 feet. A narrow snake like path precariously wound around the edge of the mountain on the western side. The hazardous walk took forty-five minutes to complete in good weather.

"This must be one of the best views I have ever seen," Nebedeus said. "The air is clear and the breeze seems to enquire who is in its domain."

"Many priests have told me that they feel a strong connection with the heavenly God when they pray at the very spot you are standing," Herod said. "One priest asked God for forgiveness before jumping to his death. He knew I wasn't ready to forgive him."

Nebedeus suddenly felt a chill run through his body. Could Herod have found out that he only had food poisoning? He fought his emotions and took a deep breath.

"I can't believe how well you look after your severe illness," Nebedeus said.

"You mean poisoning?" Herod said. "I owe you and Theudas a great debt."

"Not at all, Your Highness," a relieved Nebedeus said.

"I am investigating the matter, secretly and thoroughly before I act. Heads will roll and I will appoint you High Priest within four months."

"Four months," Nebedeus exclaimed.

"There needs to be a court case and Theudas will be required as a witness."

"Excuse my outburst," Nebedeus said, "I meant only four months. I am betrothed to Hannah and we plan to marry and spend some time in Alexandria before my appointment."

"Congratulations Nebedeus. Hannah is a fine young lady. I look forward to an invitation to your wedding."

"Now that I find myself with a slightly restricted schedule, I wonder if I could be bold enough to ask if the wedding could be held here at Masada."

"Nebedeus my friend, if it is your wish you can be married Sunday night in a special ceremony amongst my most loyal friends. I also extend a warm invitation for you to stay at my southern palace for two weeks before you tour Egypt."

"I accept your gracious invitation to stay and for the wedding ceremony to go ahead on Sunday," Nebedeus said.

Herod invited one hundred guests for the banquet, and organised adult entertainment which included musicians, jesters and dancers. Children had not been invited, making Hannah, at the age of fifteen the youngest guest. Herod warned his staff that Nebedeus would be escorting a young lady, betrothed to him, and they were not to think she was his daughter. Hannah was dressed in a fine white silk robe, and Nebedeus wore his ceremonial Chief Priest robe. The couple walked to the reception room and were escorted to their chairs in the banquet hall, seated next to Herod as his guests of honour.

Midway through the banquet, Herod clapped his hands, and twelve scantily clad maidens danced provokingly in front of Nebedeus in their veiled garments. The dancers finished their routine and were applauded and cheered as they curtseyed and ran out of the room. The resident priest appeared, and the betrothed couple were called to the raised platform for the marriage ceremony. Hannah beamed with delight when Nebedeus placed a gold ring on her finger, lifted her veil and kissed her. She was in a teenage dream as the thirty-five year old Nebedeus walked her to a private portico in the heated bath-house. Nebedeus undressed Hannah and took off his robe. He picked her up in his strong arms and waded into the warm water. Nebedeus kissed Hannah, holding her mouth tightly against his lips. At that moment, he performed his marital duties for the sake of his family dynasty. Hannah tried to scream, but Nebedeus' kiss stifled her breath.

Herod was surprised to see the couple returning to the table within half an hour. Nebedeus flashed a fleeting smile and nodded before sitting, indicating to Herod that the marriage had been consummated. Hannah sensed her fairy-tale wedding dream was over, and a glimpse of a long, unromantic life ahead filled her senses.

The couple barely talked to each other for the rest of the evening. Hannah consumed several glasses of sweet *mulsum* wine and chatted with the woman beside her while Nebedeus talked at length with Herod. The two men bonded, both having similar characters and ambitions, and agreed to meet in Jerusalem on the first day of January for the High Priest ceremony.

Nebedeus received Joseph's message and delayed the courier for a few days before responding. He wanted to ensure he had departed Masada before a second message could reach him. The courier would most likely inform Joseph of his marriage to Hannah, and the urgency and secrecy of the event would be deliberated. Nebedeus called for the courier and decided to give him false verbal information, which he could repudiate later.

"Inform Joseph that Mary is in Bethany and performing the duties of midwife."

The courier recited the message to Nebedeus, who nodded and released him with a nonchalant wave.

Hannah fell pregnant on the third night. Her mother had advised her that conception may alter her taste and that she would probably experience morning sickness, but that was natural and nothing to fear. Hannah had already felt a strange craving for moist clay and could no longer tolerate the smell or taste of wine. She had to eat a particular type of clay which was used in the potters' workplace. Hannah's urge to eat the potters' clay was so strong that she filled up enough containers for the upcoming journey to Egypt.

***

Qumran, Dead Sea
23 August 745 A.U.C.

The courier ran up the outer stairs to the upper monastery lobby. Stefan answered the loud knocking on the door.

"I have an urgent message for His Holiness from Nebedeus," the courier said.

"Come in, I have been advised of your errand and we have been waiting for your arrival for a few days," Stefan said.

The courier apologised to Joseph for the prolonged delay, explaining that Nebedeus had married Hannah at Masada and did not offer him an audience for three days.

"Nebedeus stated Mary was performing the duties of midwife in Bethany."

"Did Nebedeus tell you the family name of the pregnant woman?" Joseph asked.

"No sir. That was the complete message. In fact, he made me recite it."

"Thank you, that will be all."

Joseph didn't show his emotions to the courier, but he had been taken by surprise that Nebedeus had married. He recalled how the Chief Priest had written to Hannah and had opened her scroll before opening King Herod's. Nebedeus had obviously planned the marriage hurriedly, but why the secrecy? Joseph rang Daniel's office bell.

"Yes Your Holiness."

"Daniel, please arrange for a horse for Gabriel. I want him to take a message to Mary, who is working as a midwife in Bethany."

"I will have the horse ready for sunrise," Daniel said.

"The message is urgent. I will give Gabriel permission to ride on the Sabbath, and I will tell him to avoid the strict Sadducee sect in Jerusalem. Thank you, Daniel."

Joseph grabbed an apple from the dining room table and walked out to the northern balcony to look for his parents. He spotted them in one of their favourite areas, walking among the rows of grapevines. He threw the apple core to gain their attention and beckoned them to come inside.

Stefan prepared a jug of weak *mulsum* and placed it on the dining room table, together with three tumblers and wooden bowls containing fruit or sweetbread.

"Thank you for the invite Joseph," Miriam said. "The food looks delicious."

"I just received a message from Nebedeus," Joseph said.

"Hence the flying apple core," Jacob said. "What is the news?"

"Mary is in Bethany and Nebedeus has married Hannah, his fifteen year old niece."

Jacob stood up, walked away, scratched his head, and then returned and sat down.

"Did Nebedeus discuss his wedding plans with you," Jacob asked.

"Not with me or anyone else for that matter," Joseph said.

"I know what he is doing," Jacob said. "Nebedeus wants the High Priest position in Jerusalem when Simeon retires and heirs to bolster his position."

"Not only that, Nebedeus probably sees your child as a possible rival in the future." Miriam said.

"That certainly explains the need for a quick, secret wedding," Joseph said. "All I want to do is find out where Mary is staying in Bethany so that I can visit her."

"We will come with you," Miriam said. "From there we can travel to Hebron and discuss your wedding reception with Mary's relatives."

"Gabriel is riding to Bethany at first light," Joseph said. "When he returns with Mary's address and has acquired suitable accommodation for us we can all travel."

Gabriel wasn't keen to ride on the Sabbath for he would be breaking the religious laws of the two major sects. In his youth, he had been seen gathering food from his garden on a Sabbath by a visiting Sadducee Chief Priest and whipped severely the following day. As a consequence, Gabriel decided to leave two hours before sunrise and rode to Ain-Feshkha under the cover of darkness and kept close to the foreshore. He dismounted at the oasis where the horse could graze and drink while he waited for the first grey light of dawn.

Gabriel led the horse through the darkest section of a gorge that converged with the Mird *wadi* and then mounted when the light improved. He followed the dry *wadi* until he reached a major fork, the same one Nebedeus took to avoid the bandits two months earlier. He dismounted and goaded the horse until it traversed the higher bed of the *wadi* that led to the open arid plateau. He rode past the Justus family land-holding in the fertile soil of the Ramah valley and entered the Kidron River *wadi,* guiding his mount along the shallow river bed. Gabriel stopped for a meal at Emmaus, a small village situated on the slopes of the valley, seven miles south-east of Jerusalem. The village was named after the hot mineral spring that is fed from deep below the earth's surface. The monks and hermits lived in hand cut cave homes that dotted the southern cliff face. Weary travellers bathed in the large man-made pool used for healing and relaxation. The community supplied travellers with food, overnight shelter, and prayer services. In return, the guests donated money, gifts, wine, cloth, goats, hens, food or other tradable goods.

Gabriel continued his journey along the *wadi*, making sure he took the next two right-hand forks that led to Jerusalem. Two miles from the city, more than the permitted Sabbath walking distance, he turned onto a track that led to Bethany. His first port of call was the village synagogue. Gabriel entered the foyer, stopped for a short silent prayer, and walked down the aisle towards the pulpit. A young lady in her teens was placing fresh flowers in the clay pots, and the priest was rolling a scroll, selecting the passage for today's sermon.

"Excuse me," Gabriel said. "I apologise for interrupting you, but I have been sent on an errand by His Holiness at the Qumran Monastery."

"Welcome to our village, how can I be of service?" the priest said.

"I am looking for a woman called Mary. She came to Bethany to work as a midwife for a lady that is well into her seventh month of child bearing."

"I know everyone in the village, and there is no woman so advanced. One woman is four months pregnant and another woman gave birth two weeks ago."

"Thank you," Gabriel said. "I will return for your evening sermon."

"I will ask the congregation about Mary and pray for the success of your mission."

Gabriel booked a room at the Inn and ordered grilled fish for his evening meal.

"Excuse me, sir. I am looking for a woman called Mary. She came to Bethany to work as a midwife for a woman late into her pregnancy."

"I know most people in the village," the innkeeper said. "I have not heard of any visitors arriving recently or women matching your description."

The next morning, Gabriel returned to the monastery and informed Joseph that Mary was not residing in Bethany or the nearby hamlet of Bethpage. Joseph interviewed the first courier again. Satisfied that the town in question was Bethany, Joseph had no other option than to send another messenger to Nebedeus asking for more details, including the pregnant woman's surname.

Four days later, the courier returned with news that Nebedeus had left Masada because his bride had fallen pregnant and was experiencing chronic morning sickness. Hannah was seen eating potters clay and had asked to be taken home to visit her mother. Nebedeus had apologised to King Herod for leaving his gracious host earlier than expected. Herod understood his predicament and granted him leave on the condition Nebedeus attended the annual meeting in the great hall of Jerusalem on the first day of January.

Joseph rang the bell to the Chief Priest's office.

"Yes, Your Holiness," Daniel said.

"I am taking my parents to Jerusalem tomorrow. I will require a two horse drawn carriage for daybreak."

"Will you require a driver?"

"No thank you Daniel. I will take Stefan."

Joseph informed his parents that Nebedeus and Hannah had left Masada before the courier arrived and were staying at her parent's mansion in Jerusalem.

"I don't believe his sudden departure is only for his wife's sake," Joseph said. "I believe Nebedeus is avoiding contact with me but I don't know why."

"I just want to find out where Mary is staying," Miriam said.

"Tomorrow Stefan will drive us to Jerusalem," Joseph said. "We will talk to Nebedeus and then visit Mary."

"In that case, may I suggest we have an early dinner and an early night?" Jacob said.

Stefan woke to the sound of neighing horses. He dressed in his driver's robe which he wore with great pride and prepared breakfast for the Justus family before waking Joseph. While they were eating, Stefan loaded the carriage for the five day trip. He felt excited about getting away from the monastery and loved his new master for the freedom he bestowed on him knowing he would have been detained in the basement by now if Nebedeus had remained Chief Priest.

Joseph and Stefan assisted Jacob and Miriam climb on board. Stefan quickly sat on the driver's bench and grabbed the reins.

"Any quicker than that and we will have to call you Jehu," Joseph joked.

Jacob and Miriam laughed.

"Who is Jehu?" Stefan asked.

"A king of Israel who was notorious for furiously driving his chariots," Jacob said.

"Head north Jehu and don't spare the horses," Joseph said.

Stefan jiggled the reins and the horses ambled forward, slowly gaining speed to a trotting pace that was comfortable for man and beast over the long journey. They followed the sandy coastline until the river village of Nahal Kalya. From there, they followed a clay track that led north-west and linked up with the road to Bethany and Jerusalem. Three miles out from Jerusalem, Joseph felt uneasy about the unscheduled meeting with Nebedeus.

"Stefan, when we reach Bethany stop at the Inn for a while."

"Yes, Your Holiness."

Joseph booked two rooms and asked the innkeeper if he knew the whereabouts of a pregnant woman in her eighth month with a midwife called Mary in attendance.

"You are the second person to ask about the women. I am sure they are not staying in Bethany as I hear most of the gossip in the village."

"Thank you for your time. I wish to book a table for four, at dinner and for breakfast."

Joseph beckoned to Stefan to move over while he took the reins. He knew the address of Hannah's parents and would answer the Roman guards if they were challenged at the gate.

"We will stay overnight in Bethany, I have booked rooms and meals. The innkeeper has not heard of anyone matching Mary's description."

"Nebedeus has a lot to answer for," Miriam said.

The guards waved the group through, asserting that two elderly people and a youth with a priest was not a threat to the city. Joseph avoided the Essene community and headed towards the Pharisee section of the city. He stopped the carriage in the shade inside the mansion grounds and asked Stefan to remain with the horses.

Joseph knocked on the door and a male servant opened the door as far as the safety chain allowed.

"We have come from Qumran to visit Hannah and Nebedeus," Joseph said.

"I am sorry sir, nobody is at home at present," the servant said.

Joseph turned towards his parents and expressed his of frustration in silence.

"When do you expect them home?" Jacob asked.

"The owners will be home this afternoon."

"When can we see Hannah?" Miriam asked.

The servant looked at the three people standing in front of him and hesitated to ponder if he should give out further information. Joseph sensed the servant was reluctant to go on.

"I know we have never met," Joseph said. "However, my parents and I have known Hannah and her parents for many years and it is important that we see them before we return to the monastery."

"Hannah and Nebedeus are going overseas. They left early this morning to board a ship at Gaza."

"What time is the ship due to depart?" Joseph asked.

"I would say they have left port and are on their voyage to Alexandria."

The servant couldn't help notice the disappointment in their facial expressions.

"After six weeks touring Egypt, I believe the couple are visiting friends and dignitaries in Rome. They are not expected to return until the December solstice festival."

"We didn't know they would be leaving Jerusalem this soon," Jacob said. "We could visit Mary before returning home, but we are not sure of her address."

"I know a few Mary's," the servant said. "What is her surname?"

Mary is Salome and Heli Eliam's daughter," Miriam said. "She is a midwife."

"I am sorry," the servant said. "I do not know the woman or her whereabouts".

"Thank you for your time," said Joseph. "Please pass on to her parents our congratulations for Hannah's wedding and the early conception. We will be staying overnight at the Bethany Inn should they know of Mary's whereabouts."

"What to do now?" Miriam asked.

"You must be tired after travelling, do you want to rest at the inn?" Joseph asked.

"We are fine," Jacob said.

"I would like to see Theudas before we leave," Joseph said.

They passed the city walls and took the fork in the road that led to Joppa. Theudas villa was within walking distance of the city, yet it had a peaceful country atmosphere. The nurses heard the carriage arrive, and two came out to greet the visitors.

"Welcome, Your Holiness, welcome Mr and Mrs Justus. What a surprise," Rosina said.

"You must be Stefan," a teenage nurse said. "Come in after you tend to the horses."

The guests were ushered into a large dining room and refreshments served. The room was soon filled with chatter and laughter. There was a lot of news to catch up on.

Rosina sat opposite Joseph and they discussed the day's events.

"From the sound of things, your timing is out of kilter," Rosina said. "You have also missed Theudas by less than half an hour."

"Do you know how long he will be away?" Joseph asked.

"Mira wanted to place flowers on Jenah's grave and Theudas accompanied her."

"I feel like a walk, if I leave straight away I should meet them at the cemetery or along the cliff track."

Mira placed the flowers near the headstone, and Theudas knelt beside her and weeded the mound.

"Jenah liked you very much Mira. She would appreciate your remembering her."

"I can't believe it has been two months since Nebedeus—"

Mira stopped mid-sentence, realising what she had nearly blurted out.

"What do you mean since Nebedeus?" Theudas asked.

Mira looked at Theudas and broke down and cried. He hugged her and told her everyone missed Jenah, as a friend and a nurse, but especially her sense of humour and laughter.

"That is not why I am crying. I saw Nebedeus throw Jenah down the stairs."

"What are you saying Mira," Theudas demanded.

"I should have been with her on that shift," Mira shrieked.

"You can't blame yourself for Jenah's death. Tell me what happened."

Mira broke down again and cried hysterically while Theudas stroked her hair to calm her down.

"I am saying Nebedeus murdered Jenah and threw her down the steps," Mira cried.

"But why would he kill Jenah?"

"She was convinced Herod was only suffering from a chronic bout of food poisoning combined with long term dietary arsenic consumption."

"Do you believe Jenah told Nebedeus that Herod wasn't poisoned deliberately?"

"Yes, that is what I believe, so help me God," Mira said. "I saw Nebedeus carrying Jenah, her dead eyes staring at me."

"Why didn't you tell Uzziah or me?"

"I was scared. It would have been my word against the word of a Chief Priest."

Theudas kissed Mira on the cheek and wiped away her tears.

"I believe you Mira. I promise I will avenge Jenah's death."

Theudas held Mira by the hand and began the trek home. Theudas walked, deep in thought. *He would journey to Masada on the premise of checking Herod's health. He would take Mira and three other nurses with him. Tell Herod that his poisoning was accidental and that Nebedeus had murdered Jenah and should face trial.*

Theudas looked ahead and could not believe his eyes. Nebedeus was approaching in his Chief Priest robe. Theudas saw a chance where he could easily dislodge Nebedeus and make him fall of the narrow track. He would fall to the rocks below, just like Jenah's body. Theudas braced himself for the deed he knew would be fitting retribution. Nebedeus waved as he approached within one hundred yards, and as he came closer his facial appearance changed from a mental image into a visual image. Theudas was dumbfounded, it wasn't Nebedeus at all. It was his friend Joseph. They hugged each other and shook hands.

"You saved me from committing a horrendous act," Theudas said. "I will explain the whole saga on our walk home."

Joseph listened intently and then told his account over the same period, only omitting the fact that Mary had conceived. The two men realised how ruthless Nebedeus had become in his ambition to attain the High Priest position.

The next day, Theudas planned his trip to Masada. He had a heavy schedule over the next two weeks with the autumn festival and seasonal council meetings to attend. Mid-September he had several herbal treatments to administer, however, his nurses could perform those duties, freeing him for several days that he required to visit King Herod.

Joseph and his parents travelled south towards Hebron. Stefan had managed to gain control of the reins and was enjoying the role of Jefu, albeit at a much slower pace. The horses were rested just outside the outskirts of Bethlehem where there was grass and water. Joseph asked his parents if they wanted a rest break when they reached the inn.

"We are fine," Jacob said. "Let's press on."

"I am looking forward to seeing Mary's relatives," Miriam said.

"Jehu, it is time we hit the road again," Joseph said.

The next town was Tekoa, halfway between Bethlehem and Hebron. Joseph insisted they stop and freshen up at the small inn. They enjoyed cold *mulsum* drinks and bagel rolls.

Joseph paid the innkeeper and thanked him for his hospitality.

"We are heading for Hebron to visit friends," Joseph said. "They have a niece named Mary who is a midwife for a woman eight months pregnant. She is working in towns away from home. Have you heard of her around these parts?"

"Sorry, I can't say I have. There is only one woman pregnant in this village and she is now five months. That I know because she has entered into the home seclusion stage."

Hebron was the next stop. They passed some ruins on the way, and Stefan was inquisitive.

"I have never been along this road. What is this place called?"

"It is called Beth-zur," Jacob said. "It is in ruins now, but one hundred and fifty years ago the Hasmonean Maccabees fought a battle against a Grecian army."

"Who won the battle Mr Justus?" Stefan asked.

"The Grecian army was far superior in numbers and weaponry, but the Maccabees and descendants of King David held the higher ground and the fortress had two solid walls surrounding it. The inner wall was lower than the outer wall and unknown to the invading enemy. When they broke through the outer wall the enemy soldiers rushed into a confined space and were annihilated by the Maccabee archers."

"Why didn't they retreat and regroup?" Stefan said.

"The enemy couldn't retreat because of the horde of soldiers attacking behind them. The trumpet sounded, and the soldiers outside the walls scattered. Most of the survivors found their way back to the base camp before nightfall. The enemy commander sent men under the cover of darkness to spy on the Maccabees activities. Some returned to inform the commander that the walls were being rebuilt."

"Did the enemy attack again the next morning?" Stefan asked.

"The enemy had been lulled into thinking the Maccabees where still defending. During the early hours of the morning, they assassinated the remaining spies and attacked the enemy base camp. They rolled burning bundles of hay down the hill and into the tents. The soldiers that tried to fight were struck down by a hail of arrows. The commander was captured and beheaded. The women and male survivors were made slaves."

"That was a dramatic story, Mr Justus."

"War stories usually are," Jacob said. "The Maccabee casualties were sustainable and their army liberated Jerusalem to give the Jewish people full autonomy over Israel."

Stefan remained quiet for the remainder of the journey. His hands controlled the horses, but his thoughts were of the raging battles and the bravery of soldiers fighting for the right of self-government and to practise the religion of their choice."

Joseph took over the reins after they entered the main thoroughfare of Hebron. The town was the largest in the hill country and higher above sea level than Jerusalem. The town attracted many wealthy families and Mary's uncle and aunt were among them. They lived in a two storey mansion with two married servants. Joseph drove the horse drawn carriage along the long leafy driveway, through an arch and onto a circular stone courtyard.

Stefan and the manservant unhitched the horses while the maid escorted Joseph and his parents inside.

"This is an unexpected surprise," Mary's aunt said as she hugged Miriam and the uncle shook hands with Jacob and Joseph.

"What brings this honour to our household?"

"We have come to discuss family matters," Jacob said.

"You make it sound quite serious, come into our dining room and we will talk over refreshments."

"Unfortunately Nebedeus has made matters very serious," Joseph said. "He arranged for Mary to act as midwife for a woman in Bethany, but neither woman is known there. To make matters complicated, Nebedeus married his cousin Hannah and has left for Egypt."

"Surely the priestess knows the whereabouts of Mary?" Mary's aunt said.

Joseph discussed the whole story covering everything that had happened over the last two months. Beginning with Herod's poisoning and ending with the search for Mary.

"I gather you were hoping we knew where Mary was working," Mary's uncle said. "I am afraid this is the first we have heard, and I am now very concerned for Mary's wellbeing."

"We assumed Mary was still in the Abbey," the aunt said. "Mary did not send word that she had consummated her betrothal or resigned and taken the midwife position."

"I believe Nebedeus and Ilana convinced Mary that I was arranging the marriage and wedding ceremony with her parents and my parents," Joseph said. "That would mean Mary is expecting to hear from us, with the belief that we know where she is staying."

The conversation continued all afternoon with all options and ideas raised and deliberated. Joseph and his parents stayed overnight and resumed discussions over breakfast. Joseph promised he would send out messengers to search every town in Judea to locate Mary's whereabouts. He advised them not to worry as he was sure Mary was in good care and would be located soon. In the meantime, they could compile a list of guests from their side of family and friends for the marriage ceremony. Miriam and Jacob would do the same. Joseph would book the facilities at Ain-Feshkha and hire staff and a priest. He would contact Mary's parents in Nazareth and advise them the betrothal had been consummated.

The journey back to Qumran was hot, dry and uncomfortable. From Hebron, they travelled east on rough tracks that followed dry *wadis* to the Dead Sea town of En-Gedi. Jacob made enquiries about Mary but had no favourable responses. The northerly route between En-Gedi and Mazin was along the damp sand close to the water's edge. The horses coped well and pulled the carriage along at a fast pace and prompted more Jehu remarks directed at Stefan from the passengers.

At Mazin, the group had refreshments at the inn while the horses rested. Joseph asked about Mary but no one had seen her. Jacob and Miriam were taken home to Ramah. The horses were unhitched and left to graze in a paddock close to the house, while everyone washed, ate lunch and rested for two hours.

The last leg of the journey was across the Buqeia Plateau to Qumran. Stefan arranged for the horses and carriage to be washed, and then climbed the outer stairs to the apartment to join Joseph.

"That was a very exhausting trip," Joseph said. "You handled the horses well, Jehu."

"Thank you, Your Holiness. I really enjoyed the experience."

"Well Stefan, I am retiring for an afternoon nap and I suggest you do the same."

Joseph slept for twelve hours. The travel, heat and stress had used more of his energy than he realised. The bedside lamp was burning. Stefan had rekindled the hearth fire in the kitchen using a friction bow and lit the night lamps in the bedroom and dining room. Joseph rang the bedside bell twice and Stefan appeared with a sweetbread and warm lemon juice. He bowed and left the room for five minutes, returning with massage oil. He knew Joseph would either dismiss him or make a gesture to join him. Stefan wanted to reciprocate the generosity of his Holiness, and sexual pleasure was a good way for him to show his appreciation. Joseph knew sunrise was an hour away and wanted to be pampered.

Two hours later, Joseph met with Daniel.

"I require a scroll with a map of Judea, showing all the towns and roadways," Joseph said. "I want to dispatch Gabriel and four scouts to locate Mary's whereabouts."

"I will hire four celibate men from the Essene community," Daniel said. "I can have them available by the seventh hour."

"That will give me time to write out the routes, towns and the women's description," Joseph said. "The scouts must return within three weeks, Gabriel can search Jerusalem."

"Joseph, there is something else you need to know," Daniel said.

"Concerning Mary?"

"Concerning all citizens," Daniel said. "We have received notification from Rome that Emperor Augustus has decreed a worldwide census of all adults will be conducted in March next year. King Herod decreed that all men must register their families in the town of their birth"

"That will be an administration and logistical nightmare," Joseph said.

"Furthermore, each province must hold a census every fourteen years henceforth."

"Thank you Daniel, I will send the four scrolls down the chute before noon."

Gabriel and the four men received their instructions from Daniel and set off on their missions. One man went north to search in the towns within a radius of twenty-five miles from Qumran. Another man went south, and three men went in westerly directions.

Two weeks passed. Not one of the men had returned. One of the scouts walked past a villa and saw a man and four nurses on a carriage. He hailed the driver to stop.

"Excuse me sir, I was wondering if you or your nurses know of a midwife by the name of Mary? She is staying with a woman now in her eight month."

The nurses chatted among themselves, and the scout thought they may know Mary.

"Is Joseph still looking for Mary? My name is Theudas. Tell his Holiness I will ask King Herod if he knows Mary's whereabouts. In the meantime, good luck with your search."

Theudas cracked the whip, and the two horses responded, pulling the carriage onto the roadway and turning towards Jerusalem. The journey to Masada would be undertaken in two days. Theudas wanted to stay overnight in Hebron and arrive at Herod's palace the following afternoon. He had four of his concubine nurses to keep him company. Mira was a witness to Jenah's murder and beautiful thirteen year old Emma was Jenah's replacement. Two other nurses were selected by ballot, leaving eight nurses to cook, clean, water the vegetable garden and tend to the farm animals.

Theudas booked a large room in the Hebron Inn and Emma was asked to prepare refreshments in the kitchen. Three nurses followed Theudas into the bedroom which had two double beds. Theudas and Mira stripped and laid face down on the beds while the other two nurses oiled and massaged their bodies. Half an hour later, they changed positions with their partners and they were oiled and massaged. Mira came to Theudas and hedonistic sexual acts were performed, followed by Mira straddling Theudas and whipping his thighs like a rider trying to get her horse to go harder.

Emma had stopped making the drinks and was peering in through the open door, left open so that she could learn about life's pleasures. The other two nurses where in the nun's position known by the Grecian women of Lesbos Island as a 69. Emma noticed that both pairs were enjoying themselves so much that they laughed uncontrollably when they finally stopped wriggling and collapsed next to one another.

Emma finished making the lemon drinks and took the tumblers and placed them on the bedside tables. Theudas smacked Emma on the bottom as she walked out.

"That is for watching, you are too young to participate."

"I am thirteen now, the age Jewish law allows for a woman to be married."

Theudas had succeeded in convincing the girl she was ready to participate. He knew there was nothing better than to tell a woman that she couldn't have something. Yes they could.

That evening the three nurses were asked to prepare and cook a feast fit for a king. Emma was asked to oil and massage Theudas, who in turn oiled and massaged Emma. His oiled hands slid gently and softly over her smooth olive skin. Theudas massaged her neck, shoulders, back, bottom, and down her long legs. He ran his fingers from Emma's ankles to her thighs, moving higher on every upward stroke, until she murmured with delight. Emma's body moved rhythmically, searching for the source of pleasure. Theudas gently smacked her on the bottom and placed a robe over her beautiful young body.

"That is all for today," Theudas said, "it's time to enjoy the feast."

The next day Theudas and his nurses arrived at the gates of King Herod's fortress, built on a plateau high above the Dead Sea. The guard challenged the group.

"State your name and business," he said.

"My name is Theudas. King Herod is expecting us."

"Open the gates at once!" the guard yelled, "escort Theudas to the northern palace."

The King was advised of the arrival of Theudas and the nurses were shown to their rooms in the western palace. Theudas approached the King and bowed. He was being fed grapes by one of his concubines on the ground floor portico that overlooked the great Dead Sea Lake.

"Good afternoon, Theudas. We meet again under more favourable circumstances."

"You have fully recovered from your illness and look fit and healthy," Theudas said.

"You mean the poisoning. I am gathering information before I question the culprits."

"I need a word with you regarding that matter, if you would be so kind to grant me a private audience," Theudas said.

"I owe you my life," Herod replied. "Any request by you will be considered in good light.
Come with me to my private library on the second terrace."

Herod and Theudas climbed a rock staircase cut into the cliff-face that linked all three terraces. Herod ordered his personal guards to remain outside the room and ushered Theudas inside where they sat on cushioned chairs, separated by a table with bowls of fruit, a jug of wine and glasses.

Herod poured the wine into two glasses and offered Theudas a bowl of grapes.

"What are we about to discuss that my concubine and guards can't hear?"

Theudas felt nervous as the King's authority and status overwhelmed him.

"I am here because one of my nurses shed some light on your poisoning."

"Does she know who is responsible?" Herod asked.

"Not who, but what." Theudas exclaimed. "We now believe you suffered from two types of poisoning at the same time."

"Was it snake poisoning as well as arsenic poisoning?" Herod asked.

"We believe you have consumed arsenic through your normal food chain over a long period of time, probably from the salt gathered from the Dead Sea."

"I do like salt on my food," Herod said. "What about the snake poison?"

"There was no snake poison," Theudas said. "When you were in Jerusalem you ate seafood that was not fresh and it caused a bad bout of food poisoning."

Herod drank his of wine and refilled the glass. Theudas followed the procedure, needing to moisten his dry throat and calm his growing nervous disposition.

"This is good news," Herod said, "but Nebedeus said Simeon and Mariamne's sons poisoned me and you agreed with him."

"At the time, you thought that and we agreed with your assessment," Theudas said, "however, since the death of Jenah, more details have emerged."

"You must explain the whole story from the beginning," Herod said.

Theudas took a deep breath and gathered his thoughts.

"We believe Jenah my most experienced nurse, told Nebedeus that food poisoning was the main cause of your illness and that you would fully recover."

"Nebedeus never mentioned that possibility with me," Herod said.

"Nor with me either," Theudas replied. "Nebedeus killed Jenah because she knew you hadn't been deliberately poisoned. He broke her neck and threw her body down the steps, making it looked like an accident.

Nebedeus would have fooled us all, except another nurse overheard Jenah talking to someone in your room. Then she witnessed Nebedeus carry Jenah's prostrate body and throw her down the stairs. He placed one of her sandals at the top of the stairs and left the scene."

Herod was relieved that Simeon and his family had not tried to assassinate him. He had gathered enough circumstantial evidence and motive to have Miriamne and Simeon arrested.

"If what you say can be verified, I have been deliberately misled by Nebedeus and he will pay dearly. I will dismiss him from all religious ceremonies and deport him to Cyprus."

"Mira, the nurse that witnessed the incident accompanied me here," Theudas said.

"Good, I will interview her tomorrow," Herod said. "In the meantime, you are invited to a feast tonight. I want you to be my guests at Masada for a week."

Theudas accepted the offer, not knowing whether he really had a choice.

"Thank you for your kind offer, my nurses will be thrilled," Theudas said.

At the banquet, Theudas was seated next to Herod as guest of honour. The nurses were introduced to the King and his wife Mariamne. Herod was interested in Mira and kept a close watch on her to evaluate her personality and demeanour. Herod clapped his hands to officially open the night's festivities. The King ate a leg of chicken and tasted the wine, Mariamne followed, and then the guest of honour ate. The other guests commenced eating and the entertainment began. Light music filled the air and twelve scantily dressed dancers wearing long silk veiled costumes entertained the revellers with their first provocative dance routine.

"I see you enjoy the dancers Theudas," Herod said. "Choose two and I will have the courtiers escort them to your room."

"I like the Asian girl and the red haired fair girl," Theudas said.

"Fine choices Theudas. They are both good performers. The redhead is from Britannia and is very fiery, and the Chinese girl will pamper you all night long."

"Could I be bold enough to ask for a room away from my nurses?" Theudas said.

"You are welcome to stay in a room here. We will be seen to leave the banquet together," Herod said. "Now tell me about yourself and your sect."

"I am the Chief Priest of the Therapeutic sect. I have twelve concubine nurses and hundreds of spiritual followers. We believe in a heavenly God, an afterlife, good and evil spirits of our ancestors and practice our faith in home gatherings. We are the only sect that does not take monetary donations. We source our income by supplying herbal medicine and treatment for the sick."

"Your herbal medicine certainly saved my life," Herod said. "I understand you paid a heavy price with the loss of your nurse. I will arrest Nebedeus in January when he attends the annual meeting in the great hall. He is expecting to be anointed as the new High Priest, but will be defrocked and exiled instead."

"That will not bring back Jenah, but at least some justice will be done," Theudas said, "Nebedeus will not attain the position he went great lengths to achieve. All his lies, devious scheming and treachery will not be rewarded in my lifetime."

"Come," Herod said, "it is time we departed and enjoyed the fruits of life."

Theudas was shown to his quarters on the second terrace. The Asian dancer had already prepared a hot scented bath and was ready to join him in the tub. The red haired dancer was lying provocatively on the bed, like a lioness waiting for the prey. Theudas dropped his robe and stepped into the tub. He turned to the Chinese girl and bowed.

"My name is Theudas."

The Chinese girl bowed, clasped her hands and smiled.

"*Chewthis*, you like I bath?"

"Her language skill is limited to her own vocabulary, but she has many skills that you won't need to interpret," the redhead said.

Theudas sat and beckoned the girl to join him in the bath. She dropped her silk robe and stepped into the bath. She washed his back and massaged him with scented oil. Theudas enjoyed the pampering, but his thoughts were focused on the fiery redhead. She was obviously well educated and spoke with a high-class accent. Theudas stood and was towelled down. He motioned to the

Chinese girl to stay in the bath. Theudas pulled the redhead into a sitting position on the bed with her long white legs over the side.

"Hello Theudas, my name is Maur—"

Theudas grabbed her firmly by her head and pulled her open mouth towards him. He didn't want to know her name. He wanted to perform the *movaan* sexual act that he had missed so much since Jenah's demise. Theudas' sexual stamina was phenomenal, prolonging the act by performing foreplay on Maureen between the three positions. The Asian girl stepped out of the bath and knelt beside Theudas. She ran her tongue along Theudas thighs and buttocks, and when the opportunity came she swung his body around and performed fellatio on him. Theudas accepted the gesture for a while, but his thoughts were still on the conceited redhead that he wanted to tame. He dismissed the young girl and turned his attention back to Maureen who had edged away when she saw the opportunity. Theudas pulled her back, turned her over and smacked her for being disobedient. Maureen arched her buttocks in stubborn defiance, only to be sodomised and hand whipped until Theudas and the consort were exhausted.

***

Qumran Monastery
Dead Sea

Gabriel returned to the monastery in mid-September with news of Mary. He reported directly to the Most High.

"I saw the Chief Priest at the temple," Gabriel said. "He said Zechariah wrote on a blackboard that his wife was eight months pregnant and Mary was her midwife."

"How can that be?" Joseph said. "His wife Elizabeth has tried to conceive for years and was thought to be barren."

"I was sent to the temple ten months ago by Nebedeus," Gabriel said. "I was told to tell Zechariah his prayers had been heard and Elizabeth would become fertile for one year."

"What knowledge did Nebedeus base his prediction on?" Joseph asked.

"I believe Nebedeus was given advice by a wise woman that said barren women could conceive during the women's change of life period," Gabriel said.

"Thank you Gabriel, you have performed your duties admirably."

Joseph felt overwhelmed with relief that Mary's location had most likely been discovered. He advised Daniel of the good news and then asked Stefan to bring him a strong *mulsum*.

At sunrise the following day, Joseph and Stefan mounted their horses. They rode across the Buqeia Plateau desert wilderness on Arab horses bred for hot arid environments. They crossed over the Qumran *wadi* and the Mird *wadi* and headed straight for Emmaus. If they had been walking, the men would have taken the longer shaded route following the Qumran and Schacha wadis to Mird. The horses were rested by the Kidron River while Joseph and Stefan bathed in the warm spring fed baths. Stefan enjoyed himself as he frolicked in the water and dived to the bottom to pick up rocks. Joseph was content to relax and let the force of the warm current massage his body as it swirled up from a crevice directly between his feet. Stefan surfaced in front of Joseph and in the excitement of the moment Joseph pulled the youth towards him and kissed him on the mouth. Joseph had never kissed any of his other boys and for the first time realised this relationship meant more than hedonistic sexual pleasure. Joseph and Stefan looked into each other's eyes, totally nonplussed.

"Forget that kiss happened," Joseph said. "It was just a spur of the moment thing."

"I understand, Your Holiness," Stefan said. "I appreciate your kindness towards me."

"I have been celibate all my life, but soon I must marry," Joseph said. "I have to continue the King David dynasty and father male heirs."

"I understand, Your Holiness, I know my time with you will end soon."

"That kiss will be our last moment together," Joseph said. "From this day forward I have to pledge my life to Mary. I will continue your service as head servant."

"Thank you sir."

"There will be a few changes. Mary will need a maid," Joseph said. "The maid will help you in the kitchen and dining room, and will be company for you."

Joseph and Stefan dried and dressed. They ate at the travellers cave, and Joseph gave a donation to the Monk standing at the entrance. Emmaus was halfway to their destination, but the route was more difficult and followed several *wadi* beds and gorges. They entered the Nahal Gorten and followed the dry creek bed until it petered out on the broad slopes of a hill. On the other side of the hill, they rode past the small hamlet of Juhazm and into *Wadi al-Arias*. They passed Hujayala and Bayt Sahur and into a dry gorge that led on to the main road on the outskirts of Bethlehem. Joseph galloped his horse over the last mile.

Mary was in the front garden drawing water from the well when she heard the horses approaching fast. She raised her hand above her eyes and peered at the riders. The person in front was waving. Mary dropped her bucket in astonishment when she recognised the rider was Joseph. She ran down the path and out to the road, her arms wide. Joseph dismounted, handed Stefan the reins and hugged Mary tightly.

"We have been looking all over Judea for you," Joseph said.

"I have been in Bethlehem as you wished," Mary said.

"That was not my idea. Nebedeus and Ilana wanted you to leave the Abbey to avoid any controversy over your conception."

"I was told to assist my aunt Elizabeth who is due to give birth any day now."

"Nebedeus married and is touring Egypt with his wife. He informed me you were staying in Bethany, instead of Bethlehem."

"The poor man obviously had too much on his mind," Mary said. "Come inside and meet Zechariah and Elizabeth. I must warn you Zechariah has taken a vowel of silence until the baby is born to honour God answering his prayers."

Stefan led the horses to the back yard and unsaddled them. Joseph was introduced to Zechariah and they shook hands. Joseph congratulated him and blessed Elizabeth and her unborn child. Mary prepared refreshments and Zechariah indicated to his wife to invite the men to stay overnight. Stefan excused himself from the table after satisfying his appetite and went outside to chop wood and attend to the farm animals. Joseph assisted Mary prepare the evening meal in the kitchen while Zechariah and Elizabeth had an afternoon rest.

Joseph and Mary discussed the events of the last two months, marvelling at the many things that had occurred in those few weeks that would change their lives forever.

"We will get married as soon as Elizabeth's baby is born," Joseph said.

"I have pledged my support for a further month as Elizabeth will need my assistance until she has fully recovered her strength," Mary said.

"That will give me time to prepare our wedding arrangements," Joseph said. "I thought the venue at Ain Feshkha would be an ideal setting."

"That is an excellent location, between the cliffs and the blue lake," Mary said. "I would marry you tomorrow if it was possible."

"On my way home I will call in on my parents and ask them to visit you," Joseph said. "They can stay until the baby is born and then report back to me."

"I will be able to leave three weeks after the birth," Mary said.

"I will send a messenger to your parents in Nazareth, letting them know we have consummated our betrothal and will visit them in October."

Stefan knocked and entered the kitchen, dangling a freshly plucked rooster and some herbs from the garden. Mary asked Stefan to gut the rooster as she was feeling queasy and couldn't bear the smell of the uncooked flesh. She had preferred fish since her conception.

Joseph and Stefan departed early the next morning before the heat of the day made their journey uncomfortable. Joseph asked Stefan to lead at any places where a choice of direction was required. Stefan would have to know his way through the wilderness on his own. They stopped at Emmaus for refreshments and relaxed in the thermal pool. Joseph led the way along the Kidron River *wadi* until they reached the narrow track heading for Ramah, where they dismounted and led their horses onto the plateau above. Joseph stayed with his parents overnight and reached the monastery before noon the following day.

***

**Bethlehem,
28 September**

Elizabeth was in her last stages of pregnancy and experiencing regular contractions. She was squatting in a communal tub filled with warm water. Several women stood in readiness, holding towels and various instruments. Mary climbed in the tub to assist with the birth and grab the baby before it took its first breath. Elizabeth screamed and pushed with all her remaining strength. The baby rose to the surface, and Mary held the baby above the water. The experience of cold air touching warm skin made the baby cry and draw breath.

"It's a boy," Mary exclaimed.

"His name is John," Elizabeth said. "Gabriel, our Lord's messenger, promised us a male child."

Two women rushed to Zechariah's house to deliver the good news to the men. Zechariah had taken a vowel of silence that was to last until the baby was born alive and healthy. He wrote on a blackboard. His name is John. The men were surprised. Some said there was no one among your relatives with that name.

Zechariah broke his vow of silence. He praised God and celebrated the birth of his son. Mary stayed with

Elizabeth for another twenty-eight days, and then travelled by carriage with Joseph and Stefan to her parents' house in Nazareth.

Heli and Salome hugged Mary and congratulated her on consummating her betrothal. During the week, Heli and Salome wrote out their family guest list and everyone agreed the wedding should take place on Friday, the first day of November. Joseph wrote out a second copy of the names to give to his parents. Salome marked the names of the guests they could deliver the invitations to in Galilee and wrote the addresses of the guests living in Judea. Joseph would arrange accommodation in Mazin for guests to stay, including the bridal party. Mary stayed in Nazareth with her parents as she could not see Joseph again until the day of their wedding.

***

Ain-Feshkha
November 1

The guests began to arrive after the third hour of daylight for the wedding of Mr and Mrs Joseph Justus. Theudas and his twelve nurses were among the early arrivals. Theudas was chosen as best man and the twelve nurses were bridesmaids dressed in yellow robes. The villagers of Ain Feshkha were invited to witness the wedding and had organised tables and chairs around the outside of the shelter. They gathered near the courtyard, leaving the southern and northern ends clear for the bride and groom to enter the courtyard on horseback and chariot. The tables under the communal shelter had white table cloths decorated with sprigs of yellow olive tree flowers. Ribbons and streamers fluttered in the light sea breeze, the sky a brilliant blue.

The synagogue bell tolled five times and the guests looked north and south, hoping to glimpse one of the bridal parties. A group of boys on top of the cliffs yelled and pointed north. A lone rider was galloping towards them on a white horse, about a mile away. The crowd cheered, clapped and whistled. The boys yelled out again and pointed south. Then they ran down a track along the cliff face to join in the celebrations. Heli had timed his run to perfection. Two white horses and a gleaming white and gold four wheeled carriage appeared from behind a bend in the cliffs. Heli was the charioteer, sitting on the front bench seat with Jacob beside him. Miriam and Salome sat behind them, with Mary sitting in the middle dressed in a pure white silk robe. She wore a gold tiara with a gold sash around her waist and in her hands was a bouquet of yellow and white flowers. Her long black hair flowed in the breeze and her demeanour shone of royalty.

Joseph slowed his stallion to a trot. He was wearing a white robe and a ceremonial headdress mitre with a gold sash over his shoulder and across his waist. Both parties entered the courtyard together and circled around slowly three times. The bride and groom looked into each other's eyes, unaware for a moment of anyone else being present.

The chariot stopped, Jacob and Heli alighted and assisted their wives down. Joseph dismounted, handed the reins to a deacon standing nearby, and assisted Mary from the carriage.

The bride and groom were escorted by their parents to Daniel. The Holy Spirit prayed over the couple, anointed them with scented oil and announced them man and wife. Theudas handed Joseph the wedding ring which he slipped on Mary's finger next to the signet ring he gave her at his Chief Priest ceremony on the first of July. Joseph lifted Mary's veil and kissed her on the mouth. Mary placed Joseph's wedding ring on his left-hand finger next to his High Priest ring, and they kissed again, this time for longer. Mary threw the bouquet over her shoulder and turned to see Emma jump higher than the other bridesmaids to snatch the flowers. The guests clapped and cheered, wishing the couple well.

The bride and groom were escorted to the row of tables on the eastern side of the shelter. They were seated in the middle with their respective parents on each side. Daniel, four Bishops and eight priests sat on Joseph's right. Theudas and the twelve bridesmaids sat on Mary's left. The other guests sat at the other two rows of tables facing the bridal party. The townsfolk gathered around the guests, sitting and eating just outside the covered shelter, but still feeling very much part of the celebrations. The bride and groom talked and laughed, ate and drank, made speeches and listened to speeches. The choirboys and girls sang songs in the background after they had eaten and the speeches had given way to jovial conversations. Joseph placed something in Mary's hand. Mary smiled, slowly slipped on the silk underwear, and whispered to Joseph.

"Does this mean you want to have your signet ring returned?"

"It means our secret love pact is over," Joseph said. "Our love story will be known throughout the kingdom and spread to every corner of the earth through our newborn child."

"You are so romantic. I love you Joseph."

"I love you Mary, and the miracle baby in your womb that is four months old today."

"I know the exact day I conceived, Monday the first of July," Mary said. "Our beautiful baby is one hundred and twenty-four days old."

The wedding celebrations and wedding feast came to a close when the synagogue bell rang out nine times. All country functions ended mid-afternoon so that patrons had three hours to find accommodation before nightfall. The final toast was given to the bride and groom, and the guests formed two lines, holding hands above their heads with a person opposite to form a long archway. Joseph led Mary by hand, slowly walking through the crowd to the waiting carriage. The proud parents kissed the newlyweds goodbye and wished them a long and happy life together. Jacob gave Joseph the reigns and whispered some last minute advice.

Joseph kissed Mary on the cheek and steered the horses toward his palatial apartment. They would stay at Qumran for three days before leaving on a voyage to Athens for six weeks.

"Was that some last minute instructions from your father?" Mary asked.

"Yes, how did you know?" Joseph asked.

"I was given advice from my mother," Mary said. "Apparently we cannot have coital sex said after the four months conception period under Essene-Jewish laws."

"That was what my father said, that will teach us to have warm baths together. However we can try oral sex."

"You mean—"

"Yes," interrupted Joseph, "we can certainly talk about it."

Joseph felt the full force of Mary's slap on his arm, making the horses pull to the left until he relaxed the reins.

Mary grabbed Joseph.

"Perhaps we don't need these seeing that they have done their job?"

"I thought you wanted eight children," Joseph said.

"A woman can easily change her mind."

Joseph steered the horses past the monastery gardens and tied the reins to a post near the tower stairs. Mary offered her hand to Joseph for support as she stepped down the first rung of the carriage ladder. Joseph slipped one arm behind her thighs and carried Mary up the stairs to the lobby entrance. Stefan opened the door, allowing

Joseph enough room to carry Mary across the threshold. The bedroom had a huge bed covered with yellow petals and the room was lit by ninety small candles and two large candles, one on each bedside table.

"The two large candles represent you and me, and the other ones represent our family and guests," Joseph said as he laid Mary gently on the scented petals.

"The setting is unbelievably beautiful and the aroma of the flower petals is very sensual," Mary said as she looked adoringly into Joseph's eyes. "I hope those candles don't have eyes, as I do believe I need to show you my appreciation."

CHAPTER 5: Flight to Safety

King Herod sat in the comfort of his palanquin surrounded by his entourage and waved to the crowds lining the streets of Jerusalem. Today, the first day of January was one of the most important days in the Roman occupied territories when the leaders of each province selected their most loyal religious advisers. King Herod, who was not in the best of health, was assisted down from the palanquin to the steps leading to the great hall. He waved to the cheering crowd and then commenced the twelve steps to the grand entrance. Each step represented one of the twelve tribes of Israel. At the sixth step, the King waved again, and the crowd responded with great enthusiasm. Herod just needed the rest break. He continued climbing the steps until he reached the basilica podium where he turned and saluted the crowd.

The crowd erupted in a long thunderous applause. King Herod turned to Simeon, the High Priest.

"To my loyal subjects, I am more than their King, I am their God," he said.

The High Priest bowed to the King, but refrained from commenting. Instead, he ushered the King towards the huge wooden doors that were swung open as they approached.

Inside the great hall sat most of the prominent citizens of Jerusalem—politicians, religious leaders, Sanhedrin judges, solicitors, physicians, scribes, high ranking soldiers and men of wealth. Together, they rose as one body and applauded until the King and the High Priest reached the podium and held their hands up, requesting the crowd to become silent.

The High Priest asked the audience to be seated. Nebedeus and Hannah stayed on their feet longer than most other members, applauding the King. They were eagerly looking forward to the announcement of the next High Priest and the changeover of religious power to them.

The King sat on a chair next to several high officials and let the High Priest give his annual speech. Simeon then removed the High Priest ring from his finger and handed it to the King, thus ceremonially ending his twelve month tenure. Simeon, a Pharisee priest had actually held the position for the last fifteen years, and the King had always reappointed him. This year the rumours were it was time for change, and Nebedeus had recently rented a large mansion in Jerusalem, fuelling the rumours. Even Simeon was expecting a fall from grace because of the recent riots and increasing hostility towards Emperor Augustus first census of the Roman world.

King Herod accepted the ring and placed it on a certificate lying on the pulpit. Simeon sat down with the other officials, feeling despondent. He had enjoyed his tenure as High Priest and Herod's political adviser, and had hoped it was for life. The King looked around the great hall and then began his speech.

"Chief Priests, distinguished guests, gentlemen and ladies, I will announce shortly who will be my religious adviser for the following twelve months. As you are aware, there have been insurrections lately against Roman soldiers and authorities. Two days ago I received a written request from the Roman Emperor, Caesar Augustus. He has asked me to quell these illegal actions, and to round up the ringleaders. Anybody found guilty will be sent to the sulphur mines for life, chained to the labour gangs. Under these trying times, it would be inappropriate to change the priestly leadership, we need certainty and continuity. I hereby reappoint Simeon ben Boethus as the High Priest for a further twelve months."

King Herod looked at Simeon, and the audience stood and applauded loudly. All except Nebedeus, who remained slumped in his seat, shocked and flabbergasted that he wasn't nominated as prearranged at Masada. Before he could gather his senses, four soldiers escorted Nebedeus and Hannah out of the hall. They were ordered to leave the Kingdom of Israel for twenty years or face treason charges to be laid against them by King Herod. They must forfeit all their property and must reside on the island of Cyprus. They were fortunate to escape with their lives, some jewellery and gold coins, any citizen below Chief Priest would have been charged with murder and treason.

Simeon rose from his chair, acknowledged the crowd and bowed to King Herod. The King placed the High Priest ring on Simeon's finger and handed him the certificate, stating the nomination for another twelve month period. Simeon raised his right hand.

"I hereby swear on the Holy Book of Moses that I will uphold the office of High Priest to the best of my abilities, honour Roman authority, honour your monarchy and to uphold the will of God."

Herod congratulated Simeon, but also warned him that his stay in office depended on quelling the riots and bringing the offending culprits to justice.

In the audience, two sect leaders were quietly discussing the outcome of King Herod's reappointment. Theudas congratulated Joseph.

"This means you will have complete control over the Monastery and its finances without Nebedeus' interference."

"Yes," replied Joseph. "But I still have to overcome any objections from the panel of thirteen celibate clergymen. There has never been a married person overseeing the celibate monastery."

"I know you are a staunch nationalist, another thing we have in common, you must find a way to remain in the Most High position. It is also a major step forward for the King David heir line to regain regal power in the future."

Joseph wanted to change the subject as this was not the place to be discussing such matters.

"Today's decision was vindication for the murder of Jenah. I know you would have preferred a death sentence for Nebedeus, but that would have caused political upheaval."

Theudas sat in silence for some time, in memory of Jenah before continuing his conversation.

"Neither death or deportation will bring Jenah back, but I will not let her sacrifice be in vain. Nebedeus is a Pharisee but from now on I will pledge allegiance with your Essene sect.

Joseph shook Theudas hand.

"I have heard enough and the meeting is in its final stages. Are you ready to leave?" he said.

"Yes, let's go before the doors are blocked by the mass exit."

The annual meeting was nearing its close and the two friends exited the great hall among the early leavers, mainly disappointed people that supported the Sadducee sect for the appointment to the highest religious position.

Two nurses met Theudas in the street and the group of four walked out of the walled city and towards the villa. They came to a fork in the road where Joseph had left his white horse with a blacksmith. Joseph said goodbye to his friends and then paid the blacksmith for shoeing his horse. He stroked the horse on the neck and whispered, *time to go Reuben*.

Joseph untied the reigns and mounted. He waved goodbye to Theudas who was three hundred yards down the other road and galloped towards the Kidron *wadi*. Joseph entered the *wadi* and slowed the horse to a walk as there were people bathing, washing their clothes, and children playing in the sand. Everyone watched Joseph ride past. Many were Essenes and knew who he was and waved, bowed, and cried out, "Good morning, Your Highness."

Joseph acknowledged the crowd, but was intent on seeing Mary and his parents at their house in Ramah, and so he didn't stop. As soon as the crowd thinned, he spurred Rueben into a trot and followed the sandy track running parallel to the creek that wound around the arid hills.

The Kidron creek cut deep into the red clay and past the limestone layer that showed the men with knowledge that the area was once under seawater. The horse was brought to a walk as there were fallen trees, large boulders and many water crossings to negotiate over the next four miles. Joseph was enjoying the ride. He liked horses and so did Mary, but she wouldn't risk riding until after their baby was born. At that thought, the sunshine shone on Joseph's face and lit up the valley for the first time in the trip. Joseph knew it was a sign from above. It meant that it was now noon and he had been riding Rueben for three hours. Joseph could hear the Emmaus monks chanting, the chants reverberating out of the caves and echoing down the valley.

Joseph dismounted and led the horse into the creek to drink before tying the reins to the branch of an olive tree. Joseph waited until the chanting ended before entering the communal cave to enjoy the midday meal in the company of the monks. Joseph remained at Emmaus for two hours, discussing the procedures and outcomes of the Jerusalem symposium.

Joseph rode into Ramah valley at dusk, reaching the house half an hour after sunset. Mary squeezed Joseph tightly.

"You made it just in time for dinner, darling. We waited for you."

"How did it go at the meeting? Was Nebedeus appointed as expected?" Jacob asked.

"Firstly, I am washing my hands," Joseph replied. "Then I will tell you all about it."

Jacob said grace, broke the bread into four and passed pieces to Joseph, Mary and Miriam.

"The bread we are about to eat is the embodiment of God almighty and our family."

Joseph then told the family how Simeon had been reinstated as High Priest and how Nebedeus had been arrested and exiled to Cyprus for twenty years. Caesar Augustus decreed all insurrections had to be quelled, leaders captured, crucified or sent to the mines. Herod officially announced a worldwide census would take place during March.

"Well," Jacob said. "Good news and bad. We have to be very careful how we plan future demonstrations against the Roman atrocities, especially as Herod is supporting Roman authority more than ever before. Thankfully, the Pharisee sect has retained the religious power over the Sadducee sect that supports Emperor Augustus."

"Best of all, Joseph will keep the position of Most High at the Monastery now that Nebedeus has been defrocked," Miriam said.

"I will have to gain the approval of the Holy Spirit, Bishop, two of the four Priests and at least three of the other committee men or my position will be untenable," Joseph replied. "There has never been a married Chief Priest overseeing celibate men before so I am creating a precedent that will cause some controversy."

"I am sure you and Jacob will discuss the matter very carefully and come up with the right strategy, please excuse us though, Mary and I need to talk about women matters," Miriam said.

Mary and Miriam sat on the upper porch chairs and discussed names for the unborn baby. They had already decided the name Jesus if it was a boy. But what if the baby was a girl?

"To tell you the truth," Mary said," I just figured the baby was going to be a boy. I haven't even considered a girl's name."

"Are there any girl's names in the family that you like?" Miriam said.

"Yes, I like Salome, Joanna, Miriam and Mary."

Miriam loved the choice of names and they talked for hours. Mary found the right time to confide to her mother-in-law that she was still a virgin and had abstained from coital sex during her pregnancy as required by Jewish Essene custom.

Joseph and Mary stayed overnight, had an early breakfast of fish and eggs, and then prepared for the trip to Qumran. Two Essene staff attended to the two white horses and the chariot that was given to Joseph and Mary as a wedding present from Heli and Salome. Miriam insisted that Mary should have a maid, for household help and also for female companionship. Alexis, a distant relative to Mary pleaded for the position and was given the opportunity. Joseph and Mary enjoyed their married life on the third floor of the monastery. Joseph convinced the thirteen man committee that his position as overseer of monastery procedures would not interfere with their daily routine, and in fact, he intended to report less information to the Roman authorities than Nebedeus had. The committee voted eight to five in favour of Joseph with a condition that the position would be for a twelve month period ending on the 31st of December each year, with the entitlement of reselection, the same as the High Priest.

Joseph accepted the conditions and advised the committee that he intended to use the spare room for his page boy Stefan and the second bedroom for the maid, Alexis. Days turned into weeks, weeks into months. Mary was almost eight months pregnant and she was feeling nervous about the birth, especially when a woman in the nearby town of Ain-Feshkha died during childbirth. Mary pleaded with Joseph to take her to her mother's house in Nazareth before she gave birth to the baby. Unknown to Mary, Heli and Salome had sold their house to reside closer to their daughter. They had bought a mansion in the mountainous region of Hebron, within walking distance of Salome's sister.

King Herod had decreed that all head males in each household had to register in the towns of their birth. This meant that Heli had to remain in Nazareth until at least the first of March and Joseph had to register in Bethlehem. Heli asked Joseph and Mary if they would occupy the new house until they registered. Joseph accepted the proposal as it would be convenient for him and Mary would have good access to midwives in the town. Joseph made some alterations to the four-wheeled chariot so that Mary could lie down on the trip whenever she felt tired. He boxed in the chariot floor using twelve inch wide planks. He filled it with straw and placed a mattress on top. Satisfied with his efforts, Joseph called Mary to the barn to inspect his creation. Mary was pleased with Joseph's thoughtfulness and gave him a tight hug, which made the baby inside the womb roll over and kick.

On the twenty-fourth of February, Joseph and Mary said goodbye to Salome and Heli and began the first leg of their journey. They travelled to Jerusalem, staying overnight at Theudas' Villa, where they hired a nurse. Theudas insisted Joseph take his most experienced midwife with them to Hebron. The nurse, called Rosina, examined Mary and told her she estimated the baby was due in a month. Rosina then sought out Theudas.

"I don't know what method they used to get her pregnant, but Mary is still a virgin."

Theudas was astounded, but refrained from asking Joseph about his sex life. Emma, on the other hand, wanted to become pregnant.

"Mary, do you think I am old enough to have a baby?"

"You are still young Emma. I believe you should enjoy life for the present and reconsider your options after you turn eighteen."

"That is what Theudas advised. Besides, he prefers to use the *movaan* method, which prevents unwanted pregnancies."

Emma explained what that entailed and Mary vowed to herself to try the *movaan* method with Joseph, in three months' time.

The next morning Joseph, Mary and Rosina travelled into Jerusalem to visit the city markets before heading for Hebron. On the way Mary suffered stomach pain and experienced some early contractions. Joseph discussed the situation with Rosina and they decided to take Mary to the Essene commune where travellers could book a room. They stayed for a month until Rosina was satisfied Mary had stabilised and passed the point of miscarrying. Mary insisted that they leave for Hebron so that she could be with her mother. Her parents had left Nazareth after them but arrived well ahead because of Mary's unscheduled delay. Rosina examined Mary and advised Joseph that it was safe for Mary to travel provided they stopped for a rest at regular intervals on the twenty-five mile journey.

Joseph stopped at Bethlehem and asked the town blacksmith to check the left hand wheel as the iron rim sounded loose. Joseph unhitched the horses and led them into the stable yard at the back of the workshop. He paid the smithy for the chaff and oat feed and joined the women for lunch. The inn was crowded and the patrons were vocal and animated. The innkeeper was asking for calm. Mary felt claustrophobic and so they decided to leave as soon as the Blacksmith had completed his task. Joseph paid the man and thanked him for repairing the wheel ahead of schedule.

Rosina escorted Mary to the buggy, but before they reached it, Mary experienced a major contraction. Rosina sat Mary on a wooden crate for a rest. Three minutes later, Mary had another contraction, followed by more contractions every three minutes. Mary called for Joseph, and Rosina told him to get towels and hot water, the baby was arriving. Joseph placed the mattress on the hay in the stable, helped Rosina make Mary as comfortable as possible and went to the inn for towels and hot water. Five hours later Mary gave birth to a baby boy. They named him Jesus Immanuel Justus, the new heir of the King David line. Joseph talked to the inn-keeper.

"My wife has just had a baby, could I hire a room for the night."

The inn-keeper laughed.

"It is census month and all my rooms have been double-booked for weeks. If you intend to stay the night you will have to fill out the census by order of Emperor Augustus.

"I forgot about the census," Joseph said. "We have a maid, page and a nurse travelling with us. Are we required to enter their names with our details?"

"Yes. This census includes all the population from all the countries under Roman rule. This is the first time, all men, all women and all children must be counted, and you must list your parents' names and your place of birth."

"The Romans are interfering more and more with our way of life. Where will it all end?" Joseph unintentionally uttered out his thoughts in the spur of the moment.

"Sir, I agree with you but be wary of what you say. There are Roman scribes staying here. They will report any protests, or record your information if you can't write."

"I can write."

Joseph reached for a pen and ink and jotted down the details, including the newest Jewish citizen, Jesus, born on March 29th, 746 A.U.C. Joseph paid three messengers, and sent them to the homes of Jacob, Theudas and Heli to report the news that Mary gave birth to a healthy boy at Bethlehem.

Joseph returned to the stable with a bowl of stew and a jug of juice. He told Mary and Rosina about the new census conditions while they ate. They despised the concept of being numbered and heavily taxed by the Roman authorities.

Mary breast fed her baby, wrapped the newborn Jesus in a white cloth and placed him in the manger, a wooden feed trough filled with hay. All three of them slept for four hours.

Two breastfeeds later, Joseph, Rosina, Mary and baby Jesus were ready to leave for the final leg of their journey. They stayed with Heli and Salome at Hebron for one week, and then travelled to Jerusalem. The eight day old Jesus was presented to the Essene doctors for circumcision and Joseph booked a sanctifying ceremony at the Temple. Rosina was taken home to Theudas where Joseph and his family stayed overnight.

The next day, Jesus was taken to Ramah to be held and loved by Jacob and Miriam. The Holy Grail, the King David bloodline had been extended into a new generation.

On the second Sabbath, the tenth of May, the Justus family and their friends attended the Temple in Jerusalem. Daniel, revealed to the High Priest, Simeon Boethus, that the baby, christened Jesus Immanuel Justus, was a first born child descendant of King David. The High Priest blessed Jesus, and then he took him in his arms and praised God for the healthy firstborn Royal male.

After the ceremony, Simeon handed the baby to Mary and told the proud parents that Jesus was destined to cause the falling and rising of many in Israel. On their way back to Qumran, Mary and Joseph marvelled about what was said during the consecrating ceremony. They enjoyed their lifestyle at the monastery. Mary also found the right moment to tell Joseph about the *movaan* sexual technique which prevented unplanned pregnancies. When Mary gave birth sixteen months later, to a boy named James, word quickly spread that the King David line had been extended.

King Herod's mental health had deteriorated dramatically over the last two years. He was suffering from chronic kidney disease and gangrene genitals. Herod's condition caused him great distress and he became ill tempered, cruel and paranoid. He thought two of his sons, Alexander and Aristobolus, were attempting to assassinate him for the throne. King Herod travelled to Rome and sought an audience with Emperor Augustus where he accused his two sons by his wife, Mariamne, of high treason. The Roman court found the two sons guilty and they were summarily executed. King Herod's mental state worsened over time and he became more agitated and even more paranoid.

He charged Antipater, his son from his marriage to Malthace with his attempted murder. Emperor Augustus upheld the death penalty and Herod had Antipater executed. Herod's advisors warned him of another threat to the throne. Joseph and Mary Justus, from the King David line had two sons from their marriage. The Sadducee sect had recognised Jesus as legitimate, even though Mary had conceived the baby for more than the ninety day period allowed between betrothal and a dynasty marriage. The Pharisees believed James was the legitimate heir, because he was consummated after the wedding. The danger was that a Roman Emperor could select the next King from the David Justus line instead of Herod's line of sons.

King Herod was advised by his spiritual advisers, who saw the rise of the Justus power through religion, to eliminate the two sons. Herod ordered the death of the two boys. His soldiers killed every boy they found in the Bethlehem area aged two years old or less. The Jewish community called the callous act, 'the massacre of the innocents.'

Mary's sister Rachel fled to Ramah with her husband and their two young boys. Herod's soldiers, however, tracked the family down, and killed the father who had tried to protect his children. The two boys were murdered in front of their mother.

Jacob sent a messenger to Joseph warning him about the death warrant on his sons. Miriam mourned with Rachel who wept for three days without sleep, refusing to be comforted over the loss of her family.

Joseph resigned from his position as Most High, the Essene God at the monastery, only informing his trusted friend Daniel. The family fled from the monastery during the early hours of the morning, about three hours before sunrise. Stefan hitched the two white horses to the four-wheeled chariot while Alexis packed food from the pantry into boxes. Mary organised the clothing and bedding for the boys so that they could sleep on the trip.

Joseph and Daniel went to a secret storage area on the second floor near the Chief Priest's office. Joseph was given two bags of gold coins, his entitlement for twenty years of monastery service. Severance payments were given to members who had to leave the monastery to marry and father children under the dynastic rule, as was the case with Joseph.

"Stay inside the monastery as I don't want anyone to know which route I will take, and I haven't yet decided whether to head north or south," Joseph told Daniel.

"Good luck and God speed, I will pray for your families safety and new life," Daniel replied.

Joseph met with the others and placed the gold coins under his bench seat. He checked the wooden board and branches he had tied at the back of the chariot, designed to cover the cart and horses' tracks during the sandy leg of the route.

Joseph decided to go north to Jericho. He was planning his escape on the run. If he didn't know his final destination, neither did anyone else. Joseph stopped the chariot near the small village of Nahal Kalya, cut the board and branches loose and hid it behind some bushes. Joseph looked along the foreshore of the great lake. The contraption had done a good job of covering their tracks, and if the Roman soldiers didn't search the area before the second hour of daylight, the local foot traffic would obliterate all other traces of their movements.

After twenty miles, Joseph rested the horses stopping under the shade of a large tree and near a slow running creek, about five miles north-west of Jericho. Stefan and Joseph unhitched the horses and tied them to saplings on long leads so that they could graze and drink near the creek. Mary woke the sleeping Jesus and let him run around. He walked down hill to see his father, stumbling twice on rocks hidden in the knee length grass.

Alexis placed a rug on the grass and placed the fruit and water on wooden crates, ready to eat. Stefan took Jesus by the hand and sat with Alexis on the rug, letting Jesus eat some grapes. Mary looked at the sleeping baby and decided to leave James asleep until she had something to eat. Mary walked down to the creek to wash her hands and to see Joseph.

"Joseph, I am thirsty, but the creek water may be contaminated," she said. "I would prefer the living water if you have some."

Mary knew from the ascetic monks that the living water was pure and gave more energy and strength than creek water. With two young boys still suckling milk, Mary needed as much strength as she could muster.

The group ate, drank and rested for nearly an hour, and then it was time to hitch the horses to the chariot. Mary fed, washed, and changed James during the next leg of the journey. Joseph rested the horses again near Shechem, a town nestled between Mount Ebel and Mount Gerizim. The fugitives had managed to outrun any Roman soldiers that may have been searching for them.

"I was thinking of going to Galilee, but the Roman soldiers would track us down eventually. What do you think if we lived in Egypt for a while?"

"I will live anywhere you can keep our boys safe from that mad tyrant Herod," Mary replied. "The further away the better."

"Well," Joseph said pointing northwest, "That city on the coast is Caesarea. We can sell the horses and chariot and buy a fishing boat."

They arrived in Caesarea at nine bells. The trip had taken twelve hours including the two rest breaks for the horses. The sixty mile route had ended with the relative short term safety of the group, as they could now mingle with the crowded city folk. Joseph chose an inn near the harbour that had a blacksmith and stable nearby. He booked two rooms, one for Mary, Alexis and the boys, the other for himself and Stefan. When everybody had eaten their afternoon meal in the dining room, the women returned to their rooms. They both slept with one of the boys. Mary slumbered with baby James and two bags of gold in her bed.

Joseph and Stefan walked to the blacksmith's barn.

"Where can I sell my horses and four-wheeled chariot, preferably as one unit and at a fair price?" Joseph asked the smithy.

"Right here sir," the smithy said with a smile. "I can see the chariot is finely built and the horses are a fine breed. They are capable of being ridden or used to pull the chariot."

"You are correct in what you say. The slightly taller horse is called Rueben, the other one is Asher. My wife and I regret having to sell at any price; however we need the money to start a new business."

"I understand," the smithy said.

The men discussed the matter and finally reached a satisfactory deal for both parties. Joseph and Stefan shook the man's hand and left with a small bag of coins. They walked three miles north to the harbour district and looked for a suitable fishing vessel to buy. They asked several fishermen, but no one wanted to sell their boats as it was their only livelihood.

"That seaworthy schooner is for sale with an eight man cabin, the captain lives on board," a fisherman said.

"Thank you," Joseph said, "I will enquire about the vessel, but it looks far too large for my requirements."

Joseph introduced himself to the captain who shook his hand and offered him a drink.

"My name is Zebedee; I am the master of this vessel."

They talked for over an hour. The two men bonded immediately, their ages and personalities being very similar.

When Joseph found out Zebedee had to sell because he lost his sister ship and cargo during a fierce storm, and owed financiers money, he offered Zebedee a deal.

"I am willing to be equal partners with you if you stay on as captain and are willing to show me the ropes," Joseph said opening up to the captain.

"Why do you want to go to sea?" Zebedee asked, "I can tell by your hands and skin that you are a scribe."

"I will explain that tomorrow when we sail for Egypt," Joseph said. "In the meantime, we will need to work together in mutual trust. I can start by giving you this bag of coins for a deposit, and the balance tomorrow, before sunrise."

The two men discussed the deal thoroughly and agreed to meet early tomorrow, with intensions to sail as soon as the creditors were paid. The matter to be kept strictly secret between themselves or the deal could not proceed. Zebedee understood Joseph had some concerns about privacy and gave his word he would not leave the vessel until they met in the morning. Joseph shook his hand and patted him on the back. It felt like they had been mates for years. Joseph climbed up the ladder to the top deck and found Stefan fishing off the bow.

"Look at the fish I have caught," Stefan exclaimed.

"Well done, we will ask the innkeeper to cook them for our dinner."

The next morning, after breakfast and as soon as Joseph settled the account, the six fugitives were on the move again.

They walked to the pier and boarded the schooner. Joseph paid Zebedee, who counted out the amount owed to his creditors.

"Make yourselves at home in the cabins below, I will be back within half an hour," he said.

Zebedee returned to find Joseph and Stefan waiting on the pier near the gangplank.

"Looks like you are keen to sail," he said. "Well, now is a good time with the breeze at our backs."

"What can we do to help?" Joseph asked.

"You can come aboard and raise the gang plank," Zebedee said. "Stefan, you can undo the hawser from the fore bollard, and using this pole, push the bow seaward."

"Aye aye captain," Stefan said.

"By the way," Zebedee said, "There are eight soldiers in town asking shop owners and inn-keepers if they have seen a man in his mid-thirties with a twenty year old lady, teenage boy and girl, a two year old boy and a nine month old baby. They didn't ask me though."

"Good thing they are not looking for us two men and a teenage boy," Joseph said. "But let's cast off and get the hell out of here."

"Stefan, you heard the man, undo the aft hawser and using the pole between the pier and the vessel pole vault on board," Zebedee said.

"Aye aye sir."

Zebedee grabbed the brails and hoisted the foresail.

"It's a good omen that the Etesian winds are blowing from the north-east. We can make the coast of Egypt in two days if this weather holds."

The vessel slowly gained speed and was guided out of the harbour by Zebedee. He manoeuvred the single square mast vessel by using one of the two large oars at the stern. When he had to veer portside, he would let the port oar drag in the water, turning the vessel left, or paddle with the starboard oar. He would use the opposite technique to veer to the starboard side. When he passed the last moored vessel in the harbour, Zebedee lowered the foresail and hoisted the larger square mainsail.

Joseph had only sailed on Lake Galilee and the Dead Sea, never on the open ocean.

"My family have never experienced sailing. I will go below and make sure they are all right."

"Don't worry," Zebedee said, "I will sail in sight of land and we can anchor near the coastline at night."

"I appreciate that," Joseph replied. "I will tell the women."

Joseph need not have worried Mary and Alexis and the two boys were fast asleep. Yesterday's travel and the two early morning rises had deprived them of much of their sleep.

Joseph also felt tired, more from stress than lack of sleep. He lay on a bunk, just to rest for a while. Within moments, he was fast asleep. Joseph had saved Jesus and James from execution by King Herod's henchmen. Unfortunately, in the last six days, many innocent boys, all two years old or younger had been taken from their parents and slaughtered.

Two hours into the sea journey, the soldiers discovered the horses and four-wheeled chariot that belonged to the Justus family. They interrogated the blacksmith for an hour, but when he produced the sack of coins proving the deal was a genuine sale, they released him without further questions.

The smithy knew nothing about Joseph except he had a teenage boy with him. The soldiers soon found the inn where the fugitives had stayed overnight. The inn-keeper was more forthcoming with information.

"Yes, several people matching your description stayed overnight. They were touring the area and went fishing. I cooked their fish for dinner."

"Which direction did they travel after checking out?" the soldier in command asked.

"That I can't say, they paid their account and departed early in the morning. That is the last I saw of them."

The soldiers continued searching and enquiring, but no further trace or sighting of the fugitives were found. The soldiers split up into pairs and drew lots for areas to continue searching. Two soldiers stayed in Caesarea and searched house to house, taking down the names of any boys under two years old as they searched for the Justus family. The other soldiers mounted their horses and rode towards Haifa to the north, then Joppa to the south, and later, Nazareth to the east.

On board the schooner, the crew changed positions. Zebedee and Stefan retired to their bunks for a nap, and a refreshed Joseph steered the vessel, making sure he was well in sight of land. Mary came up on to the main deck and sat next to Joseph, giving him a hug and cradling James in her left arm.

"Darling, you are my hero, my sailor, my lover and prince charming. I love you more than all the drops in this ocean."

Joseph gave Mary a long kiss on her mouth.

"You are my beautiful queen and I know we will be happy where ever the wind takes us. As long as we are together, we have bread on the table and a roof over our heads, we have all we need."

Alexis poked her head up through the open hatch.

"Jesus is climbing the ladder, and is determined to do it by himself. Is it all right for him to come onto the deck?"

"Yes," Mary said. "We can tie a rope around his waist, and as long as someone has hold of the other end, he will be safe."

Jesus found his feet on the swaying deck and ran towards his parents. Mary and Joseph both laughed, not knowing who Jesus was hoping to reach as he zigzagged towards them.

Finally he fell into Joseph's arms and climbed on his father's lap. From there he could reach the handle of the steering oar that was resting well above sea level. The prevailing wind was blowing the schooner in a south-westerly direction, on course for the coastline of Egypt.

"Looks like he will follow in your footsteps and become a sailor," Mary said.

"That's the plan," Joseph laughed. "At least until he is fifteen, then he will be enrolled in a monastery for religious study and priesthood as did his forefathers.

Alexis joined the group, bringing a tumbler of water for Jesus.

"Does anyone want refreshments? I can fetch water and sweetbread if you like."

"I would like some grapes," Mary said.

"Yes, I would too," Joseph added, "and a drink of water."

Mary breastfed James and enjoyed the gentle rolling motion as the vessel cut its way through the water at a steady five knots per hour. "The weather is perfect at this time of the year, the blue sky with barely a cloud, the sun warm and it is not too hot."

"Yes, I have always liked the weather in the months of Nisan, Iyyar and Sivan, or March, April and May, according to the Roman calendar," Joseph replied.

Alexis and Stefan came with refreshments and asked if they could stay.

Most surely," Mary said. "In fact, while we are away from monastery life. I am sure life will be more cordial and far less regimental."

Zebedee came on deck and scanned the landscape for features that would show their present location. Unable to see any prominent markings, he filled a container with water and simultaneously threw a string over the bow with a short piece of wood tied to the end.

"Why is the captain letting the string out? Is he fishing?" Stefan asked.

"No, he is not fishing," Joseph replied. "The water container is called a *clepsydra*. It has a hole on the bottom edge which allows the water to flow out. When the container is empty, it means one minute of time has passed. Zebedee will stop the string at that point and rewind it. The string has nine knots along its length at regular intervals. When he counts the number of knots, the total will show him how fast the vessel is travelling per nautical mile."

"That's remarkable," Stefan said. "I wonder who invented that."

"Seamen came up with the idea when their vessels went past stationary driftwood and after a while distanced themselves from the floating object. Today's method is more refined and more accurate," Joseph said.

Alexis was listening to their conversation and was intrigued. She had never been sailing before and she found the whole experience very exhilarating.

"Excuse me, Your Holiness," she said.

"From now on, do not use that title under any circumstances," Joseph interrupted. "You are old enough to call me Joseph, or if you prefer sir during working hours. We must not reveal ourselves as being religious leaders or leak our previous identities to anyone. I must be referred to as Joseph of Arimathea, the name of the landholding in Ramah."

"I am sorry, sir. I will be more careful in future," Alexis said.

"I don't want to be called Madam, or by my Abbey rank of Virgin Mary, both names make me feel old and sterile,"

Mary said. "I will be happy if you just call me Mary. Now, what were you going to ask His Nastiness?"

They all burst out laughing. It was a great feeling to be free, no need for pomp and ceremony, no more regimented procedures that were only relevant to the power mongers.

"Why does the captain need to measure the vessel's speed, we are not racing other boats?" Alexis asked.

"The captain wants to find our present position on the map," Joseph replied. "Then he will work out where we can safely anchor overnight, probably in a natural cove or inlet."

Zebedee estimated the schooner was sailing at just over six nautical miles an hour and they had been at sea for five hours, making the distance travelled thirty nautical miles. He unrolled a map and measured the distance from Caesarea.

"We should see the towns of Tel-Qasile and Joppa soon, separated by the Nahal River," he said as he walked towards the others. "If the wind remains favourable we can reach a safe inlet about ten miles past Gaza by nightfall."

"That is good news indeed," Joseph replied. "Then if the weather holds overnight, can we make Alexandria the following day?"

"I believe we could reach Tamiat, a trading port on the nearest river fork of the Nile. If the wind remains steady and we are prepared to take a little risk on the voyage."

"What sought of risks?" Mary asked nervously, instinctively holding James tighter.

"We will have to venture a little further out to sea and travel on a straight course. We will need to start our journey earlier, and I will have to navigate by the stars like I always do on long voyages when the weather conditions permit."

"We trust your expertise and judgement Zebedee and we feel safe in your hands," Joseph replied.

Several hours later, within an hour of sunset, the schooner sailed into a protective cove. Zebedee dropped the mainsail, and when the vessel slowed, Stefan dropped the stern anchor. The schooner slowly turned in the current, and Joseph released the bow anchor. The vessel was now ready and pointing in the right direction for tomorrow's night voyage.

Mary and Alexis had prepared the evening meal and the famished men were ready to eat and celebrate the mutually beneficial partnership with a tumbler of fine wine.

An hour later, everyone on board was fast asleep in their bunks. Mary woke up after four hours, breastfed James and then fell back into a deep sleep. When James wanted another feed about five in the morning, Mary realised the schooner was moving.

"Are you awake Joseph?" she asked.

There was no answer. The men had risen earlier and the schooner was heading for Egypt, Zebedee navigating by the stars in the clear night sky.

The voyage to Tamiat was in choppy seas and all four landlubbers were feeling varying degrees of seasickness. Joseph managed to stay on deck with Zebedee, but the others rested on their bunks, with buckets nearby.

Zebedee wanted a discussion with Joseph in private to talk about the partnership and personal matters, and this was a good opportunity.

"I am not sure where you want to live in Egypt, but I think it would be advisable to avoid Alexandria because of the Roman garrison based there."

"To tell you the truth, we haven't discussed any town. I would like to live among a Jewish community where there is a synagogue," Joseph said.

"I know a town, exactly like that, with an inner harbour, quays, and slipways."

"That sounds perfect, what is the name of the town."

"It is called Apollonia. The port for Cyrene, my wife's hometown," Zebedee said.

"Great, we will even have friends in town. We haven't talked about your family yet, have you any children?"

"Yes, we have one son and one daughter. My wife's name is Sharma, James is three, and Candace is fifteen months old."

"I am looking forward to meeting them. Do you think we could find a house to rent in Cyrene?" Joseph asked.

"I can ask at the synagogue and the marketplace, I will soon find suitable accommodation for your family and staff."

Thirteen hours passed, and the schooner sailed up the Damietta, one of the rivers of the Nile delta and docked at Tamiat. Joseph booked two rooms and ordered two large tubs filled with warm water. They all spent about half an hour each in the bathwater, all except Jesus, who stayed in for an hour, splashing and blowing bubbles, sharing the tub with Mary or Alexis.

Later, they ate a three course meal in the dining room, enjoying the warmth of the open fire, and talking about their new life away from Israel. Zebedee and Joseph decided to buy oil, wine, fabric and other goods first thing in the morning to sell at the Cyrene markets. Two hours later, rest beckoned and they retired to their rooms where they slept soundly all night, Mary only waking once to feed James when he cried and then she fell back to sleep.

The next morning, after breakfast, the three men walked along the wharfs, searching for goods to purchase. Zebedee was a well-known trader and was very good at haggling over prices and knowing what fetched the best prices in Cyrene. When the schooner was fully laden the women met them at the prearranged time of three bells, with fresh food for the next leg of the journey.

"Eye Mama, eye," Jesus said pointing to the bow of the schooner.

"Yes, a beautiful eye," Mary answered, who also took notice of the vessel's name for the first time.

It was named *Accyrenia*, an anagram of the province Cyrenaica, their new homeland. All schooners had eyes and feminine names, giving the vessels a living soul and female presence for the lonely sailors on long sea voyages.

The *Accyrenia* sailed north along the Damietta River to the open Mediterranean Sea, travelling at six knots on the river current and light breeze. One mile past the Nile delta, Zebedee changed course to a north-westerly direction and headed for Apollonia. The schooner slowed to four knots, the wind no longer blowing directly behind them, the cargo making the schooner lower in the water. The weather remained fine for the whole journey, and eleven days later, at midday, the vessel sailed into the sheltered inner harbour of Apollonia and docked.

***

Herod's Palace
Masada

Nine hundred miles away, eight Roman soldiers returned to the fortress of King Herod in Masada. They informed Herod how they tracked the six fugitives from Qumran to Caesarea, and found where they had stayed overnight. They located their abandoned horses and four-wheeled chariot, but lost all trace of their whereabouts. The soldiers had searched the city and surrounding towns in all directions, but no further sightings were made.

"Your Royal Highness, we believe they are hiding with friends or have sought sanctuary within the Pharisee sect who has close connections with the Essene sect," the commanding officer said.

King Herod was furious.

"Caesarea is on the coast you bumbling fool," he yelled. "They would have sold their belongings and fled on a vessel. They could be anywhere by now, Rome, Athens, Alexandria or any of the islands."

"We did inquire along the piers, but no one saw anybody fitting the description of the six fugitives."

"Did you board any of the larger vessels docked in the area?"

"No sir, but we asked the masters if they had passengers aboard."

King Herod had heard enough.

"Arrest this idiot and escort him outside," he shouted.

Herod marched out with the soldiers, grabbing a heavy sword from his personal guard standing at the doorway. The shaken officer was ordered on hands and knees, and with one almighty swing of the sword, the inconsolable King decapitated the soldiers head.

"Bury the body in the pauper's cemetery outside the fortress walls, without a headstone," he said then issued a death order for the four Justus Fugitives.

***

**Cyrenaica
Northern Egypt**

The port of Apollonia was bustling with activity, the docked *Accyrenia* attracting interest from the merchants and traders. Zebedee sold the oil and wine to the highest bidders, making a handsome profit for Joseph and himself.

"We have sold the heavy items, Joseph. The fine fabric and perfumes we can trade at the Cyrene markets for a good price."

"I have much to learn about our new partnership, I am completely reliant on your trading expertise and seamanship."

"We will become the best traders in the Mediterranean. I will never forget how you financed this schooner after I fell into debt when my sister ship, the *Cyrenia* sank."

"It was meant to be," Joseph said. "You saved my family from that tyrant, King Herod. Now we have a mutual bond for life."

Zebedee hired two carts and donkeys to haul the remaining cargo to his house in Cyrene. Stefan volunteered to stay overnight on board the schooner. Alexis and James sat in the first cart, with Zebedee leading the donkey on the eight mile trip home. Mary and Jesus sat in the other cart being led by Joseph. Three hours later Zebedee made it home where his dog Pal announced his arrival with a high pitched howl. Sharma ran towards Zebedee with her arms outstretched and fell into his arms.

"I was so worried about you. The recent storms were the worst in living memory, thank god you are safe."

"I lost the *Cyrenia*, the whole crew and its cargo. I only saved the *Accyrenia* by ordering the crew to throw the cargo of wine and oil overboard. The storm was devastating."

Sharma whispered, "I see we have guests, but I have very little food to offer them."

"We have brought food for consumption and goods for the market."

Zebedee introduced Sharma to Joseph's family and Alexis, and mentioned that Stefan was guarding the schooner overnight. Zebedee and Joseph led the donkeys into the barn and unhitched them. The women took the food into the house and Jesus was introduced to three year old James, who was playing on the floor with wooden blocks and carved animals. Candace was having a nap, and Mary breastfed James, and then nursed him to sleep. Later the two families joined together for prayers, ate the evening meal and chatted for hours, getting to know each other and talking about the past and the future.

During the next two weeks, the families joined together, selling the fabric, incense and perfume at the market. They searched for a suitable house to rent in Cyrene, but there were none available. Joseph found a large house in Apollonia for rent. It was eight miles away from his friend's house, but it would suffice until a new house could be built on Zebedee's vacant adjoining block. Zebedee asked a cousin, named Jeremiah, who was about the same age of Stefan, to join the crew. Joseph, who had trained as a carpenter while in the lower ranks of monastery life, revamped the schooner's cramped eight berth cabins into two twin cabins, more comfortable and more suitable for longer voyages.

The two men planned their next voyage, happy in the knowledge that the women and children could stay together in the larger house while they were away.

"I would like to send a message to my parents as soon as possible," Joseph said. "They must be worried sick. They would have heard about Herod searching for us, and know that we hastily left the monastery. I need to let them know we are safe, but not let them know where we are living."

"We can harvest the giant fennel herb Silphiuffi, it fetches high prices in Corinth and Athens," Zebedee said. "Then we can cross over to Ephesus and meet with one of the schooner masters I know. When he sails to Caesarea, he can employ a messenger to visit your parents. We can leave as soon as the southerly *ghibli* winds blow. At this time of the year they are quite mild, but later in the season the wind reaches gale force with dangerous squalls."

"What is the fennel herb used for?" Joseph asked.

"Mainly for contraceptive use by the temple prostitutes, But it can also be used for abortions if used in stronger doses."

"Would we trade between Athens and Ephesus?"

"I have never left any port empty, unless under duress from local hostilities," Zebedee replied. "We need to trade heavily, earn good profits, and then buy a sister vessel so that we can sail in tandem to Britannia. You will need to gain at least two years seamanship skills before we venture out past the straits, through the gates of Hercules."

Over the next three years, Joseph, Zebedee, Stefan and Jeremiah traded between the ports in Egypt, Greece, Italy, France, Spain and Turkey. On the first docking at Ephesus, Joseph gave Zebedee a parcel to give to his contacts. It contained locks of hair from Mary, Jesus, James and himself, with a note: *'We are safe and well. We will return when it is safe to do so. We love you and miss you.'* There were no names mentioned, no contact address given, but it was a message that would bring hope and joy if delivered.

They traded in fine linen, silk fabrics, oils, wine, pottery, herbs and spices. The trading voyages became longer and more daring with the crew more experienced in the open sea. Zebedee and Joseph bought another schooner from their huge profits and named the vessel *Pollonia*. They now skippered their own vessels and hired two more deckhands for both schooners. Joseph was at sea during the births of his next two children.

In the house at Apollonia, Mary gave birth to another son named Josephes, Joses as his siblings called him. Eighteen months later, she gave birth to a daughter named Mary. Her friend Sharma, and Sharma's mother, a trained midwife, were both at her side during the crucial months before and after each birth. Sharma also fell pregnant with her third child, a boy they named John, born three weeks before Mary's daughter.

Eight months later, the two schooners, *Pollonia* and *Accyrenia* sailed into Apollonia, fully laden with goods. News of their arrival soon reached the crews relatives and before the stock was unloaded onto the wharves many happy reunions took place. Joseph and Zebedee hugged their wives and held their newborn babies for the first time. Stefan was greeted by Alexis and the two walked away, holding hands and unashamedly kissing in public. Absence had made their young hearts grow fonder, and the close friends had fallen deeply in love.

Zebedee and Joseph stayed in the province of Cyrenaica for the next six months. Joseph and Mary moved into the newly built house next door to Zebedee and Sharma. They even designed the house with a large connecting room where they could all eat together whenever they desired. They always ate together on the Sabbath, after attending the morning service at the synagogue, and on the third day of the week, they would usually discuss business after the evening meal.

"I have learnt so much about the world religions since I left the confined walls of the monastery," Joseph said confiding to Zebedee.

"Like what?"

"Well, since I have been at sea, I have realised how ridiculous the Sabbath rule is that you can't work on that day."

"You mean like not being able to throw over cargo in a storm to avoid sinking?"

"Exactly," Joseph replied, "and the farmers still have to milk their goats and cows on the Sabbath."

Zebedee laughed.

"At least the herdsmen can lay back and watch the wild animals kill their goats. Why should they risk being ostracised by clergymen who make up rules to grandiose themselves and their manmade beliefs?"

"It's the same as the Roman senators, voting on how much they deserve be paid for their hard earned court gibberish," Joseph said.

The two men laughed at the idea of men in their own trades making up rules and regulations that greatly benefited themselves. They compared it to releasing a small snowball at the top of a mountain and watching it grow bigger by adding more snow to itself as it rolled along. The men changed the subject and talked about repairing the vessels sails and cleaning the hulls in preparation for their longest voyage ever planned.

The voyage included ports in Italy, southern France, Spain, and for the first time for Joseph and the crew, Britannia.

Over the next four years, Joseph and Zebedee traded between ports in Cornwall and Rome. Mary dreaded the trips Joseph and Zebedee took outside the gates of Hercules, and insisted the men visit home after unloading the tin and iron cargo at the Italian ports. In the same period of time, Mary conceived again and gave birth to a boy in the house at Cyrene. She named him Simon after the synagogue Rabbi who comforted her through the most trying times.

The next voyage on the agenda was a short one to Alexandria. Joseph and Zebedee decided to take their eldest sons, Jesus, now aged seven, and James eight for some seafaring experience and sightseeing along the Nile.

They visited the pyramids at Giza, and Jesus was allowed to accompany a priest into a passageway that led under the Sphinx. Inside was a room about thirty feet wide and forty-five feet long, with murals painted on the walls and ceiling. Jesus was amazed at the stories and history depicted, and the rows of timber shelving holding bamboo baskets full of scrolls and ancient clay tablets. The priest told Jesus about some of their Gods, their beliefs and traditions. Jesus was particularly interested in the sun god Ra, and how the Pharaoh Ramses named himself the son of Ra, the Son of God.

On the way back to the schooners Jesus discussed the matter with Joseph.

"Father, the Egyptians think the sun is a God, but we only face the sun to praise god for light and warmth."

"Yes son," Joseph replied, "The Roman's also think the sun is a god, and like the Greeks and Egyptians, they believe in hundreds of Gods, which include planets, animals, sea, wind, even thunder and lightning."

"Is that why the first day of the week is called Sunday by the Romans?"

"Yes Jesus, followed by other gods, the second day is named after the moon, Monday.

The seventh day is named after the planet Saturn, Saturday. We believe in only one almighty God that created Heaven and Earth, and all things."

"Have you seen God at the monastery?"

"No son, nobody has seen God, but I have felt his presence many times. It has been prophesied that God will one day send a Messiah to Earth and we will behold his likeness, power and glory."

Joseph looked down at Jesus lying on his lap. It had been a long day and the boy had drifted off to sleep, probably dreaming of the things he saw in the underground library.

They reached the docks an hour before sunset, checked that the new cargo had been loaded as arranged, and found suitable accommodation nearby. They ate dinner at a waterfront restaurant and went to bed early.

The next morning Joseph was paying for the overnight accommodation when a sailor approached him.

"Morning sir, I am inquiring about a job. My name is Jacob Justus."

"Pardon?" Joseph said.

"I am looking for a job, sir," the sailor repeated.

"And your name is Joshua?"

"No sir, Jacob. Jacob Justus."

"Come with me. I have a friend who needs a deckhand."

Joseph and the sailor boarded the *Accyrenia* and met with Zebedee and the crew in the cabin. Joseph asked the sailor to sit at the table and poured him a wine.

"This man is looking for a job, his name is Jacob Justus."

Zebedee glanced at Joseph.

"That's your—"

"Exactly," Joseph replied.

Zebedee questioned the sailor, "I know of Jacob Justus, and you are not that person. What is your real name?"

"Sir, my real name is Tyrone. I was sent by Jacob Justus to find his son, believed to be living in Egypt. I was hired to approach any man near forty and tell them my name was Jacob Justus. Eventually, I would get a reaction and that man may be the missing son or a friend."

"What were you to do if you got a reaction?" Joseph asked.

"Give the person a message if he could answer two specific questions."

"What questions?" Zebedee asked.

The man looked at Zebedee and Joseph, not knowing whom to ask.

"The first question, what is the name of your favourite horse?"

"That's easy," Zebedee said. "It's "Star."

"Sir, that is not what I was told."

"What about Rueben?" Joseph said.

"Yes, that was one of the horses mentioned."

"Now you tell me. What was the other horse's name?"

"I was told if 'Asher' was the name given, to ask for a second horse's name."

"What was the other question?" Joseph asked.

"You need to confirm your eldest son's middle name," Tyrone said.

"I can give you his full name, Jesus Immanuel Justus."

"Sir, Immanuel is correct."

"Well," Joseph said, "You have found the person you are looking for, but now you have to convince us who you are, and who really sent you."

"I am telling you the truth. Jacob paid me to find you, and I have been searching for two years."

"How do we know if Jacob sent you or someone else?"

"King Herod passed away, and Jacob told me it was reasonably safe for your family to return home."

"What else did Jacob say?"

"Do not return to Jerusalem, Ramah or to the monastery, but send a message, date and meeting place."

Joseph was convinced the man was telling the truth, for he had not entered Jesus's middle name on the census form. Only his immediate family and Simeon, the High Priest knew of the name Immanuel. Joseph thanked Tyrone and gave him a generous bonus for his diligence in delivering the original message.

Joseph turned to Zebedee.

"I am going to take my family back to Israel as soon as I can."

"I too would like to return to Israel," Zebedee said. "I have family in Capernaum, on the shores of Lake Galilee."

The crews sailed the two schooners to the port of Apollonia and greeted the rest of the family with the good news. Mary was so delighted that she broke down in tears and hugged Joseph for ages, not daring to believe her ears.

"Oh darling, tell me again. Is it true? Can we return home at last?"

"Yes darling, as soon as we sell the houses, we will return home."

"I want to see our parents," Mary sobbed, "I want to kiss them, hug them, and tell them how much we missed them. They haven't seen Jesus and James for so long."

"They don't even know about Joses, young Mary and Simon, or our new friends Zebedee and Sharma," Joseph replied.

"Oh, I haven't thought about losing our friends," Mary cried.

"Well don't," Joseph replied.

Mary looked at Joseph in disbelief. The family had been such good friends and it was out of character for Joseph to be so callous.

Joseph saw the look on Mary's face and smiled.

"They want to come with us. Zebedee has family in Galilee and Sharma will take her mother with her. She is her only relative here besides her three children. It has already been discussed and decided. Everyone is happy."

"I will be glad to go home," Mary said. "The Jewish people here are a minority and the nomadic tribes are becoming more hostile and quite aggressive at the markets."

That night the families met in the adjoining room between the two houses and happily talked all night, planning their future lives, rejoicing and drinking, celebrating until their tired eyes and bodies forced them to retire for the night.

A few months later, a rich merchant bought both properties. The families said goodbye to their friends and promised to meet up whenever they docked overnight in Apollonia.

Zebedee, his family and his crewman boarded the *Accyrenia* with all their belongings, and prepared to sail. Joseph, his family and crew boarded the *Pollonia* with their belongings, and prepared to sail. At sunrise the breeze strengthened and they sailed out of Apollonia Harbour.

Nine days later the two schooners docked at the port of Caesarea. Joseph noticed two Roman soldiers patrolling the wharf and immediately felt worried about his family's safety. He knew his family were still on the wanted list until the warrant for his arrest was dissolved by the highest court in the land, the full bench of the Sanhedrin. Joseph asked his family to stay on board while he talked with Zebedee.

The two men discussed the situation. They decided Zebedee would find overnight accommodation in a nearby inn, and Joseph's family would remain in their cabins, out of sight. Zebedee arranged the accommodation and asked the innkeeper who was crowned the new King of Israel.

"There is no longer a King of Israel to rule our land," the man said.

"What?"

"The Roman Senate, acting on Emperor Augustus orders, divided King Herod's kingdom into smaller provinces to reduce the power of the appointed rulers and to reduce the power of the people."

"What is going on?"

"We are now in the province of Judea, under the rule of Archelaus Herod, who was appointed Ethnarch, not King. Herod Antipas was appointed Tetrarch of Galilee, and Philip Herod Tetrarch of Ituraea."

"What has been the reaction by the major religious sects over this Roman interference in our nation?" Zebedee asked.

"There have been many secret meetings, some organised protests, and there have been many people arrested. The word on the street is the Pharisee, Essene and Therapeut sects are against the subdivision of Israel into smaller provinces. The Sadducee sect which also includes most of the judges, scribes, doctors and the wealthy are tolerant with the Roman authorities and the protection provided by their soldiers."

"So the nation is divided and weakened. Just what the Romans authorities intended."

Zebedee thanked the innkeeper for the information and returned to the schooner *Pollonia* to talk to Joseph. When Joseph heard that Archelaus, the erratic son of King Herod was appointed Ethnarch of Judea, he became more frightened for his family's safety.

"Let's replenish our fresh food and water supplies today, stay overnight and recuperate, and then sail for Galilee tomorrow."

"I agree," Zebedee replied. "Galilee under the more tolerant rule of Antipas would seem a better choice at this stage."

Joseph escorted his family and friends to the room at the inn and then walked to the nearby blacksmith. Joseph was delighted to see the same smithy that bought his two horses several years ago.

"You may not remember me, I—"

"I remember you very well. I bought the two white horses and carriage from you."

"Yes, that's right," Joseph replied. "You gave me a fair deal under trying times."

"Times were hard under that tyrant King Herod, but may become even worse under Archelaus I fear."

"You are the only man I know and trust in town. I was wondering if you could do me a favour. I will pay you for your troubles."

"I'm sure I can help. What do you want?" the smithy asked.

"I need a reliable messenger to give a verbal message to my parents in Ramah."

Joseph drew a map showing the homestead at Ramah and told the smithy the verbal message, stating their overseas relatives will be attending the synagogue at Shechem on the third Sabbath of next month.

The smithy was pleased with the payment and vowed the message would be delivered within three days. The next day the two schooners sailed away from the wharf at first light and headed north towards the port of Haifa situated on the mouth of the Pishon River.

CHAPTER 6: The Family Reunion

Joseph and Zebedee's families settled in the province of Galilee. Zebedee bought a house in Capernaum on the foreshore of Lake Galilee. Joseph settled on his grandfather's farmstead on the outskirts of Nazareth. The property was run down and virtually abandoned, only being used by local herdsmen to graze their flocks. Joseph and Mary had fond memories of the farm as many years ago they met here with their families during the harvest festivals.

They vowed to restore the old farmhouse and then have a larger dwelling built near a crystal clear spring-fed stream. Joseph bought a horse and four-wheeled cart. He made two trips back to the schooner with Stefan to collect their belongings. Stefan and Alexis stayed on the moored schooner on the second trip and made it their home until a house could be built for them on the property.

On the third Sabbath of the month, Joseph, his three month pregnant wife Mary, Jesus, James, Joses, Simon and their sister Mary, travelled to the town of Shechem. They arrived two hours before the noon service begun at the synagogue and Joseph searched the town for any sign of Roman activity before stopping at a restaurant for refreshments. Joseph left Mary with the children and went to find overnight accommodation. He found an inn with three rooms available and a paddock for the horse to graze. Joseph returned to the restaurant and waited for the arrival of the children's four grandparents. Mary and Joseph had no way of knowing if the message had been delivered.

Two hours later, the children were getting restless. Joseph and Mary changed plans and went to the rooms at the inn for a rest. Joses, his sister Mary, and young Simon went to sleep, while Jesus and James played with the several small wooden animals Joseph had carved for them while he was away at sea. Every voyage, Joseph would bring back at least two more carved animals for his children.

Joseph looked down the street towards the synagogue. The local congregation were milling around in the front yard, and some were walking towards the open doorway. Joseph asked Mary to stay with the children while he went to the synagogue. Joseph stepped outside and peered down the main road which stretched in a straight line for ten miles. He could see something approaching a long way off with a trail of dust. Joseph walked towards the oncoming object praying it was a horse and chariot carrying his parents. Joseph walked until he came to the yard where his horse was grazing contently. He could see two white horses and a white four-wheeled carriage, with four people on board, it had to be them. *It was them!*

Joseph waited until they were closer and then waved them down. Joseph couldn't believe it. Jacob had bought back his beloved horses and wedding chariot from the smithy in Caesarea. Jacob slowed the horses to a walk and stopped beside a railing where he tied the reins to the rail. Suddenly, Joseph was besieged with arms hugging him all over, Miriam, Salome, Jacob and Heli, all hugging him, crying with joy and not letting go. This moment had taken six years to unfold, no one wanted to let go on the family reunion.

Joseph suggested the horses should be led into the paddock and unhitched, so they could greet Mary and the grandchildren.

Mary watched from the upstairs room window and waited until she heard the footsteps in the corridor. *Close enough!* Mary opened the door and flung her arms around her mother. They hugged and cried from sheer joy. The six adults hugged each other and talked for quite some time. Then the focus turned to Jesus and James playing quietly with the toy animals.

"The boys have grown so much," Salome said.

"It has been six years since you last saw them," Mary said. "Before I re-introduce you follow me, I have something to show you."

Mary led them into the next room. There was a collective gasp as they saw three more children sleeping soundly in their beds.

"God-parents, please meet your other grandchildren, Josephes, Mary junior and baby Simon," Mary said proudly.

"I can't believe you have five children Mary," Salome said.

"I thought Joseph was all at sea," Heli joked.

"He obviously came home a few times," Jacob added smiling.

"Only last week one of the Nuns mentioned to me, *'I often wonder what the Virgin Mary is doing,'* " Miriam said with a smirk. "I will inform her Mary has been very busy."

"You know how much I love children, and I have more good news. I am three months pregnant," Mary said.

"I can't believe how slim and beautiful your figure is Mary, what is your secret?" Salome asked.

"Well," Mary said. "I exercise a lot, mainly from running away from Joseph, but also running after the boys."

The whole family laughed and then went to talk with Jesus and James, reintroducing themselves to their grandchildren. Jacob and Heli talked to Joseph while the women caught up with years of gossip and prepared refreshments.

"We have applied to the full bench of the Sanhedrin for the withdrawal of the arrest warrant ordered by King Herod," Heli said. "The judges overwhelmingly agreed to have the warrant rescinded and will send a delegation to discuss the matter with Archelaus later this month."

"I do not trust Archelaus any more than I would his father," Joseph replied. "He is irrational at the best of times. I am refurbishing the old farmhouse at Nazareth. We will live there until a larger house is built near the creek. Work is scheduled to start in a few weeks."

"I am glad to hear you want to live on the family farm," Jacob said. "We had many good times there, especially on family reunions during the festivals of Pentecost and Dedication."

"I also met Mary at one of those festivals," Joseph said.

They heard a voice coming from the far corner of the room.

"And I was betrothed to you there, on my thirteenth birthday, not that I had any say in the matter, darling."

"Not trying to change the subject," Heli said in a loud voice, "but Jacob and I have a present for Jesus and James."

The two boys ran towards their grandfathers and stood nearby.

"Listen carefully boys," Jacob said. "Both presents are similar, only the colours are different."

"The colour you pick is the one that will belong to you," Heli said. "You cannot swap from day to dry, is that clear?"

The boys nodded in agreement.

Joseph gave both boys a blackboard and chalk.

"I want you both to write down three colours. Go on opposite sides of the bed and come back here with your answers."

While the boys were writing, Jacob and Heli picked up one object each and held it behind their backs. Jesus came back first and handed his father the blackboard, with the three written words, green, blue and white. James followed. His words were spelt as red, wite, and blak. The men looked at each other and nodded.

Heli gave James a ball that had been stained red and white. Jacob gave Jesus a ball that had been stained blue and white. The two boys both hugged their grandparents and ran off to play with the balls. They bounced them, threw them, kicked them and rolled them. Mayhem ruled in the room until the adults organised a group throwing challenge. The rules were: if you dropped the ball once, you knelt on one knee, twice two knees, third drop you were out. They played two games. Jesus won the first game, James won the other. The adults congratulated the boys on their catching and throwing. Then it was time for refreshments.

Later, the two black boards were cleaned and wrapped. When Josephes and young Mary woke they were given the blackboards and chalk by Miriam and Salome. Baby Simon was given a silver coin which he grasped tightly, but at his age he was happy just to be held and breastfed by Mary.

"All your children are about eighteen months apart in age, have you always had enough breast milk?" Salome whispered to Mary.

"I haven't given it much thought. I have been breastfeeding since Jesus suckled. I have always had a good supply, and I don't completely wean the children until they turn two."

"Don't you get sore? I mean, when you breast feed two children?"

"Not at all," Mary replied. "In fact, I like it when my nipples become erect and sometimes I have an orgasm as well!"

"Well good for you," Salome said wishing she had not raised the question. "I had better clear these plates now."

The family stayed together that night and talked on into the early hours of the first day of the week. One by one, tiredness overcame them and they excused themselves and found somewhere to sleep. When Jacob was alone with Joseph, he brought his son up to date with the political scene.

"Son, a lot has changed while you have been in Egypt over the last six years. King Herod died in agony and Archelaus was appointed Ethnarch of Judea."

"I heard that, but who is the High Priest?"

"King Herod sacked Simon ben Boethus when his daughter Mariamne and her two sons were involved in a plan to poison the King. They just wanted to put him out of his misery and suffering. The King had his two sons executed and appointed a Sadducee, Matthias son of Theophilus as High Priest."

"So we have a Sadducee as High Priest. I have been informed that they are tolerant toward Roman rule and occupation."

"Yes they are, but when Herod died Archelaus dismissed him. Matthias refused to give Archelaus the title of Supreme Priest because he had not been granted the kingship. He then appointed Joazar ben Boethus as the new High Priest."

"So we have a Pharisee as High Priest?" enquired Joseph.

"Yes we do, but not Joazar. He was dismissed for the same reason. His brother, Eleazer, and Joshua ben Sie followed suit in quick succession."

"So who is the High Priest now?" Joseph asked, completely flabbergasted."

"Well, Joazar changed his ruling and anointed Archelaus Supreme Priest. Joazar was then restored as the High Priest."

"So the erratic and unstable Archelaus has religious and political control of Judea."

"Yes, unfortunately," Jacob said. "Archelaus has already enforced the Julian calendar on Judea, banning the use of the Jewish calendar."

"Couldn't the full bench of the Sanhedrin overturn the ruling?" Joseph asked.

"They tried, but their ruling was dismissed, and Archelaus threatened to dissolve the Sanhedrin if they did not comply."

"Is Archelaus allowing the use of our Jewish months for religious ceremonies?"

"Yes, at least for now. All written items must be dated under the Julian calendar, and verbally, Jewish months must be associated with the appropriate Julian month."

"So when we near the end of Shebat that is the middle of the Julian February? The end of February is halfway into Adar. The two calendars seem at odds with each other."

"There is one more thing you need to know about the calendar," Jacob said.

"I think I'm ready for bed, but tell me anyway."

"When Archelaus was anointed Supreme Priest, he decreed the new calendar years would start from that day."

"Pardon, that flew straight over my head."

"Archelaus decreed January the first as 1A.D. Today's date is February 5th 1 A.D."

"What about all the previous years from the date of creation until now, don't they count?" Joseph asked.

"Believe it or not, Archelaus and his advisers came up with a solution of sorts.

Those years would date *'Backwards to Creation'*. Last year would be 1B.C. and ten years ago, 10B.C."

"That means Jesus was born on March 29th 8 B.C. and our next child will be due around August, year one."

"Yes, the year will be written *'After Dedication'*, 1 A.D."

"Father, on that note it's goodnight from me, and goodnight to you. I will see you later in the morning. Goodnight and God bless."

"Goodnight son and God bless you and your family, and it's great to have you home at last," Jacob said hugging Joseph.

Four hours later, six month old Simon woke up hungry and cried. That woke James and Jesus who played with their air filled goat bladder balls, encased in goat leather. The balls soon landed on Joses and two year old Mary and woke them. Mary was in bed breastfeeding. Miriam and

Salome looked at each other, shrugged their shoulders and wearily struggled out of their warm beds to greet the cold winter morning. The children ate breakfast first, and later when the men rose, the adults ate sweet-bread and drank water or juice.

All too soon the family had to part; they agreed to meet in Shechem on the first Sabbath of each month. Jacob wanted to give Mary and Joseph their white four-wheeled chariot, with their horses, Rueben and Asher, but Joseph declined the offer.

"We need the work horse on the farm," Joseph said. "When the new house is built we would love to take up your offer."

Everyone had a last round of hugs and then the two parties split, one heading for Nazareth and the others for Hebron and Ramah.

Joseph shook the reins, and the work horse broke into a trot. That was when young Mary screamed and started crying.

"What's wrong Mary? What's the matter?" her mother asked.

Joseph slowed the horse to a walk and looked around, looking at the three boys, thinking they may have upset her.

"I left my blackboard under the bed," Mary sobbed.

Joseph slowly shook his head from side to side and turned the chariot back to the inn.

"Don't cry darling, I will get it for you," Mary said comforting her daughter.

"Let Jesus run and get it," Joseph said.

"I will see the innkeeper and check out both rooms for anything else that may have been left behind," Mary replied.

Mary found the blackboard, chalk and a blanket belonging to Heli. She grabbed the keys to the room, closed the doors and headed for the stairway.

When Mary regained consciousness, she was lying in the doctor's surgery with Miriam and Salome holding her hands and comforting her.

"Don't try to talk Mary," her mother said softly. "You are all right, but you had a nasty fall down the steps."

"You will be sore and bruised, but you didn't break any bones," Salome said.

Mary tried to speak, but Miriam asked to sleep for a while as the doctor had given her medication for pain and it would also make her feel drowsy. Mary drifted off to sleep, and the doctor had his nurse swab the blood on her legs. Mary had miscarried.

Joseph had borrowed the innkeeper's horse and caught up with his parents after he took Mary to the doctor. They rebooked the rooms in the inn for another day as Mary would need to be in the doctor's care for at least twenty-four hours. They discussed the accident and decided it would be best if Miriam told Mary about the miscarriage.

Miriam was holding Mary's hand when she stirred.

"Hello darling, you are looking better, but you will feel drowsy so take it easy."

"Mum? Is the baby all right? I feel sore."

"Darling, the doctor couldn't save the baby."

"Oh no Mum. I think it was a girl this time. No Mum, no!"

"Mary, you must get well. Think of your lovely family. You have been blessed with lovely, healthy children."

"Mum, was the baby a boy or a girl?"

"Darling, the baby was a girl, just as you thought, but the doctor has assured us that you can conceive again later."

"Mum, you don't understand. I wanted to name her Miriam."

"We will name her Miriam, and she will be with you on the farm in Nazareth, I promise."

Miriam hugged Mary, and they cried together, until Mary drifted back into a restless sleep.

The next day the two chariots headed for the farm at Nazareth. Mary was laying on a straw mattress, covered with Heli's blanket, her mother by her side. In the back of the second chariot was a heavy box. Inside the box was a small wrapped body of baby Miriam. She had been given a traditional Jewish ceremony in front of Mary and all the family. Then her little body was placed on the soil and covered with more soil. The box was sealed, ready to be transported to the farm at Nazareth.

Mary selected a position for the gravesite near the creek, about one hundred feet from the site of the new dwelling. The men dug the grave, and Miriam and Mary planted an almond tree at the head, leaving room for a headstone and for the growth of the tree. The box was lowered into the grave while Joseph prayed Mary and the children threw in almond blossoms. When the mound had been shaped, everyone stood in a circle, held hands and sang hymns.

Later in the afternoon, Joseph carved a head-stone with the words, 'Miriam Justus, stillborn February 6th 1A.D. God bless you, Rest in peace, in God's care'. Joseph placed the headstone and Mary cried softly, "Thank you Joseph."

***

Jerusalem

Two Sanhedrin delegates were sent to see Archelaus after their scheduled monthly meeting held at the great hall in Jerusalem. Among other matters, they brought to his attention the possible withdrawal of the outstanding warrant for the Justus family arrest and the possible pardon for the exiled Nebedeus and Hannah who had a son called Ananias.

Archelaus was not in the mood to make decisions, and so he informed the delegates he would discuss the matters that King Herod had decreed with Philip of Iturea province, and Antipas of Galilee, before handing down his decision.

Joseph disregarded the warrant and decided to take his family to Jerusalem to celebrate the Jewish Passover festival in the Jewish month of Nissan, and according to the Sadducee sect the 3965th year after the Biblical creation of the earth. Now decreed to be 1A.D., year one of Archelaus' Dedication and anointing as Supreme Priest of Judea. Joseph would use the occasion to pray in the temple for his family, have his new home blessed and especially have the grieving Mary blessed and consoled.

Mary had continually blamed herself for the death of baby Miriam and had fallen into depression. The whole family had suffered over the last month and Joseph wanted to celebrate with the extended family and friends to convince Mary to enjoy life again. Joseph knew his business partner had been patient and understanding, but Zebedee had already re-established his family in Capernaum and needed to trade again to produce income. Joseph decided to let Zebedee know he would be ready to sail after Passover, and to arrange for suitable trading stock for the destination of his choice.

Joseph would take Jesus and James with him on the voyage, and ask Heli and Salome to help Mary at the farm. Hopefully Mary would miss him and want to love again.

Joseph looked out of the kitchen window and saw Mary sitting near Miriam's grave. He decided to comfort Mary and join her in prayer, knowing how inconsolable she had been since she had her miscarriage. On the way, he picked a wild barley stem that was growing near the track.

"Hello Mary, I would like to join you in prayer," he said.

Mary didn't hear or acknowledge Joseph. She was in a trance. Joseph showed Mary the head of the barley.

"The barley is ripe. We are in the month of Nissan, near the end of the Roman month of March. It will be Jesus' eighth birthday in three days."

Mary was staring at the headstone, focusing on 'Miriam'.

"I was hoping you would like to see your parents in Jerusalem during the Passover festival."

Mary looked at Joseph but didn't answer. Joseph held her hand and prayed. Mary broke down and cried. Joseph lifted Mary to her feet and hugged her tightly.

"It was not your fault Mary. It was an accident. You must regain your strength for the children. We all need you darling."

Mary looked into Joseph's kind eyes and hugged him.

"Yes, I need to look after my children."

Joseph walked Mary back to the house. "We will be visiting your parents in three days' time to celebrate Jesus' birthday, will you be able to travel?"

"I will be fine. I want to celebrate Passover with you, my family and friends I haven't seen in over six years."

On the second day of the week, the Roman's Monday, the Justus family left the farm for Ramah to stay with the four grandparents. The Passover festival began after the Vernal equinox, on the fourteenth day of Nissan, on the first night of a full moon. The seven day Spring Festival had two main Holy days, at the beginning and on the seventh day, with the intervening days of the festival called Chol HaMoed. It was the best Passover the Justus family had experienced, and for Jesus and James, their most impressionable religious festival. The experience would inspire their entire adult lives, and later spark a fierce rivalry between the two brothers. During the week, the Qumran Most High approached Joseph in the Temple.

"It is good to see you again my friend," Daniel said. "You are looking very healthy and tanned."

"I have been travelling the seas of the world. I now captain a schooner and trade as far as the coast of Gallia and the southern ports of Britannia," Joseph said.

"What is Britannia like?"

"It is a free land with little interference from the small Roman occupation. They call me Joseph the tin merchant, because I trade in metals."

"I envy their freedom," Daniel said. "Joseph, I have been informed by the High Priest that you can obtain a pardon for your family from Archelaus on one condition."

"And that is?"

"You can retain your title as the David crown prince, and your seat on the Sanhedrin Council, but you must relinquish any rights to the throne and ambitions to become High Priest."

"Archelaus has no right to impose those conditions."

"Joseph, many things have changed over the last six years. Your family is in grave danger at the moment."

"I think it is a high price for freedom, but I believe you are right. Tell the High Priest, Joazar ben Boethus, that I accept Archelaus' most generous proposal and conditions."

"I know it is hard Joseph, but as usual, you are making the correct, calculated choice. I am sure you will have a great influence in other ways for the direction of our beloved country and traditions."

"Thank you Daniel. You have always been my most loyal and trusted associate and friend. Please pass on my acceptance as swiftly as possible. My family's immediate safety is of the utmost importance."

Joseph left the Temple and met Zebedee who was talking with several scribes and priests.

"Good morning, brothers," he said.

"Talk to this man, ask Joseph's opinion." Zebedee said in a frustrated voice.

"Yes, how can I help?"

"Zebedee says there is a problem with reversing the years from 1B.C. to creation," one of the scribes said. "We disagree. We actually like the system."

"What do you feel is the problem, Zebedee?" Joseph asked.

"Well, generally it is all right verbally, but it is not accurate when written and compared with other dates."

"Can you give me an example?"

"Let's see. When were your first two boys born?"

"Jesus was born in March 8B.C. and James in July year 7B.C.

"How many months apart are their ages?"

"Sixteen months."

"Now write down the dates on this slab."

Joseph wrote James 27/7/7 and Jesus 29/3/8.

"Now, if a stranger read those figures, what would be his answer for the gap in months?"

"As written, the gap would be five months remaining in 7B.C. plus three months to March 8B.C. But that is only eight months, which is not correct."

"That is my point, the years go backwards, but the months in each year remain forward. It is a mathematical nightmare."

Zebedee and Joseph parted from the group of scribes as they were hotly debating the problem.

"Can you be ready to sail, two weeks from today?" Joseph said.

"I will have to check my tight schedule," Zebedee joked. "Oh, look at that."

He pointed to his palm.

"I was ready a week ago."

Joseph invited Zebedee and his family to stay overnight at the farm in Nazareth when the Passover festival ended. The boys were full of energy and played a game of football in the open space behind the house. James Cleopas, Zebedee's nine year old son, and Josephes aged five, versed Jesus eight, and James seven. The rules were simple: no handling the ball, kicking only. Two large rocks placed three strides apart at each end were the goals. Jesus and James team scored the most goals, but it was all about having fun. That is, until the ball was accidentally kicked over Miriam's grave and upset the grieving Mary.

Two weeks later, the schooners, *Pollonia* and *Accyrenia*, sailed towards Cyprus, with the final destination being ports in Italia. Among the crew aboard the *Accyrenia* were the two James's and Jesus, all learning sailing skills from Zebedee.

Ten months later, after many successful trades, the sailors returned home and celebrated with their families. Zebedee bought two small fishing boats and taught his sons net trawling on the inland freshwater Sea of Galilee. Joseph used his skills as a carpenter to make cabinets and cupboards for the new house, which the builders had almost completed. Jesus and James helped their father and became good carpenters over time.

Passover came round again and the Justus family reunited in Jerusalem for the annual spring festival. Joseph met his old friend Theudas, from the Therapeutic sect. Theudas had several children from his harem of wives. His oldest boy nearly seven was named Barabbas. Joseph congratulated him and mentioned he had five children around the same ages.

The Chief Priest approached Joseph.

"Good news Joseph," he said. "The warrants for the arrest of yourself, Mary, Jesus and James had been rescinded by Archelaus, and the full bench of the Sanhedrin has ratified your position on the Council."

The new house was spiritually blessed in the Temple and after the Passover feast the family moved in.

One month later, Jacob passed away, aged seventy-eight. Joseph was now officially The David, and Jesus, being the eldest son, the Crown Prince. Joseph was an Essene, which was a branch of the Pharisee sect. Both sects believed in one Almighty God, spirits and eternal life after Earthly death, however, the Essenes only ate vegetables, eggs, white flesh of chicken and fish.

Unfortunately, the Pharisees decided James should be the Crown Prince as Jesus had been conceived more than the ninety day betrothal period allowed before marriage. To complicate matters, the Sadducee sect and scribes of the written law declared Jesus was the legitimate Crown Prince. This caused conflict within the family as both Jesus and James became rivals, both wanting the title of Crown Prince, and both having support from powerful religious sects.

Mary never forgot baby Miriam. Every morning and at sunset prayers, she prayed at the graveside. Joseph thought the best medicine for Mary was to have another child. Mary had decided, without consulting with Joseph, to avoid having more children, even though originally she wanted eight.

Joseph had noticed Mary always shifted one of the twenty-eight stones on her side table each night and avoided coital sexual acts when the black stones were at the front. Joseph decided to move some of the white stones every now and again, which resulted in Mary loosing track of her fertility cycle. That month Mary became pregnant. Nine months later, on the sixteenth of August 3A.D. Mary gave birth to a healthy daughter named Salome. From that day on, Mary lived life to the fullest, and Joseph never had to touch the stones again.

Heli, his wife Salome and Miriam came to visit the new baby, and Joseph asked them to stay in the renovated house while he sailed to Britannia with Zebedee.

The ocean voyage took eleven months. The three boys visited Rome twice and the southern ports of Britannia. They learnt the importance of the seasonal winds that were crucial in navigating through the straits, the Gates of Hercules. The Levanter winds blew easterly between August and October, and then the stronger Vendavale winds blew south-westerly between November and February. Joseph and Zebedee had planned the passage through the straits for October and December, gaining maximum wind assistance for each voyage.

During the four week stay in Cornwall, Jesus talked to the men in the tin mines and was very interested in their Celtic religion. They were called Druids and they held three beliefs in high esteem in their religious doctrine.

The druids believed God was light, heat and pure. God existed in the Circle of Space, Cyleh y Ceugant.

Mankind came from the circle of space, from light, and entered into the Circle of Evolution after birth, Cyleh y Abred. After death, mankind entered the Circle of Happiness, Cyleh y Gwynfyd if their life in Abred had been good, or reincarnated back to the circle of Abred to gain goodness.

James, the brother of Jesus, tried to disparage their faith and said his religion believed in one almighty God that created man and earth. When the Celts asked James about his God James said, "No man has seen him. He is invisible."

The Celts laughed and thought James as an imbecile, but held Jesus in respect for his tolerance of other faiths. James Cleopas was less interested in the faiths and more interested in the wealth of the tin mines. One of Jesus strongest traits in his youth was the ability to listen, without interrupting. When he returned to Jerusalem for the Passover festival of 4A.D. Jesus listened to the priests, gaining as much knowledge as he could about the Pharisee and Essene Faith. Through Joseph, his father, Jesus had seen most of the known world by the age of eleven. He had experienced happiness and hardship, acceptance and rejection, love and hate, life and death, and witnessed pagan and pious ceremonies. Young Jesus had gained knowledge beyond belief.

***

Passover
Jerusalem
5 A.D.

The Justus family and friends travelled to Jerusalem for the Passover festival in the year 758 A.U.C. of the Roman calendar. Herod Archelaus' calendar for Judea was 5A.D. Countries outside Roman control and many religious sects still used their own calendars, or a combination, which included solar and lunar types. For the Sadducee sect, the year was 3969 after creation, and the Pharisee sect year 3945, the twenty-four year discrepancy between the two sects often caused great upheaval when great events didn't fall on prophetic years. The High Priests were vulnerable in those years and could be replaced by priests of another sect. The years 3969 and 4000 were regarded as a prophetic years, when great changes or great events were predicted by the two major sects. These years would fall on 5A.D. and 36A.D. for the Sadducees, and 29A.D. and 60A.D. for the equivalent Pharisee prophetic years.

Jesus was eleven years old but on the last day of the festival he celebrated his twelfth birthday. Jesus went to the temple with a priest and recited the Torah reading for his Bar Mitzvah after which he was pronounced an adult.

The rest of the family and friends were unaware Jesus had decided to recite the Torah in Jerusalem, and had arranged for a family gathering for his Bar Mitzvah ceremony at the Nazareth Synagogue for the following

Sabbath. When they reached home, Mary looked for her children among the other relatives but could not find Jesus. After a thorough, but fruitless search, Mary and Joseph arranged for the other children to be cared for while they rode their horses back to Jerusalem.

After three days they found him in the temple courts, sitting among the teachers, listening to them and asking questions, Everyone who heard him was amazed at his understanding and his answers. When his parents saw him, they were astonished.

"Son, why have you treated us like this?" his mother said to him. "Your father and I have been anxiously searching for you."

"Why were you searching for me?" Jesus asked. "Didn't you know I had to be in my father's house?"

Joseph pulled Jesus to his feet, managing to restrain his right hand from clipping Jesus in the ear. They thanked the group for looking after Jesus and after some refreshments the relieved parents took Jesus home. Jesus rode on his father's horse with his mother behind him.

"I am sorry I caused you such worry," he said turning and looking into her eyes. "I went to recite the Torah at the temple and when I returned to our camp you had already left. I stayed near the temple so that you could find me."

Mary kissed Jesus on his cheek.

"Don't worry. I will explain it to your father."

Joseph rested the horses every ten miles, altering the load each time. On the second leg of the journey, Mary took the reins of Asher with Jesus behind her. As they approached the town of Shechem, Joseph and Mary were riding on Rueben, with Jesus riding ahead on Asher. Mary took the opportunity to explain the reason Jesus missed been taken home. Joseph was proud of his son's commitment to different elements of the three main religious sects, and during lunch he talked man to man with Jesus, encouraging him in his beliefs.

Four hours later, the tired travellers reached home and were among their relieved and elated family, talking, laughing, eating fruit and being merry.

Over the next six months, Joseph managed the farm, and Zebedee fished on the inland sea with his sons. The two schooners, both docked on the Kishon River were being repaired and oiled for another long sea voyage later in the year. In September Mary became pregnant again with the baby due in June 6A.D. Mary hoped the baby would be a girl and chose the name Joanna. Salome was two and needed a playmate younger than her sister Mary who was eight and wanted to act grown up, assisting her mother in the kitchen rather than playing.

In October, a delegation of highly ranked officials from Jerusalem arrived in Rome for a secret meeting with the Senate and Emperor Augustus. The Jewish officials requested Archelaus be dismissed as Ethnarch because of incompetence, corruption, insanity and demands to be addressed as God. Archelaus Herod was summoned to Rome to face the allegations. The Emperor heard all submissions with an open mind. However, he soon realised Archelaus had mentally deteriorated over his ten year reign, and was no longer fit to rule. Augustus exiled Archelaus and his family to Verunum in the province of Noricum. Judea was placed under direct Roman administration, and the territory was renamed Iudaea province, which included Judea, Samaria and Idumea. Two legions of soldiers from Syria, under the command of Coponius, were despatched to bolster security in the region until the new order was established. Coponius was appointed Procurator in March and immediately enforced civil stability, using his right to apply the death penalty to anyone inciting the Jewish citizens in rebellion or rioting against the Roman authorities. He dismissed the Pharisee High Priest, Joazar ben Boethus, who he suspected of inciting the Jewish community. Coponius appointed a Sadducee High Priest named Ananus, but limited his authority. Coponius even locked up the Holiest clerical vestments, only issuing them at events that had his personal approval.

Coponius needed more funds to sustain the increased payments for military and administration personnel. His request for more funds from Rome was denied, and he was forced to increase the already unpopular tax levy applied to males over 15 years of age. Coponius decreed that under Jewish law all males were deemed adults at twelve and would be taxed accordingly. He also declared the next census would be held in June A.D.6, being the required fourteen years since the first world census in 8B.C. All women above the age of thirteen would be required to pay a levy for the first time. The amount set at one tenth of the male levy was to be applied from January A.D.7.

The new tax, together with the Jewish population feeling that they had lost all independence under Roman occupation, caused a national outcry. A new sect was formed, called the Zealots. A cousin of Joseph was chosen as the leader of the military arm, and soon became known as Judas the Galilean. He fought the might of the Roman forces by using well planned ambushes on smaller enemy numbers. The Zealots would target soldiers escorting treasury funds or diplomatic messages to or from Rome, and then disperse, returning to their individual homes and normal activities. Coponius forces were normally engaged in large conflicts and found the terrorist tactics hard to defeat. He summoned Ananus and offered the Sadducee High Priest complete authority in religious matters in exchange for greater co-operation in relaying Zealot activity to his office. Ananus accepted the proposal.

On the farm in Nazareth, Mary gave birth to her seventh living child, a healthy baby boy. The doctor handed the baby to Joseph who wrapped him in a cloth and passed the baby to Mary for his first suckle.

"We were expecting a girl this time, but he is beautiful," Mary said.

"Are you feeling strong enough for the children see you?" Joseph asked.

"Yes, if they come in quietly."

Joseph found all the children lined up outside the bedroom. He ushered them in, indicating for them to be quiet with his finger held over his lips. Jesus led the way, followed by James, Josephes, Mary, Simon, and Salome. The children all took turns at letting the baby hold their fingers and then watched from the side of the bed.

"He has a strong grip for a baby," Mary the older sister said.

"I am still the youngest girl, I am glad it's a boy," Salome exclaimed

"What is his name father?" Josephes asked.

"We have not decided yet. We thought the baby would be a girl."

The baby fell asleep after feeding. Joseph kissed his wife and let her sleep too, knowing the next few days were crucial for her recovery and for her body to produce breast milk. Joseph asked the children to play outside while he organised a picnic lunch near the creek.

Three days later Joseph received an urgent message from Gabriel. He broke the seal on the scroll. It read: *The wrath of God in Heaven, we require your prayers on the Sabbath.*

Joseph handed a star shaped stone to Gabriel to give to Daniel, indicating that the David would be present. Joseph translated the simple coded message. *The Roman enemy of the Most High in the monastery, we require your presence on Saturday.* Joseph left his family in the care of Alexis and Stefan and rode Rueben to Ramah a day before the meeting.

Joseph arrived just before sunset, in time for the evening meal. Salome and Heli had visited Miriam and planned to take her to Bethlehem with them to register for the census

"I have been summoned to Qumran," Joseph said. "Has there been trouble in Jerusalem over the census?"

"Coponius has tried to subdue rioting in the streets by ordering a strict curfew during June. Citizens are only allowed on the streets during daylight hours," Heli said.

"That will only restrict businesses that are already struggling to pay their taxes."

"Let us forget politics for the moment and enjoy our meal," Miriam said.

Heli said grace and everyone said amen.

"By the way, Mary gave birth to a healthy baby boy," Joseph said.

"Why didn't you tell us?" Miriam said.

"I thought I just did."

"What is his name, you brute?" Salome asked.

"No, not brute, but you were close. It's Brutus."

"You are kidding. Brutus is a Roman name," Heli said.

"I am not kidding. I am Joseph."

Heli started laughing, realising Joseph was kidding.

"By the way, that would be a good name for a new religious sect. Both the Pharisees and the Sadducee sects are losing their way in these trying times."

Joseph laughed.

"Who would call a religious sect by the name Brutus?"

"Earlier you mentioned, 'by the way'," Heli said. "I think 'The Way' has a phenomenal spiritual connotation."

"Okay boys, you have had your fun, now tell me the name of my newborn grandson," Miriam said.

Joseph didn't seem to hear Miriam.

"Heli, that was half an hour ago, since then I mentioned Mary gave birth to a baby boy."

"He won't have a father if you don't tell me his name right now," Miriam said.

"Sorry, mother. The baby was born healthy, and Mary is doing fine, although she had a little difficulty with the breast milk."

"Did Mary try placing hot cabbage leaves over her breasts?"

"I thought Mary was doing that for my benefit, dressing up as Eve."

"I thought Adam and Eve used fig leaves," Salome said.

"You will be spending the night in the Garden of Eden if you don't tell me my grandson's name right now."

"Mother, would you pass me the salt please?"

Miriam held the bowl of salt above her shoulders in a menacing pose, ready to tip it over Joseph's head.

"Mary and I liked the name John."

"That is the name Elizabeth called her son," Heli said.

"Yes that is why we didn't call him John."

"I am warning you son, my arm is getting very tired."

"I am trying to tell you why we named the baby Judas."

Miriam passed the bowl of salt to Joseph.

"That is a good family name. You named him after your cousin, a good name indeed."

They raised their glasses and toasted the boy Judas, wishing him a great life.

If you have him circumcised in Shechem, we can visit Mary then. What date was Judas born?"

"Believe it or not, he was born on the sixth day of the six month in sixth year," Joseph said.

Heli suddenly gasped, went very pale and collapsed on the floor. He tried to talk, but could only mouth his last thoughts. He died before he could say 666 was the devil's number in ancient Hebrew mythology.

Heli was buried the following day in the Qumran Monastery cemetery. He had led a very religious life as a married Essene, was a good husband to Salome and adored his two children, Rachel and Mary. He feared Satan, but revered God. Heli didn't deserve the 666 that was carved on his headstone: Heli Eliam aged 66, 6A.D.

After the ceremony, Salome and Miriam went to the Abbey to pray. Daniel escorted Joseph to the third floor of the monastery tower.

"Joseph, I need to speak to you on confidential matters that are of National importance," he said.

"Daniel, you have my utmost loyalty and trust."

"I know that, but I will have to ask you to leave if you feel uncomfortable, or stay and take an oath of allegiance."

"At the moment, I feel quite comfortable."

"I must inform you that many local Jewish citizens and some Samaritans from your province have disappeared over the last week. We suspect Coponius is rounding up people to torture, gain information about the Zealots, and then dispose of their bodies," Daniel said.

"Has anyone confirmed your suspicions?"

"No one has witnessed a kidnapping, and none of the missing have returned home."

"What can I do to help, other than keeping my ears and eyes open for suspicious incidents?"

"We would like you to keep arm's length of any known Zealots, including Judas, because your family heir line is so important to Israel, now called the Roman province of Iudaea," Daniel said.

"Daniel, you know I can't stand by and do nothing."

"We would like you to join the Nationalist Party. It is a secret organisation where individuals report on incidents or rumours that affect Israel. You would work alone, dropping any information gained at a site yet to be determined," Daniel said.

"How do I join?"

"You will receive a sealed scroll with your drop site location. Make sure no one sees your deliveries and do not watch for clearances or instructions. No scrolls will be addressed to you personally. You will be given a number that will protect you and all involved with the party."

"I understand. But what about my long sea voyages, when I am away for months."

"You have been selected partially for that reason," Daniel said. "You may hear things while in Roman ports or as far away as Britannia. The party would like you to consider doing one other important task, probably a more important task?"

"And what would that entail?"

"The party wants you to create a new religious sect!"

"The Pharisees and Essenes want another new sect, haven't they already formed a militant branch called the Zealots?"

"Yes, the Zealots are a breakaway group that promote armed force against the Romans. However, most of us believe the Romans are too powerful to engage with force and so prefer to use religious means to educate and convert them to our way of life," Daniel said.

"I still do not understand the reasons behind introducing another religion."

"Once again, you were chosen because of your unique position in society. Your knowledge of religion and royal heritage are unparalleled, and you live among a large population of Jewish and Samaritan citizens," Daniel said.

"Now I am intrigued, please continue."

"Well, the Jewish people and Samaritans have always been at arm's length, separated in beliefs and culture. However, this Roman administration has given us common grievances." "You mean the interference with our religious customs and being taxed out of existence."

"Exactly, we are being taxed out of existence, virtually slaves working for the greed of Rome. That is why you have been chosen to spread our religious beliefs among the Galilean population, preaching to everyone, excluding no one because of their race or custom."

"You want me to convert mixed races into our beliefs, but with a less rigid format I presume?" Joseph asked.
"That is the thought behind the mission. The idea is to join all races against our common enemy."

"You didn't by chance mention any of this to Heli?"

"No. Absolutely not! Why do you ask?"

"You are not going to believe this, but the night he died, Heli commented on something I said at the dinner table."

"Now I am intrigued?" Daniel said.

"I mentioned *'By the way'* in conversation. Sometime later, Heli said, I think The Way has a phenomenal spiritual connotation. He said it out of the blue. We were actually talking about the birth of Judas at the time."

"Now I understand why you asked if I had spoken to Heli," Daniel said. "If you accept the task presented to you, it gives you the name of a new religious sect, with our blessings."

"Well, I accept your first proposal. I will have to discuss the new sect with Mary as that will impact on our lives quite a lot. It might even shorten my stint as a sailor if the sect becomes popular among the Samaritans."

"Joseph, I think that concludes our meeting. Thank you for your service to our country, and please let me know your decision about the sect. That can be the first correspondence the Nationalist Party receives from you.

Be assured, I will receive your answer confidentially. God blesses you and your family."

Joseph visited Theudas to discuss religion and how his sect in Jerusalem was growing in popularity. Theudas mentioned his membership had grown to over a thousand. He was content with those numbers because his sect, although religious based, dealt more with therapeutic healing and his close relations with his twelve live-in nurses. Joseph gained valuable knowledge about running the sect without hindrance from the other, more powerful sects. Theudas' sect survived because it did not cross religious boundaries, nor did he preach in their synagogues or churches. Instead, his elders preached in private homes.

Joseph returned home a few days later. He hugged his wife and greeted his children, giving each child a package of dried fruit.

"We missed you dearly," Mary said. "The doctor circumcised Judas."

"I am sorry Mary. It was not an enjoyable trip. I am the bearer of sad news."

Mary served Joseph a large tumbler of lemon juice and followed him to the bedroom. Joseph locked the door and sat with Mary on the bed, gently holding her hands.

"Mary, the night I visited our parents in Ramah your father passed away."

"No, oh no, father has never been ill in his life."

"It all happened suddenly. Heli was listening to me as I talked about Judas, and then he collapsed at the dining table."

"Had he mentioned he wasn't feeling well?"

"No, Heli was talking, joking, eating and drinking, and then he passed away without any sign of pain."

"I can't believe it. I cannot sense father has passed away."

Joseph hugged Mary tightly in his arms as she began to cry.

"We buried Heli in the monastery cemetery. Hundreds of his friends attended. It was like a state funeral. He will never be forgotten. His last thoughts were of you and baby Judas. I know he died a happy man. Your mother is going to stay with Miriam. We can visit them as soon as you want to travel."

Joseph gave Mary her father's religious pendant. Later, the children were told and the pendant was placed on baby Miriam's headstone. The family placed flowers on the grave and prayed that one day they would all meet in Heaven."

When Joseph discussed the idea of starting a new sect with the blessing of the Essene and Pharisee sects, he was surprised that Mary was overjoyed.

"I think that is what you have been missing in your life. I would love to have you home more. Darling, you know I always dread your time away at sea."

That evening Joseph planned his future ministry, using his vast knowledge gained in the monastery and from his world travels. Heli suggested the name, *The Way*, and that suited the theme of his religious beliefs. Joseph acted as an earthly God over the Essene Monastery and would again be a Godly figure, the way to Heaven. He would preach on the highest hill in each town. Not on the Sabbath, but the day after, Sunday the first day of the week. Every person would be welcomed, and everyone could enter the kingdom of God if they were cleansed of their sins and lived a good life. On the fourth evening, he would teach groups in the upper class areas. Whenever he found a person that was able to learn, wanted to convert and teach others, Joseph would anoint them minister for that town. The only dress code would be ministers teaching or ministering should wear white robes. Baptism should be with scented oil anointed on the forehead. Only adults should be baptised, males from the age of twelve, and females from the age of thirteen.

Joseph's train of thought was interrupted by Patch barking aggressively and a loud thud on the front veranda. He grabbed the lamp and went outside. Patch had stopped barking and was wagging his tail, holding a thick piece of branch in his jaw.

"What is it Joseph?" Mary called.

"Nothing really, I think Stefan threw a stick for Patch to play with."

Joseph wrestled playfully with the dog, pretending to snatch the stick away. On the second grab, Patch let go and the stick fell to the floor, partly dislodging a scroll rolled up inside the hollow stick. A shiver went up

Joseph's spine. The Nationalist Party had made contact and inside would be directions for the drop off point. Joseph hid the scroll under his robe and threw the stick for Patch.

Joseph had a very restless night sleep with recurring nightmares of intrigue. He was woken by Judas who cried every three hours, needing to suckle more often than the other children did because Mary was not producing sufficient breast milk. Joseph woke at daybreak, feeling fatigued. Mary and Judas were still sleeping as he put on his robe and walked to the barn. Joseph unrolled the scroll. Inside was a blank scroll with the number thirty-six circled on the bottom right hand side. The outer scroll had the directions for the drop, no other message, only the same number circled at the top left hand corner.

Joseph charcoaled his message. *The Way to Heaven will be known by all.* He rolled up the scroll and told Patch to fetch the stick.

"Good boy, that's the one I wanted. A bit chewed though. Let's go for a walk."

Joseph walked down the lane and turned towards Nazareth. He found another stick for Patch and threw it several times. Joseph found the drop zone as written. It was just off the main road, on a slight rise. He could see for miles in all directions. The site was perfect and an easy walk from the farm. Joseph searched the area until he found thirty-six drawn in an ant colony mound. He brushed the surface with his sandal, uncovering a large flat rock, and making the ants very hostile. Joseph threw the stick for Patch, lifted the rock and placed the stick containing his scroll into the hollow log. Then replaced the flat stone and covered it with the loose soil from the ant mound before Patch returned. Joseph looked around and made sure no travellers were coming. Then walked home, knowing the ants would soon repair the mound.

Mary had placed fresh flowers on Miriam's grave and was kneeling in prayer. Joseph kneeled beside her and listened to her pray. Mary asked God to unite Heli Eliam with her baby Miriam Justus in Heaven. Joseph said 'Amen'. He also prayed in silence for Holy guidance for his new religious sect.

On the following Sabbath, Joseph hitched the horses to the chariot and drove his family to the Shechem Synagogue. He was half expecting Miriam and Salome to attend the sermon, but when they didn't, he took his family to Ramah to visit them. Mary was grateful for Joseph's thoughtfulness. She really needed her mother's companionship after the traumatic period of the past three weeks, and Mary wanted to visit her father's grave.

Coponius appointed an administrator, Publius Quirinius to oversee the Iudaean census. During the first worldwide census of Roman territories, fourteen years ago, Quirinius had efficiently conducted the census in Syria. In contrast, the corresponding census in King Herod's kingdom was a complete fiasco. Herod had ordered all male citizens to register in their own towns, which caused unnecessary disruption in business and forcing some citizens to travel long distances. Many people protested in the streets, and Coponius planned to avoid a similar occurrence.

Theudas, the Chief Priest of the Therapeut Sect persuaded four hundred of his followers to leave Iudaea and cross the Jordan River. He had devised a plan for his followers to live outside the Roman provinces during the census period, and return later, avoiding the Roman tax roll. Ananus, hoping to gain favour and more authority for his religious sect, informed Coponius of the plan.

Coponius gathered a cavalry troop and intercepted Theudas at the Jordan River crossing near Bethabara on the 17th of June. He arrested Theudas, forced him to kneel and beheaded him in front of his followers. Coponius had Theudas' head placed on a lance and made the frightened eleven year old Barabbas hold the head of his father high above the crowd. The four hundred Jews were forced to follow Theudas' head back to Jerusalem. Their names were noted by Sadducee scribes, before they were publicly flogged then released.

Joseph received a scroll about Theudas' demise with a spare scroll wrapped inside. *Theudas beheaded, request your prayers on 26/6/6. E. M. J.*

Joseph told Mary he would register the family as required by law. He didn't want the Roman authorities to know he lived at Nazareth, and so he would vote in the town of Bethlehem, as he did in the previous census.

"I will probably be away for four days as I have business meeting in Jerusalem that I must attend," he told Mary.

"I will miss you, but I will be fine. Jesus is the man around the house when you are away, and Judas is three weeks old now and sleeping for four hours between feeds."

Joseph went to the Essene Monastery in Jerusalem and met with Daniel as arranged.

"Thank you for coming at such short notice," Daniel said.

"I can't believe Coponius had Theudas beheaded over such a minor incident."

"He is a tyrant. We believe Coponius has had many citizens kidnapped and killed over recent months. All have disappeared without a trace," Daniel said.

"Yes, I have heard some of the rumours," Joseph said.

"Joseph, even the religious sects are being scrutinised," Daniel said. "The Sadducees under Ananus have pledged their support with Rome and undermined our sects. Barabbas is still very shaken by the tragic loss of his father, only his youth prevented him from avenging his death."

"Does Barabbas aspire to become Chief Priest of the Therapeut sect and take over the responsibilities of the organisation?" Joseph asked.

"Most of the members have chosen to join the Pharisee or Essene sects. Barabbas has decided to stay in the villa with his mother, one of the twelve live-in nurses. I understand he wishes to continue studying therapeutic medicine."

"That is probably his best option at his age."

"Since the Therapeut sect has disbanded, the council only consists of two sects, with six Essene members and six Pharisee members."

"Leaving the council deadlocked on party issues."

"The party wishes you to represent the Galilean province on the council and to vote at the meetings."

Have the council members discussed this proposal?"

"Yes, you were chosen unanimously."

"I will accept on three conditions. Firstly, the council must officially recognise a new sect called 'The Way'. Secondly, I am recognised as a leader of that sect, and thirdly, I am seen as independent of both the Pharisee and Essene sects."

"The next meeting is scheduled for Friday the 16th at noon on the upper floor of the Tammuz building. I suggest you attend and put your proposal to the committee."

Joseph accepted the invitation and the two men chatted for a while, discussing a range of events, including the census and the new tax laws. The next day, Joseph was at the Bethlehem inn. He listed the deaths of Jacob and Heli and added the children's birth dates. His mind reverted to the last census, a much happier time, with the birth of his first son Jesus.

Meantime, Mary was thinking of Joseph and reminiscing about the birth of Jesus. She was cradling Judas in her arms while watching the children through the window. Mary noticed how the two girls played with their wooden dolls. The boys were quite different. Jesus and Joses often played together, usually drawing, reading or looking for insects. James and Simon preferred to build tree forts, wrestle or have mock sword fights.

Sometimes Simon would join Jesus and Joses, but rarely did the four boys play together. They did play together during their football matches, but James and Jesus were always rival captains. Just as they were potential rivals as heirs to the title of David Crown Prince. Mary's thoughts returned to Joseph. He would be home tomorrow. She wished he was home now, holding her and making her laugh.

Three more nights and Joseph still had not returned home. Mary was worried Joseph always kept to his schedules when travelling to Jerusalem. Something outside of his control must have occurred. She knew there was always the possibility of civil unrest in Judea. Often when this occurred, the soldiers could arrest, maim, or kill anyone on the streets.

Mary woke to the crying of Judas, the house in darkness. She lit the oil lamp on her bedside table and gently picked up Judas who immediately stopped crying. The rooster crowed. It must have been about five in the morning. The horses neighed, the dog stirred, the farm was welcoming a new day. Mary's eyes widened.

"Judas," she said. "The horses neighed, both horses."

She held Judas high in the air and swung him in a circle until the baby giggled. Mary grabbed the lamp and went to the spare room where Joseph was asleep on the bed, fully clothed. He had ridden all night to be home as soon as he could. Mary snuggled beside him. As she breastfed Judas, a warm sensation spread through her body. All was well.

Joseph slept until seven, waking to find Mary hugging him in her sleep. He rolled over, kissed her on the cheek and ran his fingers through her long black hair.

"I love you darling. I am sorry I was away so long."

Mary kissed Joseph long and hard. She straddled his hot body, riding her stallion until she was totally exhausted, collapsing onto his heaving chest.

Mary gasped.

"Where on earth have you been you beast?"

"I had meetings with Uzziah, the council, and Daniel. Then I went to Bethlehem for the census and visited our mothers."

"I was worried out of my mind."

"Well, you have a right to be concerned. Our cousin Judas is causing civil unrest in Jerusalem over the new tax laws. Coponius is searching for him, and citizens are being kidnapped. Never to be seen again."

"Are we safe here, do we need flee to Egypt again?"

"We will be safe if we stay away from Judas and the Zealots. I have been elected as a member of the council, and they have approved 'The Way' as a new sect."

Over the next two years, Joseph's new religious sect expanded rapidly throughout Samaria and Galilee. The home gatherings on Sunday evenings became a social event among the community and for the first time they had representation in the Iudaean religious council meetings. Emperor Augustus sent a convoy to Coponius in February of 8A.D. carrying important documents. He never received them as it fell into the hands of Judas of Gamala during a hit and run raid by his Zealot militia. The sixteen men, comprising of a Roman senator, three scribes and twelve soldiers were killed and buried in a mass grave. Joseph received a scroll. *Emperor requires all men aged fourteen to twenty-five for military training and service in Gaul. Clergy exempt.* Joseph used the information wisely and discreetly.

He met with Zebedee at the Nazareth Synagogue.

"I have received confidential information that concerns our families. The Romans want to conscript all young men for military action in Gaul."

"We can take the boys on a long trading voyage. The schooners will be fully repaired and ready to sail in two or three weeks." Zebedee said.

"I can't leave because of my commitments for the Party. There is another option. Clergy are exempt, and we have both wanted our children to have religious educations."

"That would be ideal, but the enrolment age is fifteen."

"The Qumran Monastery will accept males thirteen years old under certain circumstances, and I am sure Daniel will take our boys in this year's quota."

"I would prefer James and John went to the Pharisee College to study as they also have classes on astronomy and law," Zebedee said.

"The Essenes included those classes last year and more practical classes as well. Besides, you can enrol the lads into the Pharisee College when they turn fifteen."

"I agree, that is our best option and we must act quickly."

"That only leaves Stefan. Perhaps he could skipper the *Pollonia* with a new crew?" Joseph asked. "I know of some experienced sailors that are good men, and need work. I will make sure both schooners stay in close proximity. I am sure he will rise to the occasion."

"I will tell Stefan to be prepared to sail later this month," Joseph said. "I will see you again in two weeks. All the boys can ride, so we won't need the carriage."

Zebedee's family, Joseph's family, Stefan and Alexis arrived at the farm. It was a beautiful Spring Sunday and they celebrated Jesus fifteenth birthday which would fall in four days' time. They feasted on fish and chicken and used the best wine to toast the last supper that all of the families would be able to spend together.

The next day the five men rode to Jerusalem. Zebedee enrolled his son James in the Pharisee College in Jerusalem. Joseph succeeded in enrolling Jesus and James, into the Qumran Monastery. Bishop Timothy entered their names in the Book of David. Jesus and James were both born while Joseph had held the position of Most High, the Essene God.

Both boys were given notations next to their names: Jesus Immanuel Justus aged 15, D.O.B. 29th March 746 A.U.C. Enrolled 26/3/8 A.D. (*The Lamb of God).* James Heli

Justus aged 13, D.O.B. 27th July 747 A.U.C. Enrolled 26/3/8 A.D. (*The Lion cub of God*).

On the following day, the initiates were shown their quarters. They were introduced to other roommates, who all left the room after a few minutes. James and Jesus were left to their own devices in adjoining rooms, not having received any rostered duties. Five neophyte priests entered James' room and shut the door. Four priests held him down on a table while the other one sodomised him. Jesus heard the commotion and attempted to help James, but was forced back into his room by another seven neophyte priests and his door held closed.

Jesus silently prayed to God for intervention as he was gagged and his body oiled. The priests had heard Jesus was the David Crown Prince in waiting and gave him royal treatment. While he was being sodomised another priest slid under the table and performed fellatio. The twin act known in the monastery as Sodom and Gomorrah.

When James and Jesus talked about the initiation, they agreed that reporting the incident would be futile as the priests would say it was consensual. James and Jesus would be labelled trouble makers, their careers suffering from the consequences.

"It would be best to put what happened behind us," James said.

"Yes, let's put it behind us," Jesus agreed.

They both laughed and for the first time their sibling rivalry was put to one side and they bonded together as brothers.

CHAPTER 7: Armed Conflict

On the 31st of March, 8 A.D. during the early morning hours of Sabbath, Judas and his zealot band broke into Roman armouries of four towns in Galilee. Over the next fifteen months, the Zealots caused havoc in the Province, killing thousands of Roman soldiers and looting the treasury money destined for the coffers of Emperor Augustus. Coponius eventually received the information he sought from one of his tortured victims and established the whereabouts of Judas learning that the Galilean frequented a camp in Gamala on the Golan Heights.

The area was protected by strong natural defences with only one steep path leading up from two *wadis* that surrounded the camel shaped hill. Coponius knew that the town had thousands of residents and could be well defended. He waited months for conformation from his soldiers that the Zealot band and their leader had entered Gamala. Coponius deployed his men during the early hours of Monday July 8th 9A.D. Three hundred soldiers hid among rocks and bushes in the ravine on both sides of the town's only pathway. Two hundred camouflaged archers were positioned on the slope opposite the pathway to prevent any of the Zealots retreating up the hill.

At daybreak, the township was abuzz with activity. Some residents were leaving town in small groups. Most were men that led their camels or donkeys laden with pottery and other products to be sold or traded at other town markets. They walked past the soldiers, unaware of their presence. Two hours later there was similar foot traffic coming into Gamala, but no sign of the quarry. The soldiers were not used to guerrilla type warfare having been trained for open, structured battles with their enemy. Coponius knew his men were frustrated, sitting in uncomfortable positions for hours on end in the hot sun.

At four in the afternoon, about one hundred men leading camels and horses trudged down the steep pathway towards the *wadi*. Coponius waited until he saw which of the two routes they would take when they reached the gully. He presumed the leaders were the men on horseback and instructed the archers to bring down the horses so that the soldiers could capture Judas and his officers alive. They were not going to be given an easy death.

The leaders reached the ravine first and mounted their horses. They split into two groups and used both *wadi* tracks. The men following behind mounted their camels and alternated between which leaders to follow. Coponius would have preferred the whole band to leave in one direction so that he could bring up his soldiers at the rear and ambush the Zealots away from the pathway. That option had passed. His soldiers would have to attack in two separate melees. When the two groups were about one hundred yards away from the pathway, Coponius gave the order for the archers to fire two arrows each at the camel riders. Simultaneously, several of his best bowmen brought down the four horses. The soldiers cut down the few remaining enemy and captured their wounded leaders, including Judas. The massacre was over in less than fifteen minutes, with only one Roman casualty.

Coponius forces departed, leaving the gorge covered with massacred bodies and slaughtered animals that the townsfolk would have to clean up. It would be a warning to all those that supported sedition and rebellion against Roman authority. The four leaders were tortured for three days. Then they were blinded with a hot iron and crucified outside the armoury at Sepphoris until they died either from their wounds or from dehydration and exhaustion.

Joseph knew there would be repercussions over the massacre as the Zealots would become martyrs and other men would fight in their place. He would be needed in Jerusalem for urgent meetings with the National Party. Joseph moved his young family to the Ramah mansion for safety. The children loved being with their grandmothers and Mary could catch up on women's matters. Joseph went to the Qumran Monastery to see Daniel. It was obvious that word had not reached the isolated community at Qumran.

"Daniel, I'm afraid I bear bad news. Judas and one hundred Zealots have been killed by Coponius soldiers at Gamala."

"That is devastating news for the country and you personally. Please accept my deepest sympathy for you and your cousin's family."

"I believe this will escalate hostilities to a new level."

"I agree. I will arrange a council meeting at the house of Kislev. Will you be available on the Sabbath of July 20th?"

"Yes, I will be staying at Ramah for some time, and would like to see Jesus and James before returning to Nazareth."

"I will arrange a three day pass for the lads to visit you after the meeting."

"I am organising a family gathering on the 27th. Perhaps the pass could cover that period?"

"For you Joseph, that is the least I can do."

When the meeting ended, the two men stood up, shook hands and sombrely hugged each other. Both men knew that the massacre would be avenged.

Jesus and James walked from Qumran to Ramah, reaching the house without being harassed by Roman soldiers. Mary, Miriam and Salome hugged the young men. It had been sixteen months since they enrolled and it was their first three day pass. Josephes, Simon and Mary hugged their brothers gleefully. Both boys had grown close cut beards and looked very manly. Joseph carried young Salome and Judas over to their older brothers. They were shy and unsure who the strangers were. Jesus hugged Salome and lifted her onto his shoulders. James held Judas for a while and then gave him the flight of an eagle ride. Grabbing Judas by an arm and a leg he twirled him round and around until he couldn't walk in a straight line. Judas bonded with James immediately and wanted more rides.

Once the hilarity had died down, Joseph made a toast.

"Thank you God for this day. It is such a blessing to have all eleven of our family reunited under one roof. Bless this food we are about to eat. Amen."

Mary nudged Joseph under the table and whispered.

"I think you can make that eleven and a half."

After the refreshments, Joseph found a quiet time to speak to James and Jesus.

"There have been many atrocities lately and many young men have been sent to Gaul as tirones to bolster the Roman ranks. I am glad you are both safe in the monastery and obtained a good education."

"I am enjoying monastery life and I have made many new friends," Jesus said.

"Father, the neophyte priests sodomised me and I dislike the Essene culture," James said.

"I understand what you are saying James. I can apply to have you enrolled in the Pharisee College now that you are fifteen if that's what you want."

"Yes father, I would prefer the Pharisee College, I don't like the monastery."

"I will take you to Jerusalem after your birthday celebrations. Now go and enjoy yourself while I talk to your brother for a moment."

"I was sodomised as well," Jesus said, "but I realised it was just an initiation ceremony. The priests were just letting us know what monastery life was like, teaching us that the celibate oath meant resolved not to marry and that it didn't mean sexual abstinence. I have found the curriculum is very educational and interesting."

Joseph was glad his son had found peace, as swearing to a state of celibacy for ten to fifteen years would be like hell on earth, if you didn't learn to comply.

"Jesus, your life has been mapped out for you like mine was. You are destined to become the David, but the path will be steep and winding. You will gain good friends and even worse enemies. To keep the title of Crown Prince you will need to produce a male heir. To reach your full potential as a leader with worldly knowledge, you will have to complete ten years of study and five years as a Bishop.

"Father, you have prepared me since childhood and I want to please you. I want to free Iudaea from Roman rule, rename our country as Israel and set our people free."

"I have faith in you son. However, you are only sixteen and may be enclosed behind the monastery walls until your twenty-ninth birthday. If the opportunity arises, you may become Chief Priest, or Most High. That could add another six years to monastery life. You must be married by the age of thirty-six to carry on the male dynasty."

"Father, I promise you that I will marry on my thirty-six birthday."

"I can tell you from experience that it is not easy. Some men want to stay in the monastery all their lives. Their choices are easy. I suggest you change partners regularly and only use sexual relationships for hedonistic pleasure. I made a mistake of falling in love with Stefan. That nearly stopped me from marrying your mother, the real love of my life."

"I will do as you say, father. At the moment, that is happening anyway. The word has spread through the monastery that I am of royal blood and the Crown Prince. All the priests want to be with me. They shower me with affection, giving me the royal treatment including a complete oil massage, followed by the twin act of Sodom and Gomorrah."

"It sounds like I am preaching to the converted, but later in life you will find true love and that will surpass everything you have ever known."

Two days later, Joseph and Jesus rode Rueben and Asher to the monastery. Joseph saw Daniel and explained the reasons behind James enrolling in the Pharisee College. He stated that they regarded James as the heir to the David Crown Prince title and that James was not comfortable with monastery life.

The next day, with Daniel's blessings, Joseph and James rode to Jerusalem.

On the third Sabbath of August 9A.D. thirteen men attended a noon meeting on the second floor of Kislev house. They sat around a large wooden table. There were six men on the western side, all Essenes. On the eastern side sat six Pharisees. Joseph, represented The Way sect at the head of the table and was the chairman.

"Gentlemen, over the last two hours we have debated several topics covering the massacre. Most decisions have been made along party lines, with my vote being the decider. I realise one sect is more militant than the other, but remember we are here for the best interest of all of Iudaea. The next vote is for a new leader for the Zealot sect to replace Judas. I am abstaining from voting this round because I am closely related to two of the main contenders. I advocate a secret vote. Would someone like to second the motion?"

The motion was passed, and the vote took place for a leader, the other man would be his lieutenant. Zaduk, a Pharisee would remain as political head, regardless of who was elected the militant commander. The two men elected from six candidates were Judas' two sons Simeon, as leader and Jacob as his lieutenant. The other topics discussed and agreed on at the meeting were: The Zealots must regroup, retrain, and cease major conflicts for one year. The three towns of Gamla, Jotapata and Zippori would be fortified for Zealot and Sicarri forces support and refuge. The final vote confirmed Joseph was the David. However the title of Crown Prince for Jesus was in dispute. The laws of the Pharisees did not recognise Jesus as legitimate. He was consummated long before marriage, making James the Crown Prince. The Monastery Essenes were celibate and supported Jesus legitimacy. Jesus was confirmed Crown Prince with seven votes to six with Joseph voting with the Essene block.

Joseph and Mary stayed in Ramah for another six months until hostilities between the militant Jews and the Roman soldiers abated. Mary gave birth to a baby girl, Joanna Miriam Justus on the 19th of November 9A.D. That year the Jewish people rejoiced in the streets. Word had reached Iudaea that the administrator of the last census was dead. Publius Quintilus Varus had led three Roman legions into Gaul and was ambushed by Arminius' army in the Teutoberg forest. Varus committed suicide to avoid capture by the Huns of Germania.

Emperor Augustus had made an error of judgement by sending his successful administrator into what Romans thought was an area under their authority. The recruitment of men from all provinces intensified until the Roman army was again at full military strength.

Zebedee enrolled John into the monastery in 11A.D. at the age of thirteen to avoid his conscription. Jesus was a neophyte priest and together with another gentle priest gave John his initiation ceremony. They oiled the lad and then Jesus explained the procedure to the frightened boy. Four more priests entered the room to hold John over the table while he was given oral sex and sodomised. Jesus had insisted the boy was given the royal initiation. Simon preferred to fight for Jewish freedom. He joined the Zealots at age fourteen and lived in the isolated town of Gamala to avoid conscription. Josephes enrolled in the Pharisee College at fifteen.

In 16A.D. eight Roman Legions fought Arminius' army on an open plain near Idistaviso. The superior disciplined legionnaires annihilated the Germans and captured the severely wounded Arminius. The Romans had a hollow victory. They lost many soldiers in the battle and during the march to the North Sea, their prized captive escaped. On the voyage to Rome, a fierce storm sunk half the fleet, killing over a thousand soldiers. The mission was still hailed a success by the new Emperor Tiberius. The two commanders, Tiberius and Germanicus were given a hero's parade, followed by seven days of victory celebrations.

Jesus remained in the Qumran Monastery, mastering in his religious studies and rising through the ranks to the position of Bishop. He held the position for five years, and when Daniel died suddenly at the age of sixty-one, Jesus was appointed the Essene Chief Priest. Malachi was appointed as Most High and moved to the luxurious third floor apartments. Malachi leaned heavily towards the Zealot sect politically and soon lost favour with the Roman Prefect Gratus and the Sadducee High Priest Joseph Caiaphas. After fourteen months in office, Malachi was found dead by his boy servant. The Essene God had apparently committed suicide, but more than likely had been poisoned.

Jesus was anointed Most High and held the position for thirty days.

Valerius Gratus discussed Malachi's replacement with Joseph Caiaphas, the Sadducee High Priest.

"We need a suitable replacement that supports Roman authority and can report on monastery regime and policies."

"Jesus has moderate political beliefs, but he is the David Crown Prince."

"Caiaphas, we cannot appoint someone who can attract a large personal following. Malachi was an absolute disaster from day one."

"Well that rules out Jesus. May I suggest you appoint a Sadducee priest to oversee the monastery?"

"You can. You can also supply a name, but remember this, your High Priesthood rides on your choice."

"I can confidently suggest Jonathon, the son of Ananus."

"Find the man, and bring him to my office first thing tomorrow," Valerius said.

Jonathon was duly appointed Most High. Jesus was disappointed at being overlooked for the position, but developed a close working relationship with Jonathon over the years. Both men mellowed in their ideology. Jesus moved well away from the Zealot militancy, and Jonathon moved towards greater religious independence for Iudaea.

Jesus remained in the monastery until thirty-five, completed twenty years of religious studies that included four year terms as a neophyte priest, five years as a priest, five years as Bishop and six years as Chief Priest. Jesus ascended into heaven on Sunday, March 28th 28A.D. He had officially given Jonathon his notice three weeks ago, and in monastery tradition, received severance money in accordance to one that had to leave for dynasty obligations. Jesus was escorted to the outer stairs, where he descended to earth. He now stood in the world and would have to marry on or before his thirty-sixth birthday to remain the David Crown prince.

Jesus commenced his walk to Ramah the following day at three in the morning. The further he walked away from the monastery, the more he felt isolated and afraid. Jesus had left the fully closed sanctuary that had been home for more than half his life. It had been quiet, peaceful and orderly. Jesus had left his companion John Mark who would be enclosed for at least another two years. Perhaps seven more years, or even life if he remained celibate.

Jesus had heard his parents had found him a suitable bride. A distant cousin of Davidian blood who would produce suitable heirs. Simon had married her elder sister on his twenty-fourth birthday. His brother could have chosen the younger sister, but apparently had more in common with Martha. They had two boys, Alexander three years old and young Rufus, six months old. *At least he had a choice. I will have to make do with Magdalene.* Jesus kept walking and thinking about how much had changed in his life. Both his wonderful grandmothers had passed away. His mother had given birth to Joanna whom he had never seen. She must be eighteen now and may even be married.

Jesus realised that he had walked into the Mird *wadi*. He had planned to visit Ain-Feshkha for breakfast, but had inadvertently taken the route to Mird while thinking about his family. He stopped at an infamous junction where thirty six years ago Nebedeus had retreated after the scouts had encountered the gladiator bandits. Nebedeus' son Ananias was thirty-five, a Pharisee priest living in Damascus. Jesus reached for his water that was in a goatskin cask attached to his belt. He drank just enough to quench his thirst, and ate the last of his fruit. In a few hours, he would reach Ramah in time for the midday meal.

Jesus walked on, his thoughts reverting to his family and what he had heard. James Cleopas had married his sister Mary in 17A.D. They had three children; a boy aged ten and two daughters. Salome married Balak Strauss in 22A.D. He was known as Blastus and worked as head of staff for King Agrippa. They had a boy and a girl, aged four and eighteen months. His brother James was a Pharisee Bishop, but had not yet married. Josephes married on his twenty-fifth birthday on May 26th 21A.D and had two sons and a daughter.

Jesus approached the homestead with mixed feelings of loneliness and despair, combined with the stimulation and nervousness of the unknown that lay ahead in his new life. He was still celibate, but no longer physically attached to the Brotherhood. He was in the world, the married sphere, but not married. He had resigned as Chief Priest of the monastery, but still held the rank of Holy Spirit, a fully qualified Rabbi, but had no congregation to teach. He was the David Crown Prince, but without a throne to inherit. He was an uncle to children he hadn't met and betrothed to a woman he did not know.

Jesus went to the worker's bathroom, washed his robe and hung it outside on the horse rail to dry. He sat on the toilet, his head bowed, his hands clasped with his arms resting on his knees. Jesus prayed for strength and guidance before he faced his adult siblings and their partners. He washed his hands and face and sponged his body. Jesus ran his fingers through his long curly black hair and wiped his body dry. He gathered his robe which was still damp and dressed as he walked the last five hundred yards to the house.

Jesus knocked on the door. No one answered and the whole lower floor was dark and quiet. Jesus climbed the steps to the front balcony and saw his parents sitting at the table in the main room. His first impression was how much they had aged. His father was sixty-nine, his mother fifty-two. They looked up and saw their son with his arms stretched out. Mary was the first to hug Jesus then Joseph hugged them both.

"Welcome home son and happy birthday," Mary said, "Sit down and have a rest. I will get you a drink."

"Father, I have so much to catch up on," Jesus said. "I am afraid I won't fit in with the world."

"That is a natural reaction son. You have been behind the monastery walls for most of your life."

"Yes, twenty years with only a handful of three day passes."

"I would have ridden out to the monastery except Rueben and Asher died, and the Roman army have confiscated our other horses for the cavalry."

"I am sorry to hear about the horses, they were wonderful family pets. The walk was fine though. I needed time to clear my mind and think about my future."

Mary came back with a tumbler of water in one hand and leading a young lady with the other. "I have someone here you haven't met before."

Jesus looked around and stood up.

"Don't tell me you are Joanna?"

"Well then, I won't tell you that I'm Joanna."

"You are very beautiful, but where did you get your dark red hair from?" Jesus asked. "From my grandmother's side of the family I guess."

"Well, come here and give me a hug. I can't believe I have three grown up sisters."

They hugged for a long time, neither wanting to break the embrace.

"Well you have, and what's more, you can have me too if you dare."

Jesus was stunned.

"My name is Mary Magdalene, and I have been betrothed to you."

Jesus looked at his parents who smiled and nodded.

"I was not expecting this. I am in shock."

"Is that why you are hugging me so tightly, or don't you want me to get away?"

Jesus let go immediately. Then he began to laugh.

"You have our family wit. I am glad to meet you Mary, please sit down. We need to talk this over."

"I like a man who thinks he has got control," Mary said.

The next thing Jesus knew was the room was suddenly filled with fifteen adults and ten children. The children ranged from babes in arms to a ten year old boy. Jesus shook hands and greeted his four brothers and the two brothers-in-law. Then he hugged his sisters, Mary and Salome, who were both holding babies. Magda introduced Joanna and Jesus hugged her while she wept tears of joy. Then Jesus was introduced to Josephes' wife, Shona, and Simon's wife, Martha. An hour passed before Jesus met his four nephews and four nieces. Jesus was home. More importantly, he felt at ease and he felt at home.

The next day Joseph asked his eight children to accompany him in the study.

"I have something very important to discuss with you all. As you know your mother and I have loved you equally, but in different ways. Today is the first time you have all been together and you are now all adults. Your mother is still quite young, but I am near seventy. For those reasons I want to tell you about my will and final wishes."

Joanna cried.

"Father, you are very healthy, you will live for many more years."

"That is God's will to decide. I need to retire from most of my work, and spend more time with my family. I want to remain head of 'The Way' sect politically, but leave the ministering to others. I have appointed John the Baptist as Head Minister for Judea, but I need someone to minister in Galilee and Samaria."

"I would like to minister in those areas, father," Jesus said.

"Good. Now I need a captain for the schooner, who can work with Stefan."

"I would like to perform those duties," Josephes replied.

"Now I require a bookkeeper and administrator."

"I believe that would be me," James said.

"Good. That leaves the farm and three houses, none of which are to be sold. I want the farm divided into two equal lots, with one house on each property. The Ramah house is to remain in my wife's care."

"We can run the farms, father," Simon and Judas said in unison.

"Excellent. I want Judas, Joses and Simon to draw equal wages. Annual profit, after wages, taxes and expenses are deducted, to be divided equally among you all and Mary. My title of Joseph of Arimethea, which includes my position on the National Council, will go to Josephes. The Crown Prince title belongs to Jesus for life, regardless of which sect has the High Priest. My position on the Supreme Council with the Sanhedrin vote, will go to James. I do not intend to write out a will at this stage, but that is my wish and verbal testament. Are there any questions? You are all witnesses to what has been said."

"Father, I think I can speak for all of us," Jesus replied. "We appreciate the kindness and love that you have shown us all our lives. The will is fair and just, and we will carry out your will to the letter. However, you are fit and healthy, and we expect your presence around for at least another twenty years. You may not want to let mother know that though."

That comment broke the ice and the room filled with laughter.

"There is one more thing," Joseph said trying to regain his composure. "When I was in Jerusalem, I purchased a family sized tomb. It is carved in the limestone rock cliff face and there is a beautiful garden in front, called paradise. The tomb entrance is on the ground level and has a large round rock to secure the entrance. There is a pathway carved out above with smaller tombs on that row. The ground floor is where Mary and I wish our ossuary's to be placed."

"Why are you telling us this? Are you alright Father?" Salome asked.

"I am fine. I just want to put my house in order. Now let us wash for breakfast before Magda seeks out Jesus."

"Father, we have just met and we haven't had a chance to discuss anything about a binding betrothal."

Jesus heard his siblings shout.

"Hallelujah, for the wedding of the Lamb is coming."

Over the next few days, the family gradually dispersed, all leaving for their homes and work commitments. Only Jesus, his parents, Joanna and Magda stayed. Joanna had heard many stories about Jesus and admired him immensely. She had also made good friends with Magda and both women had secretly discussed their wedding plans, bonding in the process.

Jesus remained at Ramah for three months, getting his life in order and planning his ministry. 'The Way' had grown in popularity under Joseph and now had a strong following throughout Iudaea. Jesus wanted the religion taught world-wide eventually, but to do that he would need support from men of high status. Men that would be able to use the membership fees and offerings collected for the good of the community.

Jesus bought a donkey in Jerusalem and rode it to Nazareth. He visited Simon and Judas on the farm and stayed for three days. Then he travelled to Capernaum and visited Zebedee and Josephes who were planning their next voyage. It was to be Zebedee's last overseas trade before retiring to fish on the lake for his income. Jesus ministered among the towns in Galilee for nine months. His reputation as a speaker, minister and healer soon became well known. One day he was invited to speak in the synagogue in his own town of Nazareth. Jesus was handed a scroll and he read from the sayings of the prophet Isaiah.

"The spirit of the Lord is on me, because he has anointed me to preach good news to the poor."

Jesus rolled up the scroll and handed it back to the attendant. The congregation were amazed at his sermon and gracious words. However, some questioned Jesus' authority.

"Isn't this Josephs' son?" some said. "Aren't his brothers James, Joses, Simon and Judas?"

"I tell you the truth," Jesus replied. "No prophet is accepted in his own town. Even Elijah didn't help his own community in the three and a half year drought. Instead he went to Zarephath in the region of Sidon. And there were many in Israel with Leprosy in the time of Elisha the prophet, yet not one of them was cleansed, only Naaman the Syrian."

The congregation were furious at Jesus for demeaning the prophets and dragged Jesus to the brow of the hill on which the town was built. They intended to throw him over the cliff, but as they neared the summit, a huge cloud system rolled over the town. It drenched them in rain, and the thunder and lightning was so fierce the crowd cowered in fright.

Jesus used the distraction to his advantage and walked through the crowd and escaped among the first group to disperse. Jesus went back to the synagogue, mounted his donkey, and left Nazareth through the back lanes to avoid being seen. He kept riding until he reached Capernaum and the safety of his sister Mary's house. Jesus told them about his near death experience, and vowed to lower the rhetoric in sermons that included past prophets and traditions.

Early the next morning, Jesus left Galilee and went to the Jordan River near Qumran. He wanted to see John the

Baptist and be baptised by him before he married Mary Magdalene. Joseph had informed John about Jesus' intention to be baptised by him.

"How would I recognise Jesus?" John asked.

"The man you see the Holy Spirit come with and remain, he is my son," Joseph replied.

The next day, John saw Jesus and Bishop Jacob approaching and turned to his disciples.

"Look, the Lamb of God who takes away the sin of the world," he said. "This is the one I meant when I said a man who comes after me has surpassed me because he was before me."

Jesus walked into the water of the River Jordan and asked John to baptise him in the name of Christ. This frightened John, because only a priest that had been anointed with oil by the Holy Spirit could be called Christ.

"I need to be baptised by you. Do you come to me?" John asked.

Jesus wanted to cleanse himself of celibate life before marrying.

"Let it be so now. It is proper to do this to fulfil all righteousness."

After John consented and baptised Jesus as the son of God. Jesus walked to Qumran with Jacob, but didn't enter the monastery. He went to the stables to get his donkey, and then rode to Ramah to see Magdalene. He found her talking with Joanna.

"Magdalene, from now on I will call you Mary. I have been baptised into the world by John today and I am spiritually cleansed. I want you to prepare our wedding supper and formal arrangements."

"I like a man that has control over matters of importance," Mary said. "Joanna and I have arranged a double wedding at Cana on your birthday."

"A double wedding. With whom?" Jesus asked.

"With me and Chaunan, and you and Mary," Joanna exclaimed.

Jesus wrote a list of names of the men that he wanted to attend the wedding ceremony and gave it to Joanna. The rest he left for the women to arrange. Jesus had far more important dealings to attend to over the next few months. He had jotted down a list of twenty names that he wanted to consider as Apostles for 'The Way'. The men were all influential and representing all facets of society. They would become the political heads of their groups and have disciples in the faith reporting directly to them.

Over the coming months, Jesus consulted his father who supported the new concept. There were seven groups with two members each. Meetings were to take place on the first Sabbath of each new season. One person from each group must vote at meetings, making the total votes seven. The seven groups to be represented were: The Way, the married Essenes, Pharisees, Sadducees, Zealots, Monarchy, and Gentiles.

Jesus or John the Baptist represented The Way and were the chairmen of the council. John recommended Simon Peter and his brother Andrew to represent the married Essenes. Jesus recommended James and John

Cleopas to represent the Gentiles. Joseph recommended Jonathon and Mathew Ananus to represent the Sadducee sect. Joseph also recommended James and Josephes to represent the Pharisee sect and Simon and Judas the Zealots

The basis of the new religious based political party was formed, heavily represented by the Justus family, or close connections. The remaining group representing the Herod monarchy would be harder to fill. Herod the Great had ten wives and fourteen male heirs. Herod had three sons executed and others disinherited before he died of natural causes. Archelaus had been sent into exile by Emperor Augustus and his province of Judea replaced with Roman administrators. That still left several of Herod's children for consideration, including Philip, Antipas and the disinherited Thomas. The committee postponed the choice of Herods until after they could be interviewed and after Jesus' wedding.

On the third day of the week, on March 29th in the year 29A.D. three hundred guests gathered at Cana. It was Jesus' thirty-six birthday and as Crown Prince he had to marry to produce future heirs for the King David line. The event was planned at a farm on the outskirts of Cana. It was a beautiful spring day and the guests could mill about, moving between open sunny areas and the mottled shade of the almond trees. The trees were covered with pinkish white blossoms, some falling in the gentle breeze and covering the grass like patches of snow.

Joseph and his wife Mary walked to a small grassy knoll in the centre of a ring of tables, fully laden with every type of fruit. Joseph rang a bell to get the attention of the guests and to ask for silence.

"We are gathered here today for three ceremonies," he said. "The first is to wish Jesus a happy thirty-sixth birthday. He is my eldest son, whom I love dearly. With him, I am well pleased."

The guests turned towards Jesus and cheered before toasting him for a long life filled with good health and happiness.

"Now I would like John the Baptist to announce the next two ceremonies," Joseph said.

John came forward and stood next to Joseph and Mary.

"I would like ask Mr Joachim Zachar and his wife Ivana to join us."

"The proud parents of Jesus and Chaunan have asked me to minister the wedding ceremonies of their sons," John said when they came forward. "This I will do with great honour and respect, with utmost pride and humility."

The guests cheered again, even louder and for longer before John raised his arms to indicate silence.

"I ask everyone to find a seat and place their orders for the main course as the waiting staff makes their rounds. The first wedding ceremony will be for Chaunan and Joanna."

The wedding band started playing, and the guests turned toward the direction of the homestead. Joanna was dressed in a beautiful white silk robe with an almond pink sash around her waist. She was holding a bouquet of almond blossoms and was escorted by her father and two young flower girls. The bride and groom said their vows to each other and John pronounced them husband and wife.

"Now you can kiss the bride."

James smiled. *Like I haven't seen Chuza kissing Jo in the barn before.*

For a while, the happily married couple danced to the music. Then John beckoned for the guests to join in. The servants began to serve the seated guests with a seafood appetizer and white wine or grape juice. Half an hour later, a food platter of fish, salad and cheese, or a vegetarian dish was offered with fresh wine. An hour later, after several speeches and more dancing, another course was served with roast chicken and vegetables and a vegetarian dish.

At this point, Mary the mother of Jesus approached him.

"They have no more wine," she said.

"Dear woman," Jesus replied. "Why do you involve me? My time has not yet come."

"Do whatever he tells you," his mother said to the servants

Nearby, behind the barn, stood six stone jars. The type used by the Jews for ceremonial washing. Each held from twenty to thirty gallons. Jesus asked the staff to pour clean drinking water into jars. Then he asked them to juice and strain oranges and limes and add it the water.

"Now draw some out and take it to the master of the banquet."

The band commenced playing and the guests turned towards the homestead again. Mary Magdalene was wearing a long white silk robe with a golden sash around her waist and a tiara that shone like the stars in heaven. She was holding a bouquet of pure white almond blossoms. She was escorted by her uncle and the young flower girls, the daughters of Salome and her sister Mary. The bride and groom said their vows to each other and John pronounced them husband and wife which was followed by the requisite, "Now you can kiss the bride."

James frowned. He had never seen Jesus kiss anyone on the lips, especially a woman. The closest he had come was kissing his mother on the cheek. Jesus danced with Mary and was relieved when the guests circled them and all he had to do was shuffle around in a circle. The master of the banquet tasted the water that had been turned into wine. He did not realise where it had come from, though the servants who had drawn the water knew. He called the bridegroom aside.

"Everyone brings out the choice wine first and then the cheaper wine, after the guests have had too much to drink," said the master of the banquet. "But you have saved the best till now."

This was the first miraculous sign that Jesus performed and revealed his glory. From henceforth, his disciples put their faith in him. The two married couples were driven to overnight destinations in two horse drawn four wheeled chariots that Joseph hired from the cavalry in Sepphoris. Chaunan and Joanna were happy to dismount at the first stop, an inn in Cana. Jesus and Mary went on and stayed overnight in the inn at Sepphoris.

Jesus poured two tumblers of wine and handed one to Mary who was sitting on the bed.

"Here's to the task of creating a new generation of heirs."

"I hope we have healthy boys with ambitions like you and your father."

Mary noticed Jesus was deep in thought and decided to break the ice.

"Darling, would you like me to oil and massage your back? You look very tense."

Jesus took of his robe and laid face down on the bed.

"I was thinking whom to appoint for the two monarchy apostle positions."

Mary massaged Jesus for half an hour and then asked him to turn over. She noticed there had been little response from her actions. When Mary began fellatio, Jesus forgot about the Herods.

"Mary, I didn't know you knew about celibate sexual acts," he said.

"Joanna and your mother told me about a lot of things that make men happy."

Mary continued fellatio until Jesus was rigid. This was going to be his night. Mary straddled Jesus and slowly lowered herself onto his throbbing shaft. Jesus was no longer celibate. Mary had successfully started the coital transition that would change his demeanour forever, and hopefully produce male heirs. Mary spoke to Jesus when he woke the next morning.

"Darling, how did you turn the water into wine yesterday? The guests called it a miracle."

The only miracle yesterday was what you did for me," Jesus said.

"Darling, please tell me how you made the wine?"

"Well, an innkeeper told me long ago that if a man drank five glasses of wine, and then you gave him water, he would believe it was wine."

"But the water had a yellow tinge to it, like wine."

"I asked the staff to add citrus juice for flavour. The oranges and lemons must have given it the yellow tinge. Two months later Mary whispered to Jesus.

"I believe I'm pregnant,"

"Really, that is great. I hope it's a boy. I can't believe it. I have come from celibacy to heterosexual to expectant fatherhood in a few months. Mind you, my father managed to get my virgin mother pregnant with me while still celibate. My grandfather said the Virgin Mary was conceived by the Holy Spirit. Meaning the nun ranked as a virgin, conceived through the Holy Spirit, a Bishop."

***

In the first Sabbath of summer, the apostles of The Way had their first meeting. Ten Apostles, Joseph, Jesus and

John the Baptist attended the meeting held in the house of Tammuz in Jerusalem. The agenda was limited as the last two apostles had not been selected or approved yet. The positions had to be filled by the Herod family for canvassing the return of the monarchy in Iudaea. The Apostles agreed unanimously that the two Herods to be approached should be Antipas and Philip, with Thomas being a third option. Jesus was selected to talk with Philip while John was appointed to approach Antipas.

The future structure of The Way was discussed and held over for voting when the full committee had been established. It was agreed that Joseph would remain political leader, Jesus and John head of their allotted provinces, twelve Apostles representing the other six groups. There were twelve disciples for each Apostle, making the teaching and lead groups, 1-2-12-144. Each disciple would have one thousand fee paying members, a total of 144,000 followers. The joining subscription would be discussed at the next meeting which was to be held at the house of Tishrei in autumn. Jesus met with Philip Herod, the tetrarch of Ituraea. Philip was sceptical at first, but when Jesus mentioned the 144,000 fee paying members would contribute to building projects in his province he joined the group. Jesus explained that as a Herod apostle he would only have to attend meetings two to four times a year, and would have twelve of his own hand-picked disciples. They could be male or female, but must be strong leaders of noble character who believed in the doctrine of The Way.

John the Baptist met with Antipas Herod, the tetrarch of Galilee and Perea. John was making some good headway until a woman came into the room and sat next to Antipas. She was wearing a see through silk garment that barely covered her thighs.

"Darling, is your meeting nearly over?" she said as she kissed him on the lips.

Antipas moved his hand slowly up her thigh and rested his palm on her silk pants.

"Allow me five more minutes. We are about to wrap this subject up."

The woman rose and kissed Antipas on the forehead.

"Herodias, wait for me in my chambers. I won't be long."

"Herodias, isn't that the name of Philip's wife?" John said.

"No it is not. He no longer has a wife, and besides, he prefers boys."

John stood.

"I am ending this meeting," he said. "I do not think you are the right person for the position. Regarding Herodias, it is not lawful for you to have her."

Antipas was furious with John. He ordered the guards to throw him out and John was lucky to escape without punishment. From that day on, Antipas became his enemy. He wanted to marry Herodias after he divorced his own wife. John told Jesus about the unsuccessful meeting with Antipas. They agreed Philip would be named an apostle, and Thomas the other Herod Apostle, even though he had been disinherited. The twelve Apostles had now been selected, and were officially appointed at the second council meeting in the house of Tishrei.

John the Baptist heard that Antipas had divorced his wife Phasaelis and married his niece Herodias. John denounced the marriage and told everyone that what Antipas had done was not lawful under Jewish laws. Phasaelis managed to flee to her father's fortress in the neighbouring kingdom of Nabataea. King Aretas was furious, and hostilities broke out along the border of Perea and Nabataea. John preached that it was God punishing the evil Antipas. Herodias demanded that John be silenced. Antipas had John arrested and imprisoned him in his Machaerus fortress. He was afraid to kill John because he had a loyal following and had not committed a crime deserving death according to Roman rule. Antipas visited John in the dungeon and had long conversations about The Way and his beliefs. He liked listening to John, but he also feared him. John was a fiery orator and could easily persuade men to rebel. Herodias, more than ever wanted John put to the sword.

The Twelve Apostles

Jesus sent word for the twelve Apostles to meet him on the summit of Mount Arbel. Jesus climbed the mountain a day earlier and sought shelter in the limestone caves. He lit a fire and spent the night praying to God. The next morning Jesus addressed the Twelve.

"Thank you for coming to this urgent unscheduled meeting," he said. "I know you men are all very busy and so I will get straight to the point. John the Baptist has been captured and taken prisoner by Antipas. Skirmishes have broken out on the Perean-Nabataean border over the divorce of the King's daughter and may soon escalate into war. The Zealots are mobilising their freedom fighters and want to attack any Roman forces in the area to cause more instability."

"If war breaks out, Antipas will seek my army's support," Philip Herod said.

"Hopefully that won't happen. I need to know that whatever occurs we will remain united under The Way doctrine, and strive for freedom in religious beliefs and national self-rule. If you concur, I will anoint you as Apostles today. The Twelve pledged their support for The Way and to each other. Jesus reached inside his robe and produced a bottle of scented oil from a sheath attached to a sash around his waist. He prayed to God.

"Bless these men that stand before me, and guide them spiritually and in righteousness." Jesus, as the Christ, asked the Apostles to come forward when called.

"Simon Peter. With this oil, I anoint you Apostle Peter.

Andrew Peter. With this oil, I appoint you Apostle Andrew.

James Cleopas. With this oil, I appoint you Apostle James.

John Cleopas. With this oil, I appoint you Apostle John.

Philip Herod. With this oil, I appoint you Apostle Philip.

Thomas Herod. With this oil, I appoint you Apostle Thomas.

Jonathon Ananus. With this oil, I anoint you Apostle Nathanael.

Matthew Ananus. With this oil, I anoint you Apostle Matthew.

James Justus. With this oil, I anoint you Apostle James Alphaeus.

Josephes Justus. With this oil, I anoint you Apostle Jude Thaddeus.

Simon Justus. With this oil, I anoint you Apostle Simon.

Judas Justus. With this oil, I anoint you Apostle Judas."

After the ceremony, the Apostles gathered in prayer then talked for two hours, discussing all the matters raised. One of the Apostles' first tasks would be to select twelve diligent and faithful followers from their particular group.

"I will visit Antipas and ask if I can visit John," Simon Peter said. "I will take some fruit, religious writings and a blank scroll for him to write on."

"Take notice of how he is imprisoned," Jesus replied, "so that we can plan to rescue him if Antipas does not release him soon."

"I will go with Peter as I can gather information on the fortress defences and relay the information to my zealot commander," Judas said.

"Try to build up a friendly relationship with Antipas and his guards. Go regularly every week on the same day. Give John comfort and hope," Jesus said.

The meeting ended and the thirteen men dispersed, agreeing to meet on the first Sabbath in winter, on the upper floor at the house of Shebat. The Way religious sect grew rapidly and soon rivalled the two major sects. The Pharisee and Sadducee followers became jealous and complained bitterly to their Chief Priests about the loss of congregation numbers and reduced tithes. John the Baptist heard that Jesus was baptising more people than him, and he too became jealous and disheartened. However, it wasn't Jesus baptising, it was the disciples.

On April17th 30 A.D. Mary Magdalene-Justus gave birth to a beautiful baby daughter. Jesus and Mary named her Sarah Salome. Three years later, on February 24th 33A.D. Mary gave birth to another daughter named Tamara Miriam Justus. The second birth started gossip about the Crown Prince not producing a male heir.

James had married on his thirty-sixth birthday and had already produced one son, a boy named Michael Simeon Justus. The Pharisee sect, looking for more exposure among their dwindling congregation wanted James to become the nominated Crown Prince, insisting that Jesus was illegitimate.

Jesus and Mary went to the temple to read the blessings and naming for Tamara after the Torah had been read by the Chief Priest. When they exited the temple the Jews separated Jesus from his family and isolated him in the courtyard.

"Aren't we right in saying that you are a Samaritan and demon-possessed?"

"Your father Abraham rejoiced at seeing my day. He saw it and was glad," Jesus said.

"You are not yet fifty years old, and you have seen Abraham," the Jews yelled.

"I tell you the truth, before Abraham was born, I am."

On hearing that, the Jews went to find stones to stone him to death for blasphemy. Jesus hid himself under some tables until they left, then slipped away from the temple grounds under the cover of darkness. This was the second occasion when Jesus was threatened with death from an angry mob.

Joseph maintained Jesus was the rightful heir and should be given more time to produce a male heir. If Jesus died without a son, the crown prince would be passed on to James or his eldest son.

Mary wanted the next child to be a boy. She discussed the situation with her mother-in-law who had given birth to five boys and three girls

"Mother, can you tell me how to improve my chances to have a boy. I prayed for a boy last time before I became pregnant. Should I alter my diet perhaps?"

"My mother told me a story just before I married Joseph. She was concerned that the Justus men were being eliminated by the Herods because we were the rightful heirs to the throne. She wanted me to have as many sons as possible so that some heirs would survive and continue our dynasty."

"What advice did your mother give you?"

"Well, she was an observant lady. She noticed most couples produced sons early in their marriage, and later daughters. That is exactly what happened with Joseph and me."

"I don't understand. I have had two daughters and desperately want to have a son."

"If you see a boy and girl run in a race, who normally wins?" mother Mary asked.

"If they are the same age, the boy would usually win."

"Correct. Now if a man and woman have an equally healthy and happy life, which usually lives longer?"

"The wives just like in your parents' case."

"Exactly, now let's suppose the male seeds that fertilise our eggs perform in the same way."

The male seeds would move faster but die quicker. That means if I have sex more often, the male seed would be more likely to win and fertilize the egg," Mary said.

"That was my mother's theory and I put it to good use."

"I am sure you are right. Jesus enjoys having sex with me but prefers the *movaan* method. He prefers to finish in the anal position. It is only when I straddle Jesus that he can fertilize my egg. That would be only once a week, favouring a conception of a girl baby."

"When you are ready to have your next baby, remember our conversation. Explain to Jesus when the time comes. In the meantime, enjoy yourself."

"If we are correct, how long do you suppose the male seed would live?"

"I believe it could be as little as one day for males and three days for females."

"That means trying for boys will need to be a daily event," Mary said.

"Enjoy life while you can. Later, as you age, nature takes it course and you end up in a brother-sister type relationship, but with a lot of happy memories," mother Mary said.

Antipas had a birthday party at his castle in Machaerus and invited many influential guests. Herodias wanted to find a husband for her daughter Salome and so she asked Antipas if she could perform an erotic dance. The king agreed and Salome danced, mainly in front of him. Antipas was pleased with her erotic performance

"Ask me anything you want, and I will give it to you," he told Salome while he was in a drunken stupor. "Whatever you ask, I will give you, up to half my kingdom."

Salome went outside to speak with her mother.

"What shall I ask for?" she asked.

"The head of John the Baptist," Herodias answered.

At once, she hurried to the King with her request.

"I want you to give me right now the head of John the Baptist on a platter."

The King was greatly distressed, but because of his oath and the dinner guests, he did not want to refuse her. So he immediately sent an executioner with orders to bring back John's head. The man went, beheaded John in the prison cell and brought back his head on a platter. He presented it to the girl, and she gave it to her mother. Herodias spat on John's face and threw the severed head out on to a mound of vegetable scraps. The disciples heard what happened to John and collected his body from the dungeon. They gave him a martyr's funeral with a eulogy fit for a prophet.

John was buried without his head at a tomb in Sebaste, in Samaria. Joanna asked her husband Chaunan to search for John's head. Chaunan was the manager of Antipas' household and often accompanied him to Machaerus. One of his kitchen maids found the head when throwing out the scraps. Chaunan gave the head to his wife, and she gave it to Jesus. He in turn gave it to the Essene Monastery at Jerusalem, where it was sanctified and placed in an ossuary box. Jesus stayed in Jerusalem for the Feast of Dedication. A gathering of Jews saw Jesus in Solomon's Colonnade as he walked to the Temple to pray over John's demise. The Jews did not believe Jesus was the Messiah and demanded proof.

"How long will you keep us in suspense? If you are the Christ, tell us plainly."

"What my father has given to me is greater than all," Jesus answered. "The father and I are one."

The Jews began to collect rocks to stone Jesus. Some tried to seize him, but he escaped their grasp and fled into the wilderness. This was the third time angry Jews had tried to kill him.

Antipas thought the beheading of John the Baptist would solve his problems but he was sadly mistaken. Aretas declared war on Perea province and fought both Antipas and Philip's combined forces. When Philip was killed in a battle in 34A.D. his soldiers joined with the Nabataean army and completely routed Antipas forces. Antipas withdrew to the fortress at Machaerus with little more than his body guards. The following year he sent a delegation to Tiberius. The Emperor sent an order to the Syrian Governor Vitellius to destroy Aretas' army and kill or capture him. Jesus held an extraordinary meeting with the Apostles.

The Zealots were hell-bent on attacking the weakened forces of Antipas for beheading John. Philip was dead and an illegitimate offspring of the Herod family was chosen as his replacement. His name was also Philip. It was decided among the Apostles that it was better that there wasn't a name change at their level. He was a good man that wasn't in line for the throne, but still a Herod in name and blood. They did not have much of a choice as Antipas was given temporary control over Philips' Realm. Jesus was elected as the sole spiritual leader of the sect, and Joseph remained as political leader, but had very little input in operational matters.

Emperor Tiberius health deteriorated in the last few years of his rule. He moved to the Isle of Capri and was content with the senate in Rome having administration control. He was disturbed though, of the continuing reports of Jewish insurrection and anarchy in Iudaea. He sent an order to the presiding prefect of Judea, Pontius Pilate, to quell all rebellious activity in Judea and the surrounding provinces. He could ask for extra soldiers from Vitellius forces in Syria if warranted, but all rioting and rebellion must be quelled.

Pontius Pilate sought the advice of the High Priest Josephus Caiaphas.

"Who do you believe is behind the organised rioting?" he asked.

"I have no doubt it is the Zealots," Caiaphas replied.

"I am well aware of the Zealot sect, but who is organising the demonstrations?"

This was the chance Caiaphas had been waiting for. He knew about Jesus and his meetings with the Apostles through Jonathon and Mathew Ananus. They were Chief Priests in his Sadducee sect and had reported information about the two Zealot apostles, Simon and Judas. Caiaphas wanted Jesus arrested as well, as he was the biggest thorn in the side of the two major religious sects.

"I know that three Zealot conspirators will be having a meeting in Jerusalem in March. Normally they meet on the first Sabbath of each season. But I have heard this one will be held on the sect leaders' birthday."

"I want you to confirm the actual date and find one of the Zealots that will be attending the meeting. I want you and the Zealot here within a week. Is that clear?" Pilate said.

"Yes Pontius. I will have the Ananus brothers bring a Zealot apostle to me."

"Make sure he has a wife and family, and find out his home address. I want to put an offer to him that he can't refuse."

Mathew and Jonathon met Judas at the market and asked him to accompany them to see the High Priest.

"What does he want to see me about?" Judas asked.

"He didn't tell us, but it may concern *The Way* sect."

Judas followed the two apostles thinking he was in safe company. Soon he found himself in the hands of Caiaphas, Pontius Pilate and several soldiers.

"I believe you are a Zealot," Pilate said, "and as such I can have you beheaded."

Judas was petrified.

"I am a member of the Essene sect and have some spiritual connections to other sects."

"I beg to differ. I believe you have very close connections with Zealot commanders. I also understand you have a beautiful wife and young children living in a farm near Nazareth."

Judas remained silent.

"We want you to tell us the date of the next meeting that you will attend in March, also the location and exact time."

"Why do you want to know about that? The meeting is only a about religious ceremonies. You can confirm that with Mathew and Jonathon."

"We believe your sect The Way is collecting more revenue than the other sects combined. Very little is given to the Emperor of Rome. I want that lost revenue for building projects in Judea."

"You want it for yourself. The money already goes to projects in Iudaea."

Caiaphas slapped Judas over the face for being insolent. Pontius Pilate approached Judas and hit him again.

"I have placed sentries around your farm. If you mention anything about this meeting we will crucify you in front of your family. They will be tied together and thrown in the dam. You will hear them scream out for help while hanging on a cross. The young ones will drown first and their dead weight will pull your wife under."

"Tell us what you know and I will reward you with thirty pieces of silver," Caiaphas said.

Judas was deep in thought and didn't answer. Pilate slapped him again.

"I want my share of that revenue. I want your leader to agree to my demands. I want the date, time and place of the March meeting. You are to give Caiaphas the information by the end of this month. Remember, silence or you and your family will not live much longer."

Pilate turned to his guards.

"Throw him out on the street."

Judas picked himself up and looked around. No one saw him being thrown by the soldiers. He was shaken and traumatised, but not injured. Through his mind was racing the events that had occurred in the last hour. He staggered down the street, not knowing where to go, or what to do. He walked for hours and found himself on the road to Shechem. Judas had a drink of water from a creek and kept walking. His mind was numb, he was in shock. He walked on through the night, reaching the farm before sunrise. He decided not to tell his wife. His family must come first, before any amount of money. Pilate was known for his brutality and his greed, Judas knew the demands would have to be met.

Jesus and Mary were staying in the farmhouse at Nazareth for a month. Simon and Martha had gone to Bethany to renovate the home her deceased parents' bequeathed to their two daughters. The house had four large bedrooms and was situated two miles from the temple in Jerusalem. Mary heard the dog barking at Judas' house on the neighbouring farm lot. At the same time she felt the baby kick in her womb. It was January, in the 4000th year since creation according to the Sadducee sect. The year was disputed by the Pharisee sect who believed it was only 3976 years from creation. It wasn't uncommon for religious sects to change dates to suit natural or political events that occurred in their lifespan.

The Sadducees expected a sign from heaven on January 1st, the first day of the year on the Roman calendar 36A.D. When midnight passed without any shooting stars or other heavenly event they changed the night to Jesus' forty-third birthday, which would fall on Thursday March29th. A spectacular heavenly display on that night would prove beyond doubt that Jesus was the true Messiah. Mary took the Sadducee creation year as a good omen for the birth of her third child. Surely she would be blessed with a boy on this special occasion. She had convinced Jesus to let her perform the straddle sex method last June. Mary wanted to conceive that month so the baby would be born in spring. Jesus was with Mary every day and she insisted they had twenty-eight straight days of coital sex. Mary even accompanied Jesus on the three day trip to Jerusalem for the summer season apostles' meeting.

The dog kept barking and Mary woke Jesus.

"I think your brother has come home earlier than planned. Their dog sounds excited."

"I will see him in the afternoon. He must be tired after walking all night"

"The baby kicked earlier," Mary said.

Jesus placed his hand gently on Mary's bulging stomach. "I am sure this baby is bigger than the last two pregnancies were in the seventh month."

"I have been praying for a baby boy every night for the last eight months."

"I have as well. It will be a long time before I recover from those forty days and forty nights."

Mary slapped Jesus on the arm.

"It was only twenty-eight days and some nights," she said.

"If it is a boy, a gap of six years is required between conceptions. That is if the rule for monarchy heirs is enforced to the letter of the law," Jesus said.

"I think your mother and father put that rule to rest and decided on increasing the David dynasty instead."

"That is true, but look at the conflict it has caused in our family because James is only sixteen months younger than me and wants the Crown Prince title," Jesus said.

"James can only claim the title if you die without a son, or the Pharisees convince Emperor Tiberius that you are illegitimate, and he sides with the Sadducee sect."

"Would you like a warm lemon juice?" Jesus asked.

"That would be wonderful. Then I will get up and make the girls breakfast."

"Stay in bed, I can organise eggs on toast for breakfast."

"Jesus Christ. I am in heaven!"

Sarah heard her mother and wondered what she meant. That was the first time anyone had uttered the two words consecutively. After breakfast Sarah and Tamara played outside on the grass. Sarah danced around her little sister and sang a new song.

"Warm lemon juice for breakfast, I'm in heaven. Eggs on toast, I'm in heaven. Breakfast in bed, *Jesus Christ* I am in heaven."

Later that day the family walked over to see Judas, his wife Liana and their eighteen month old twins, Menahem and Maayan. Jesus noticed that Judas looked tired and fidgety and he hadn't spoken or made eye contact.

Jesus called his brother to one side.

"You looked stressed. Is everything all right?"

"I am very tired after my trip to Jerusalem," Judas said.

"I know you well Judas. Tell me what is bothering you."

"I met up with Mathew and Jonathon near the temple. They wanted me to see Caiaphas about the Passover feast."

"What did the High Priest want this time?"

"He wanted to know the date of our Apostle meeting. He told me not to discuss the matter with anyone, not even Jonathan and Mathew."

"I know there is more. What else did he want?" Jesus asked.

"He knew the meeting was in March. I didn't tell him the date. He asked me to find out the exact time and place of the meeting. If I told him he would give me thirty pieces of silver."

"That is a lot of money. It does mean that we can trust Mathew and Jonathon though, because they have obviously not mentioned the venue location."

"I don't think they trust Caiaphas, even though he married their sister," Judas said.

"That is because he was chosen ahead of them for the High Priesthood. Now tell me what else did Caiaphas want?" Jesus asked.

"He wants some of The Way's revenue to replace the tithes lost from falling membership numbers."

"Do you think he plans to attend our meeting?" Jesus asked.

"I am sure that is his intention."

"I don't trust the man. I don't believe he will hand over the silver if you tell him the information in advance. Tell Caiaphas you want the money up front. Then you will lead him to the meeting on the day. I am sure the apostles will vote against the motion and he will leave empty handed."

Three weeks later Simon and Martha returned to the Nazareth farm and Jesus took Mary to Bethany in a wagon pulled by two donkeys.

CHAPTER 8: Titius and Paul

On March 21st 36A.D. Mary gave birth to a healthy baby boy. Jesus and his mother comforted Mary, and Luke the family doctor delivered the baby. Jesus was overwhelmed with emotion.

"I have a son! I have a son! The David heir line has continued into another generation."

Jesus hugged and kissed Mary and gave her a bunch of almond blossoms.

"My favourite flowers, they remind me of our wedding. Thank you darling."

Eight days later, the baby was taken to Jerusalem and circumcised in the Jewish tradition. He was named Jesus Titius Justus. Jesus went to Jerusalem and praised God in the Temple. The Pharisees heard that Mary had given birth to a male heir and were greatly distressed. They still believed James was the true Crown Prince and his son was older than Jesus' son.

On Thursday March 29th, the Apostles' meeting was held at the house of Shebat. Outside the premises was a sign of Aquarius, holding a water jug. The twelve Apostles wished Jesus a happy forty-third birthday and congratulated him on the birth of his newborn son, Jesus-Titius who had only been circumcised that morning. Then they discussed business. Part way through the meeting, Jesus turned to Judas.

"I understand you have other business to attend. What you are about to do, do quickly," he said.

Judas went to the Temple and saw Caiaphas.

"Jesus is at the house of Shebat with the other Apostles."

Caiaphas had Judas arrested and thrown into jail.

"You had better be telling me the truth or you will die tomorrow," he said.

The High Priest joined the meeting, sitting in Judas' position. His request for a substantial proportion of the revenue to be donated to the Temple funds was debated and voted on. Jesus and one apostle from each group voted. The vote was counted. The vote was five to two against. Caiaphas looked at all those in the room and stormed out.

Jesus stood.

"Gentlemen, I do not trust Caiaphas," he said. "I suggest we adjourn this meeting and go to the Mount of Olives hall where the disciples are camping for Passover."

Caiaphas informed Pontius Pilate that he had Judas in jail and that Zealot leaders were in a meeting in the city.

"Who are they and what are their ranks in the bandit force?"

"Jesus is their spiritual leader and the most dangerous in my opinion," Caiaphas said.

"Who else is there? I need at least three Zealot leaders to ease the political tensions with Rome," Pilate said.

"The one in jail is known as Judas the Iscariot, He is a knife assassin. The two main leaders are Simon the Zealot and his brother, Josephes."

"I do not want you to be associated with the arrests. Gather the Chief Priests and officials, I will send a detachment of soldiers to the temple grounds. Make Judas identify the three men. Remind him that his family's fate is in his hands. Bring the culprits to me first thing tomorrow and I will judge them," Pilate said.

Judas, still believing it was a matter of money, led the soldiers to the house of Shebat. Not finding them there, he led them towards the Mount of Olives. At the city gates, a group of Pharisees joined them with lanterns and weapons.

"I suggest we wait until midnight," a Chief Priest said. "If there is no sign from the heavens that Jesus is the messiah, there will be less resistance from his followers."

"I don't think there will be any resistance," a soldier said. "By midnight, most of them will be asleep or intoxicated."

Jesus, Simon and Josephes were identified by their younger brother, Judas. Only Peter drew his sword, slicing the ear of Malchus, Caiaphas' servant. Jesus realising they were outnumbered told Peter to put his sword away. The soldiers arrested them, chained them together and led them away.

Jesus turned to face his disciples.

"Do not let your hearts be troubled," he said. "I will come back and stand in your presence."

The next morning Pontius Pilate questioned the three brothers. When he found out they were from Galilee, the realm of King Antipas, he ordered the guards to take them to him to be tried. The King was in Jerusalem to attend the Passover festivities, and it would be political politeness to let him judge the men.

Antipas had heard of Jesus and even suspected he may be a reincarnation of John whom he had beheaded. The King questioned Jesus, whom some people were claiming was a king of the Jews. He found that Jesus was just another religious priest causing unrest in the community. He was hoping Jesus would show him some type of miracle, but when Jesus did nothing, Antipas had him whipped. Then he had him dressed in an elegant robe and sent the three men back to Pilate. That day Herod and Pilate became friends.

Pilate had one more political act to perform. He took Jesus on to his balcony for the crowd to participate. If he had their support it would bolster his authority and popularity.

"I find no basis for a charge against this man," Pilate said.

"Take him away, crucify him," the crowd yelled.

Pilate brought out a prisoner called Barabbas. He was Theudas' son and had been imprisoned with the insurrectionists who had committed murder during a recent uprising.

"Who shall I release, Barabbas or your king of the Jews?"

"Release Barabbas, we have no king but Caesar."

Pilate wanted to please the crowd and so released Barabbas and had Jesus publically flogged and humiliated. Then he handed Jesus, Simon and Josephes over to the soldiers to crucify. The arms of the men were strapped to a cross bar with wet cowhide which would tighten as it dried. They were forced to trek outside the walls of Jerusalem to a place called Golgotha, a nearby cemetery. Simon, judged the Zealot leader, was hauled up the main post first and the crossbar was bolted into position. Jesus, with a sign nailed above his head stating, 'THIS IS JESUS THE KING OF THE JEWS' was crucified in the middle. Josephes was not a Zealot but was crucified in the place of his brother Judas. The guards ran the chain behind the posts and locked the chains on their legs

When Judas realised he had been deceived by Caiaphas, and that his brothers had been condemned, he was seized by remorse. He returned the thirty silver coins to the Chief Priests and the Elders.

"I have sinned, for I have betrayed innocent blood," he said.

"What is that to do with us? That is your responsibility," a Chief Priest said.

Judas threw the money on the floor of the Temple and left. He found a rope in a nearby yard and ran to a tree not far from his crucified brothers. He made a lasso on one end and tied it to a branch overhanging a steep ravine.

Then he made a noose and placed it around his neck. Judas yelled to his brothers at the top of his voice.

"Jesus, Simon and Josephes, forgive me, I am sorry."

His three crucified brothers watched helplessly from the crosses as Judas jumped over the cliff. The branch broke and Judas crashed down the side of the ravine, ripping his stomach open on the jagged rocks. Judas writhed in agony and was slowly bleeding to death.

Joseph and James were standing near the crosses with a large group of women. Among the weeping women were Mary Magdalene, his mother and her sister Rachel, the mother of Zebedee's sons, his sisters, Mary, Salome and Joanna. Joseph and James had heard Judas yell out and saw his horrific fall. They ran to his aid and carried him to the closest doctor's surgery. Judas lingered for hours but never regained consciousness.

Jesus had been whipped more severely than Simon or Josephes, and was drifting in and out of consciousness after nearly three hours on the cross. He opened his eyes and saw his mother standing by his beloved disciple who was holding baby Jesus.

"Dear woman, here is your son," he said. "Here is your mother," he said to his wife.

From that day, his mother and Mary lived together.

"Curse you Jesus for leading us into a trap," Simon said.

"We have been punished for our crimes," Josephes replied, "but Jesus has done nothing wrong. Jesus, remember me when you come into your kingdom."

"I tell you the truth," Jesus answered. "Today you will be with me in paradise."

Jesus had remembered the family tomb was in the garden of paradise, and he knew they would be buried there for one year before their bones would be dug up and placed in ossuaries. Jesus wit remained with him to his final hour on the cross.

Crucifixion was the most popular form of punishment the Romans used to quell uprisings. The condemned would remain on the crosses until they did not have the energy to breathe, dying of asphyxiation or dehydration. It was the cruellest public execution because the person suffered for days, even weeks if the weather was mild with occasional rainfall.

One hundred years earlier, Spartacus had led a rebellion against Rome. His seventy thousand man army was eventually routed after many conflicts. The body of Spartacus was never found. He may have escaped, however six thousand of his men were captured. The Roman commander, Marcus Crassus, crucified them along the Appin way, from Capua to Rome. He ordered the crosses to be erected by the prisoners themselves, one each side of the road, every hundred metres apart. Some of the crucified men lived for nine days before dying.

The weather had been fine in the morning when the three Nazarene men had been condemned. At noon when they were crucified a strong wind from the east blew red dust over Judea. The sun was blocked out, and for three hours, Jerusalem was covered with a dark shadow.

"I am thirsty," Jesus cried out meekly.

One of the men standing nearby soaked a sponge into a jar of wine vinegar, placed it on a stalk of the hyssop plant and lifted it to Jesus' lips. Jesus drank the juice, which was laced with poison and an analgesic mix of crushed coriander seeds, gall and myrrh.

"It is finished," Jesus said after he received the drink.

With that, he bowed his head and gave up his spirit, the crown prince title to his son.

It was the day of preparation, and the next day was to be a special Sabbath, one that fell on the last day of the month. The Jews did not want the bodies left on the crosses during the Sabbath and Passover festival. A delegation was sent to Pontius Pilate to have the men's legs broken and their bodies buried alive. He despatched six soldiers who broke the legs of Simon and Josephes. Jesus however appeared dead already, and so they used a spear to stab him in the side. Blood and water spurted out, the soldier had pierced Jesus and the water container he had on a belt around his waist. Satisfied Jesus was dead the soldiers did not break his legs.

Joseph and Luke noticed the blood spurting from Jesus body and realised he was still alive, but totally unconscious, void of pain and movement. Joseph hurried to see Pilate to ask for the body of his sons so that he could put them in his family tomb which was nearby. Pilate was busy with the Chief Priests and discussing arrangements for the Passover feast. He ordered the men be locked in a sealed tomb so that the men would suffocate overnight. Joseph asked his friend Nicodemus, to fetch a mixture of seventy pounds of myrrh and aloes and hide it in the tomb.

The soldiers cut Jesus down, and he fell heavily onto the ground without uttering a sound. Simon and Josephes had their chains removed and were cut down. They fell heavily on their feet and screamed in pain. They were dragged to the tomb by the soldiers and thrown inside. Jesus was carried by James and placed on a cut out slab. The soldiers rolled the heavy stone in front of the tomb entrance and ordered the women to collect wet clay to seal the tomb.

The Chief Priests asked Pontius Pilate to secure the tomb until the men had suffocated.

"Take a guard and make the tomb as secure as you know how," he said.

Joseph knew his sons would suffocate within eight to ten hours. He waited until darkness fell, and then brought two trusted disciples to the upper level track where the smaller tombs were located. He instructed the men to crawl into the tombs that were directly above the guarded tomb. He gave the men tools and told them to dig quietly until they broke into the larger tomb below. The two shafts would supply the entombed men with sufficient air to survive until James could arrange a rescue mission after the Sabbath. Joseph told the disciples to dig in the dark and to light and pass down the lanterns to the entombed men later.

Joseph spoke to the guard to distract him while the men crawled along the pathway above.

"Would you mind if I light a fire for the women relatives who will be arriving for the wake ceremony?" he asked.

"Go ahead, I will enjoy the warmth. Tell me Jew, is that moon a bad omen?"

Joseph looked towards the east and saw a large blood-red moon hovering over Qumran. It was caused by the red dust lingering high in the atmosphere after the dust storm.

"Yes, it is a bad omen for all those responsible for spilling the blood of innocent men."

Joseph prepared the fire and several women walked down the path towards him. He asked Mary and his wife to sing hymns to comfort the entombed men while they were still alive. He wanted to mask any digging noises from above.

Three hours later, the disciples broke through the tomb ceiling below. They cautioned the men to remain quiet as there was a guard by the entrance. They told them a rescue plan was being planned. They lit the lamps and passed them down to Simon and Josephes. Jesus was still unconscious, but alive. He had been given some of the mixture of aloes and myrrh which would act as a purgative, cleansing his body of the poison. Now that Simon could see, he could administer more medicine and watch for any sign of improvement. The two disciples silently crept away. They returned to the apostle's and disciples who were preparing for the Passover ceremony at the Mount of Olives hall.

James spoke to the two disciples about the health of his brothers and cautioned them to remain silent. He slipped away from the group, carrying a bundle of robes and some small containers of water and food. He talked with Simon and Josephes.

"I have brought you some things, how are you feeling?" he asked.

"Battered and bruised, and in pain, but still alive."

"Joseph is keeping the guard distracted. Are both your legs broken?"

"Josephes left leg is broken and the right one is sprained. Mine are the same, but the opposite legs," Simon said.

"I will bring back some bandages and wooden splints after the change of guards. Has Jesus regained consciousness yet?"

"No, but he is still breathing and we have covered him to keep him warm. I think he will slowly recover."

"Good. I will tell father. I will take over from him so that he can rest."

"What can we expect next?" Josephes asked.

"You will have to remain here until after the Sabbath. The guards will leave once they believe you have suffocated. It is imperative that you don't make any noise and keep your lamps burning low."

"James, tell father we love him."

"I will. Keep your spirits up, I will see you again in about two hours."

James returned to the tombs two hours after the guards changed duty. His sisters were now singing hymns, having relieved Mary and the first group of women. James passed down the bandages and splints to Josephes.

"Try to set the bones straight and tie the bandages tight as possible. How is Jesus?"

"Still the same," Josephes said. "We have given him plenty of the aloe mixture. His body temperature is fluctuating from hot to cold. Currently, he has a fever."

"Has he opened his eyes at all?"

"Not yet, but a while ago his body convulsed," Simon said.

"That may be a good sign. I will check with Luke. We have all had the worst days of our lives, and it has taken its toll on the whole family. I have to go now. If all goes well, I will see you before sunrise on Monday. Goodbye for now."

"Thank you, James. God bless you and all our family. We love you all," Simon said.

The word spread throughout Jerusalem. Jesus of Nazareth and two of his brothers had been crucified. Many in the crowd rejoiced until they noticed the moon. The full moon glowed white until it reached Qumran in the east. Then suddenly it turned blood red, causing the superstitious and the God fearing Jews to panic. The Jewish people believed God was going to punish them for killing his son. They all hid inside their tents and houses until sunrise, throwing the first day of Passover into chaos.

On the Sabbath, the Chief Priest calmed the crowd. Joseph Caiaphas announced the Passover festival would begin. The 'Blood-Libel' ceremony was about to proceed. The crowd erupted in applause and the blood red moon overnight was forgotten.

A nine year old Egyptian boy who had been fasting for four days was led into the Temple by four Chief Priests and placed on the altar. Caiaphas recited a short Passover prayer, picked up the ceremonial knife and stabbed the boy in the neck. As the boy bled to death, the High Priest recited the full Hallel Reading. The four Chief Priests filled four jars with the boy's pure red blood. The blood would be mixed with red wine, and distributed to the masses to be consumed with the four part Passover Seder meal.

At midday, the last soldier left his post at the tomb and was not replaced as the men were deemed to have suffocated. Joseph crawled into one of the small tombs and checked on his sons. Jesus was sitting up, aided by Simon and Josephes.

"Jesus, you have risen!" Joseph said.

Jesus smiled briefly and raised his hand. He had tried to wave, but was still too weak and looked ghostly white in the flickering light of the lamp. Joseph was happy to see his three sons cuddled together in support for each other. The Roman occupation had taken its toll on the family. Jesus and Josephes wanted a peaceful approach to

National freedom, Simon and Judas had wanted armed force against the Romans and Josephes and James wanted religious freedom. Josephes and Simon were brave, helping Jesus recover while suffering badly from broken legs and severe pain from the crucifixion.

Joseph handed down three containers of wine, unleavened *matza*, broiled fish, and the Haroseth. The fourth course being an apple and wine dish mixed with cinnamon and nutmeg.

"Enjoy your Passover Seder Joseph said."

"Thank you, father," Simon said. "You have made this Passover one to remember for all times."

"Thank you, father," Jesus said. "I will eat little, but will drink the cups of wine."

"Thank you, father," Josephes said. "We love you, we love you all. God bless."

The Jewish people sang and danced in the streets. They ate the Paschal Lamb during the Passover Seder and drank their cups of wine laced with the blood of the dead Egyptian boy. They enjoyed the festivities into the night and were joyous to see the bright pale white full moon appear in the east and rise high into the heavens. The moon travelled towards Jerusalem in all its glowing splendour. When it reached overhead it again turned blood red, sending the Jews into a superstitious panic. Once more, they hid inside their tents and houses and did not venture outside again until after sunrise the next morning.

On the first of April, before sunrise, Joseph, James, Nicodemus and two disciples arrived at the cemetery near the tomb. Joseph and Nicodemus went to the tomb to scrape away the dried clay that had sealed the tomb. James showed the disciples where he wanted the grave for Judas dug. While they were digging, James went to the wagon and picked up a long iron bar. Then he went to the tomb and with Nicodemus' help levered the stone away from the entrance to the tomb.

Simon was carried to the wagon and lifted onto the rear bench seat. Josephes was seated next. Then the men heard a group of people coming down the path towards them. They quickly moved the donkeys and wagon and hid them among the trees behind the garden. James and Nicodemus then assisted Jesus into a secluded part of the garden and hid out of sight. It was just before sunrise, and visibility was poor. There were five people in the group, all carrying something. They reached the flat area and turned towards the tombs. The leading person was carrying a lamp. Suddenly they stopped and started chatting between themselves. Then the one with the lamp ran forward and went inside the tomb.

"It's not the Pharisees," James said. "It is mother, Rachel, Mary, Joanna and Salome."

"They have brought spices and perfumes to anoint the bodies," Nicodemus said.

Joseph didn't want the women to linger near the tombs or cause a commotion so sent two disciples to the women.

"Don't be alarmed. Jesus, the Nazarene who was crucified. He has risen!"

"Where is he?" Mary Magdalene said.

"He is not here. See the place where they laid him. Tell Peter and the disciples that he is going ahead of you into Galilee."

The women left, but Mary Magdalene turned back and visited the tomb one more time. Jesus indicated to James and Nicodemus that he could walk by himself. He slowly walked into the open and waited for Mary. Mary came out of the tomb carrying the cloths used to wipe Jesus and a bandage that had covered his head wounds.

"Mary."

Mary looked up in disbelief.

"Jesus?"

"Do not hold on to me, but tell the others I will come to them later," Jesus said.

Mary gently held Jesus and cried tears of anguish, tears of relief, tears of joy. Joseph and the others gathered around Jesus and Mary.

"We have to go quickly, before we are seen by the Pharisees or soldiers," Jesus said.

James and the two disciples escorted Mary back to the Apostles at the Mount of Olives Hall. Nicodemus drove Joseph, Jesus, Simon and Josephes to Bethany where they would be cared for and kept hidden. The women found Peter and the disciples.

"The tomb is empty. No one is there," they said.

"I have seen Jesus, he has risen," Mary said.

The disciples didn't believe the women because their words seemed to them like nonsense. Peter ran to the tomb to see for himself. He saw the tomb was empty. He saw the strips of linen and the aloe skins on the dirt floor. He saw drops of blood everywhere and smelt the thick sickening odour of vomit. Peter walked back to the hall, wondering what had happened. He wanted to talk to the women again, but they were nowhere to be found. They had gone to the doctor's surgery to find Luke and then walked the two miles to Bethany.

They found Jesus asleep. He had swallowed a tumbler of wine and had collapsed from total exhaustion. The women hugged Simon and Josephes who were in severe pain. They were also exhausted and needed to drink wine. Luke attended to their broken legs, splinting their legs in place and bandaging their sprained legs. Simon and Josephes were helped to bed where they fell into a heavy sleep.

Many Jewish citizens were angry that Jesus, the self-proclaimed Messiah of Israel had been crucified with the Zealots. They marched to the temple grounds demanding Caiaphas and Pontius Pilate be dismissed from office.

An hour after sunset Jesus woke. He felt a stabbing pain where the spear penetrated his side. He sat up, his head was throbbing. His arms where aching from supporting the weight of his body while he was hanging on the cross. His back was stinging from the whippings he endured. He was weak from vomiting, diarrhoea, dehydration and exhaustion.

"Mary, I thirst," he called out.

Mary held the tumbler of water in Jesus' shaking hands and helped to guide it to his sunburnt lips.

"Thank you darling, I was dying of thirst."

"You are safe now. All you need is rest, love and care."

"I need to see the apostles and disciples tonight."

"You are not strong enough yet, please rest for another day."

"Mary, I need to talk to Joseph and Nicodemus."

"Can you help me get into Jerusalem this evening?" Jesus asked.

"Yes," Nicodemus said. "I still have the donkeys and cart we borrowed."

The Apostles and Disciples were locked inside the hall, discussing what had happened, and wondering what took place. Jesus opened the side door with his key, quietly walked in, and stood among them.

"Peace be with you," he said.

They were startled and frightened, thinking they had seen a ghost.

"Why are you troubled?" Jesus asked. "Why do doubts rise in your minds? Look at my hands and feet. It is I myself! Touch me and see. A ghost does not have flesh and bones, as you see I have."

When he had said this, he showed them his hands and feet. They still did not believe it because of joy and amazement.

"Do you have anything here to eat?" he asked and was offered a piece of broiled fish which he ate it in their presence.

"Everything must be fulfilled that is written about me in the Law of Moses, the Prophets and the Psalms," Jesus explained. "This is what is written: *The Christ will suffer and rise from the dead on the third day, and repentance and forgiveness of sins will be preached in his name to all nations, beginning in Jerusalem."*

The following day Jesus, Simon and Josephes sought sanctuary in the Qumran Monastery, under the care of the priests. Jesus was given the upstairs guest room on the third floor with access to the Most High and Chief Priest.

The disciples were told to spread the word throughout the known world.

"Jesus has risen. He is sitting on the right hand side of God, in Heaven," they said.

When Mary heard the stories at the marketplace, she walked home smiling to herself. Jesus had anointed her as one of his disciples several years ago and taught her the monastery idiom. What the people were saying was, in fact, correct. Jesus had risen from the tomb slab. He was sitting near Jonathon Ananus, the Most High, and God of the monastery. He was in heaven, the name given to the third floor of the monastery.

Joseph knew that Caiaphas and Pontius Pilot would search for the truth about the rumours. They would find out if Jesus was dead or still alive. Pilate had to quell the growing public anger, especially when the moon rose on the third night and remained white. The superstitious Jews were saying it was a sign from heaven that Jesus, the Messiah had risen. Joseph had three graves dug next to Judas' grave, one to the east and two on the western side. He had three large pigs wrapped in funeral cloth and given a traditional Jewish burial.

When the soldiers demanded Joseph show them the bodies of his sons, he showed them the four freshly dug graves. They asked him which one was the priest Jesus. Joseph pointed to Judas' grave. The soldiers dug down to the body.

"Sacrilege, you are violating our Jewish rites," the Jews in the cemetery yelled out.

The Romans sliced through the burial cloth and saw a bearded face.

"That is one of them, check the other graves," the soldier in command said.

"You cannot disturb a Jewish grave without the Emperor's consent," the crowd shouted.

More Jews arrived. The crowd had grown and were becoming hostile towards the Pagan soldiers. As the soldiers dug the crowd began to pelt them with stones. They stopped digging and dropped their spades.

"We have been ordered by Caiaphas, your High Priest, to identify the bodies of the condemned men. Let us spear the graves so that we know the bodies are buried here," one of the soldiers said.

"Haven't you tortured my sons enough?" Joseph said. "Do what you must and go. Report what you have seen and leave us to mourn our dead in peace."

The soldiers thrust their spears into the remaining three graves. The spears hit flesh and bone. When the spears were withdrawn, they were covered in blood. The soldiers left convinced the four freshly buried bodies were those of the three condemned men and the suicide victim. From that day on the disciples celebrated April the first, calling it April Fool's Day

Two months later, on the first Sabbath of summer, the Apostles held a general meeting with all disciples welcome to attend. The eleven Apostles were there, Jesus' mother and father, and one hundred and twenty disciples. Jesus was absent, for he was believed to have ascended into heaven by his followers, and needed to remain in anonymity. The plan had succeeded. The word had spread. It could not be challenged or reversed. The resurrection of Jesus after dying on the cross was entrenched in Jewish folklore. The Romans believed he was dead. The Way followers believed Jesus had risen and gone to Heaven. The Apostles knew he was alive and living at the monastery. Only venturing out on special occasions and for the Apostle meetings held at different venues, four times a year.

Peter stood up among the believers.

"Brothers, the Scripture had to be fulfilled which the Holy Spirit spoke long ago through the mouth of David concerning Judas, who served as a guide for those that arrested Jesus. He was one of our numbers and shared in this ministry. Therefore it is necessary to choose one of the men who have been with us the whole time the Lord Jesus went in and out amongst us, beginning from John's baptism to the time when Jesus was taken up from us. For one of these must become a witness with us of his resurrection."

So they proposed two disciples: Joseph called Barsabbas, also known as Justus and Matthias. Many believed Joseph, the father of Jesus, had the most right to the vacancy. However, old age was against him. Matthias was the code name for Mary Magdalene, Mary the Goddess; who was standing next to Joseph, wearing a hood.

"Lord, you know everyone's heart," Peter prayed. "Show us which one of these two you have chosen to take over this apostolic ministry, which Judas left to go where he belongs."

They cast lots, and the lot fell to Matthias. Mary had become the first woman added to the eleven Apostles. Joseph congratulated Mary who removed her hood and bowed to the bemused crowd. The women among the group clapped and cheered and other disciples joined in, ensuring the vote held. The disciples were dismissed and the twelve apostles sat to continue their meeting. Mary was involved in the discussions, but did not vote as she had replaced Judas, but she wasn't a Zealot. The meeting agreed to increase public insurrection and rebellion against the Roman governor and the High Priest. Jonathon also voted against Caiaphas, making it unanimous.

The crucifixion of Jesus became such a divisive event throughout Iudaea that Pontius Pilate had no choice but to dismiss Caiaphas after eighteen years in office. When Emperor Tiberius heard about the continued unrest in Judea, the bungled crucifixion and the escape of the three Zealot leaders, he dismissed Pilate. Emperor Tiberius appointed a new prefect, Marulius who also failed to quell the uprising. Tiberius died in 37A.D. and the new Emperor Caligula dismissed Marulius after only twelve months in office. The new prefect for Judea was a military tyrant called Herennius Capito. Jonathon Ananus was appointed to the High Priest position, becoming the Holiest of Holies, the earthly God in the temple of Jerusalem. His brother Theophilus was appointed Most High of the Qumran Monastery, the Essene God

That year Joseph passed away in his sleep. He had reached the age of seventy-eight. He may have lived longer had he not had a heavy heart from seeing his youngest son commit suicide and three of his other sons crucified. He lived long enough to guide his sons to safety and he died in peace. Judas bones were exhumed after twelve months, and his bones placed in an ossuary box. The ossuary was placed in the family tomb that Jesus and his brothers had been placed after the failed crucifixion and Joseph was buried in Judas' grave site. Next to Jesus,

Simon and Josephes, the names given to three large pigs buried there.

Jesus was anointed as the David, and his son Jesus-Titius was declared the future Crown Prince in a grand ceremony at Qumran Monastery where Jesus' religious career began twenty-nine years earlier. Jesus remained in the monastery for eighteen months. In that time, he wrote a book about his life, using the alias 'The Word'. John the Baptist, called Jesus 'The Lamb of God' because Jesus was born an Aries, son of Most High. Mary, his wife, was the first to call him Jesus Christ. Jesus' book was later named John, probably so the Church could maintain his anonymity. Most of his followers believe he had died on the cross and had risen to heaven.

His first sentence reads: *'In the beginning was the Word, and the Word was with God, and the Word was God'.* Translated: In the beginning was Jesus, and Jesus was with the Most High, and Jesus was Most High.

Jesus' book covered his life after he left the monastery in 28A.D. to the year of his crucifixion in 36A.D. It covers his wedding at Cana, at age thirty-six. The religious and political battles he had with both friend and foe.

It tells of the despair at being betrayed by his youngest brother, Judas Iscariot. He tells us about his newborn son, the David Crown Prince. It documents the crucifixion of himself and his two brothers, Simon and Josephes, the rescue from the cross and the tomb. Jesus explained the resurrection story and his book was copied by the scribes for the twelve apostles.

Two men assisted Jesus with the documentation of his book. John Mark, the young man Jesus loved while he was practicing celibacy in the monastery, and Luke, Jesus' family doctor. All three men wrote individual accounts covering the same period. Mark's book was kept in the monastery library for the Essene celibate priests and scribes to reference and make hand written copies.

Luke was a trusted confidant, a disciple of Jesus and the Justus family medical practitioner. He wrote his book, using the books of John and Mark as references. His book covered the life of Jesus until his Crucifixion and Ascension into Heaven, into the monastery at Qumran. Luke addressed a copy to *most excellent* Theophilus who was the High Priest of Jerusalem from 37-41A.D.

His opening paragraph reads: *'Many have undertaken to draw up an account of the things that have been fulfilled among us, just as they were handed down to us by those who from the first were eyewitnesses and servants of the Word. Therefore, since I myself have carefully investigated everything from the beginning, it seemed good also to me to write an orderly account for you, most excellent Theophilus, so that you may know the certainty of the things you have been taught.'*

Luke may not have trusted Theophilus completely, or he may have been concerned his book could fall into enemy hands for he was very descriptive on matters that the High Priest already knew, but vague in other areas. When he listed the genealogy of Jesus, Luke deliberately gave Theophilus the genealogy of Jesus' mother, but not his paternal father's family. When he named the Twelve Apostles, only Simon Peter and his brother Andrew were given surnames. Jesus' four brothers were listed as Simon the Zealot, Judas Iscariot, James son of Alphaeus and Thaddaeus instead of Josephes. Luke only mentioned the other six apostles by first names as well. Two of Ananus the Elder's sons, Matthew and Jonathon were not given surnames. Jonathon was named Bartholomew as he was the Most High at the Qumran monastery and his name and position could not be exposed. The Herods were only mentioned as Philip and Thomas. Zebedee Cleopas sons were listed as James and John. Luke's book was compatible with Jesus' account and both men wrote their books in collaboration and over the same time frame, 36-37A.D. when Jesus was recuperating in seclusion and safety of the Qumran Monastery.

Jesus, John Mark and Luke decided the books should be written in Koine Greek, a language they all new and could write. They were aware the books could eventually fall into the Roman's hands, and so they wrote the stories using parables and aliases. Jesus was known under many aliases, as *the Word of God, the Lamb of God, the Son of God, the Light or the Truth.* Jesus spoke to crowds in parables and even the seven miracles in his book were based on normal events.

When Jesus turned water into wine, he just added citrus fruit to water and the drunken Master of the Ceremony thought it was wine. *The miracle was Jesus replaced the wine with water and the Master didn't know the difference.*

When the aging Zachariah asked Jesus to heal his son John, Jesus confirmed his son would survive. *The miracle was Jesus had cast his deciding vote that would save the fiery preacher John the Baptist from being excommunicated after he prophesied in public about King Antipas' unlawful marriage to his brother's wife.*

Jesus made the lame man walk after 38 years at the pool. When Jesus went to Jerusalem, he warned John the Baptist, now thirty-eight years old and who baptised sinners with water, that Herod Antipas had ordered his arrest. *The miracle was Jesus blessed John and gave him permission to walk away and hide in the hermit caves at Emmaus, even though the Jewish law forbade him to walk that far on a Sabbath.*

When Jesus fed the five thousand with five barley loaves and two fish, his disciples gave each person a pinch of food on their tongue and blessed them. The people were satisfied because the poor normally only ate meals at breakfast and evening times. *The miracle was that the Disciples of Jesus were amazed that the large crowd was peaceful and satisfied; especially as they themselves ate three meals a day, their noon meal quite substantial.*

When the disciples rowed their boat across the lake in the dark and against a strong wind, Jesus walked along the coast and was waiting for them to arrive. Jesus walked over the water on a jetty and met the terrified men. *The miracle was Jesus reassured the disciples that they were safe and climbed into the boat which soon made it safely to the shore.*

When Jesus healed the blind man, he was referring to his brother Josephes who was a Pharisee and had believed James was legitimate crown prince. Josephes changed his mind when James refused to allow Gentiles into The Way sect without circumcision. *The miracle was Jesus promoted Josephes over his older brother as his deputy and appointed him prince Josephes of Arimathea, first in line for the title held by their father Joseph.*

When Jesus heard his brother had died, he wept for two days. Jesus went to Bethany and saw Martha, his sister-in-law, and Mary his betrothed who told him Simon had passed away four days ago after a fever. *The miracle was Jesus went to the tomb and realised there was no bad odours wafting out past the entry stone. He rolled away the stone and called out loudly to his brother. Simon woke from a four day coma and walked out, dressed in strips of linen looking like an Egyptian mummy.*

After Pontius Pilate and Caiaphas had been dismissed Simon re-joined the Zealots at Gamala and Josephes captained the schooner *Pollonia* with Stefan and sailed to Britannia. The seven miracles of Jesus spread among the population, growing in grandeur day by the day until Jesus' name had become so powerful the Chief Priests had no option but to call the crucified Jesus the Son of God, the promised Messiah. The Zealots increased their hostilities against Roman occupation in his name, gaining popular support and civil unrest amongst the Jewish and Samaritan communities.

The enemies of Jesus continued to search for Jesus. When rumours circulated that he may be in the monastery at Qumran he gathered his family and fled to Damascus. Jesus called himself John and found work as a carpenter, a trade he was taught by his father. He lived with his wife Mary, two daughters Sarah and Tamara, and two year old Jesus-Titius, now called Titius. John-Jesus prayed at the synagogue every Sabbath and mingled freely with the Pharisee community. He knew who they were, but they didn't know his true identity.

John-Jesus was introduced to Bishop Ananias and the two become friends. Ananias was impressed at *John's* knowledge of religion and politics and enjoyed their discussions.

Jesus found out information about himself and what was happening in Jerusalem. He also found our Ananias was the son of Nebedeus and had ambitions to become High Priest. *John* and Mary were invited to supper at Ananias house where they met his wife Sapphira. Jesus cautioned Mary to be careful not to divulge their past or true identities to their hosts.

After the meal, Mary and Sapphira talked about their children. Both women had three children of similar age and wanted at least one more child as three children was always considered unlucky. Mainly because the eldest child was introduced and the smallest child received attention, leaving the middle child often neglected. Also, the middle child would often play with either the eldest child or the youngest, leaving one child to play alone. The men talked about religious and political matters. Jesus heard how an Essene Chief Priest called Joseph had made himself Most High, God of the Essene community. Apparently Joseph and a Chief Priest Theudas had concocted a murder charge against his innocent father.

"My father was defrocked and exiled to Cyprus," Ananias said. "He died four years ago from a broken heart."

"I am sorry to hear that," Jesus said.

"I promised my father on his death bed that I would strive to become High Priest of Jerusalem and track down and punish Joseph's descendants."

"Wouldn't it be better if you became High Priest and led the people to righteousness?"

"I helped plan the capture of Joseph's sons with Caiaphas," Ananias said. "I was informed they were crucified on the cross, but somehow the three brothers escaped."

"Yes, there are plenty of stories circulating around the world about them," Jesus said.

"The plan backfired and now many Pharisees are flocking to The Way sect, those followers are now calling themselves Christians after their risen Messiah, Jesus the Christ."

Jesus and Mary thanked their hosts for the delicious meal and the most interesting conversations they had conversed in a long time. Jesus and Mary discussed their night as they walked home.

"They were a very interesting couple," Mary said. "Do you think it is time to move on again Jesus, you escape artist of high renown?"

"Not yet Mary," Jesus said, "perhaps when Sarah and Tamara are on school holidays."

Jesus and Mary invited Ananias and his family to their humble home and the families became further acquainted. Ananias informed Jesus that Agrippa, Herod the Great's grandson had been decreed Tetrarch of his deceased Uncle Philip's territories by the ailing Emperor Tiberius. The emperor died soon afterwards and Caligula became the third emperor of Rome. Agrippa and Caligula became close friends. Agrippa informed the emperor that Herod Antipas was stock piling arms and ammunition and was plotting against him. Caligula exiled Antipas to Gaul for conspiring against him. Caligula granted Agrippa rule over Antipas' provinces with the title of King. The appointment of Agrippa was not popular with the Roman senate and in January 41A.D. Emperor Caligula was murdered by his Praetorian guards.

Ananias never realised that John the carpenter was Jesus of Nazarene and often gave out crucial information about the Pharisees that Jesus divulged to Peter or Simon. At one dinner, Jesus heard that one of his followers had been detained and was to face the full bench of the Sanhedrin.

"Do you know the man's name?" Jesus asked.

"I believe his name is Stephen," Ananias said. "He is well spoken and has great knowledge of the Christian movement."

"What offence has been committed?" Jesus asked.

"He has been accused of blasphemy and is a threat because of his popular oratory."

Jesus travelled to Jerusalem to help Stephen but unfortunately arrived too late. Stephen had been found guilty by the Sanhedrin judges made up with mainly Sadducee and Pharisee members and condemned to death. The stoning group had surrounded Stephen who was given a moment to pray for forgiveness. Stephen looked up and saw Jesus as he pushed his way through the crowd.

"Look," Stephen said, "I see heaven open and the Son of Man standing at the right hand of God."

"Stone him," they yelled at the top of their voices and covered their ears.

A young man named Saul guarded the stoner's clothing while they pelted rocks, giving his approval to Stephens' death. When the crowd dispersed, Jesus picked up Stephen's crumpled body and arranged to bury Stephen in Joseph's empty gravesite after the funeral. Josephes bones had been exhumed and placed in an ossuary box next to Judas in the family tomb.

That day a great persecution broke out among the Christian community, and the followers were forced to flee from Jerusalem, all except the Apostles were scattered throughout Judea and Samaria. Saul approached the Chief Priests and asked permission to round up Christian followers of The Way Sect. They sent him to the High Priest at the temple who wrote him a letter to show each synagogue he attended in his search. Jesus heard Saul was heading to Damascus with a group of men. He met with his brother Simon at Gamala, and they planned to ambush Saul before he reached Damascus and visited Ananias.

Simon, Jesus and fifteen Zealots waited for Saul and his six horsemen to enter a *wadi* with a shallow running creek. The horses were left to graze and drink while the men sat on the grass in a semi-circle, eating their bread rolls and cheese. Simon lit the wick and threw the small pig stomach full of grey powder that he had purchased from some Chinese traders. The bladder sailed through the air and exploded above the heads of the circled men. Four men ran from the scene only to be run down by the Zealots who cut their throats so that they bled to death quietly. Three men, including Saul lay unconscious on the ground.

Jesus pulled out a handful of Tilapia fish scales from a pouch under his robe and wet them in the creek to soften. The Zealots tied the three men and blindfolded the two henchmen. Jesus placed the two large fish scales into Saul's eyes that would let Saul see light when he came to, but not see clearly.

Saul stirred and heard a voice.

"Saul, Saul, why do you persecute me?"

"Who are you, Lord?" Saul asked.

"I am Jesus whom you are persecuting," he replied. "Now get up and go into the city, and you will be told what you must do."

Saul was led into Damascus by his two men who were given instructions to take him to the house of Judas in Straight Street and remain with him. Simon and the Zealots went to Ananias' house to speak with him. Ananias recognised the Zealots and stood frozen with fear, believing they would kill him and his family. He promised he would remain silent about their whereabouts and pleaded with them to let him be baptised into The Way sect. Simon anointed Ananias with oil and instructed him to visit a man from Taurus called Saul.

"You will find him in the house of Judas. He has not eaten for three days and is blind," Simon said. "Baptise him, open his eyelids and blow hard into his eyes."

"Lord," Ananias answered. "I have many reports about this man and all the harm he has done to your saints in Jerusalem. He has come here with authority from the Chief Priests to arrest all who call on your name."

"Go. This man is Jesus' chosen instrument to carry his name before the Gentiles and their kings and before the people of Israel," Simon said. "I will show him how much he must suffer for Jesus' name."

Ananias went to the house as instructed and placed his hands on Saul.

"Brother Saul, the Lord Jesus who appeared to you on the road, has sent Simon to me with his lord's blessing so that you may see again and be filled with the Holy Spirit."

Ananias lifted Saul's eyelids and blew hard. Immediately, something like scales fell from Saul's eyes and he could see again. Saul stood up and was baptised, and after taking some food, he regained his strength.

Saul spent several days with the disciples in Damascus and then he preached in the synagogues that Jesus was the Son of God and the Messiah. The Jews were astonished when they heard him speak in favour of the Lord and questioned him about his mission to take prisoners back to the Chief Priests to face the Sanhedrin. Saul grew more powerful and baffled the Jews living in Damascus by pronouncing the living Jesus is the Christ. The Jews conspired to kill Saul and guarded the city walls day and night, waiting for their chance to strike.

Saul's followers heard of their plan and lowered him down through a hole in the wall during the night. Saul went to Jerusalem and tried to join other disciples, but they were afraid of him because of his past. Barnabas met with Saul and introduced himself.

"My name is Simon," he said. "I am Jesus' brother. Come with me and I will introduce you to my fellow Apostles."

Saul stayed closely associated with the Apostles and preached boldly in the name of the Lord. He found some fellow Grecian Jews and told them his father was Greek Pharisee and his mother a Judean, and he was born in

Taurus. Saul tried to convert the Grecian Jews to The Way sect, but they turned on him and tried to stone him to death. The Apostles heard of Saul's narrow escape and the Brothers took him to Caesarea for a while and then sent him on a mission to his hometown of Taurus, where he was well received.

Jesus left Damascus soon after Ananias was converted and before the local Jews tried to kill Saul. Jesus didn't trust Ananias after what the bishop had said to him when he thought he was *John*, and knew he would turn back to Pharisee philosophy to gain the High Priesthood. In that respect Ananias was tarred with the same brush as his father Nebedeus. Nothing would stand in their way when it came to their aggressive personal ambitions, not murder, deceit or betrayal. Jesus took his family to Ephesus where he established the first Christian church with Apostle John.

While in Ephesus Jesus heard of the good work Tertius and Sosipater had done in the community of Corinth. They linked with Jason and Lucius and were four of the seventy-two that Jesus sent out ahead of him to every town before he was crucified.

Jesus visited Corinth and liked the city and the Grecian citizens who were a mixed race of people that welcomed all races and creeds. The following year, Jesus moved his family to Corinth and bought a house next to the synagogue where Gaius and Crispus preached. Mary Magdalene, Jesus and the disciples Lucius and Timothy established a Christian community in Corinth and Athens.

Sosipater and Tertius were sent to the Isle of Corfu where they built a church and named it Saint Stephens after Stephen that was martyred in Jerusalem.

A few years later, Sosipater was appointed the first Bishop of Corfu but was later beheaded by King Kerkylinus. The King killed several Christian converts including his daughter Cereyra who had converted and given away the family jewellery to the poor. Kerkylinus and his soldiers boarded a boat and pursued a group of Christians that fled to a nearby island. The boat carrying the king capsized and all on board perished. Sebastian became the next king of Corfu, converted to Christianity and appointed Tertius as Bishop.

Jesus received word that James Cleopas had been arrested by King Agrippa and was to face the Sanhedrin court which had the authority to apply death sentences. Jesus, Apostle John and Saul returned to Caesarea on the schooner *Pollonia* for a council meeting with the Apostles.

Before they landed at Caesarea, Apostle James was beheaded. That happened before the feast of unleavened bread in 43A.D. When Agrippa saw that the Jews celebrated the beheading of James, he had Peter seized and placed in prison to be beheaded after Passover.

At the meeting, Jesus and nine Apostles discussed the demise of James, his replacement, the rescue of Peter and the need for protection for the Apostles and disciples. Jesus apologised for Apostle Mary's absence, declaring she was pregnant with their fourth child. The Apostles stood and applauded the good news. They prayed for the birth of a healthy boy, for James to rest in peace, and for guidance in their committee decisions.

"I propose Saul be anointed Apostle," Jesus said, "he has performed strongly and efficiently in Asia Minor and he is dedicated and loyal. He also represents and ministers to the Gentiles as did James, and as does his brother John."

"I second the motion," John said. "He is a disciple worthy to replace my brother."

The motion was passed unanimously, and Saul was called into the room.

"Saul," Jesus said, "You have been appointed to replace James who was martyred in the name of Christ. I hereby anoint you as Apostle Paul."

Saul, now known as Paul, shook hands with Jesus and the Apostles, and then sat next to John. "I graciously accept my anointing and promise to offer my life for the Lord," Paul said, "as did James, Stephen, Sosipater and many other Christian believers."

"Next on the agenda is Peter," Jesus said. "We have two options. We can send a delegation to the Sanhedrin pleading his innocence, or attempt to free him."

"I know most of the judges," Paul said. "They would not give you a fair hearing and would probably arrest the delegation you send as co-conspirators."

"I agree with Paul," Simon said. "I suggest we drug the guards' drinking water and use their keys to open the gates and release Peter from his chains."

The committee agreed with a show of hands that drugging the guards was the best option.

"The last item and the most difficult one," Jesus said, "is the protection of our members and ourselves. Are there any suggestions?"

"We need to show the people we can protect them," James the Just said.

"Congratulations on your appointment as Bishop by the way," Jesus said with his usual quick wit. "Excuse the pun about The Way, but we need your eyes and ears in Jerusalem."

"Agrippa won't stop persecuting us now that he has full support from the Sadducee sect and a large number of Jewish citizens," Andrew said.

"I agree," Simon said. "There is only way to stop Agrippa now. I can arrange the time and place to meet with him. We have reliable connections among his palace staff."

The committee agreed to let Simon deal with the tyrant's abysmal treatment of them and adjourned the meeting after discussing details of Peter's release.

Peter was visited in prison by a Zealot whose identity was unknown to Peter. He struck Peter on the side, woke him up and quietly removed his chains.

"Quick, get up," he said. "Wrap your cloak around you and follow me."

Peter followed the stranger out of the prison, past two sets of sleeping guards that had been drugged, and out through the inner city iron gates that were opened by two waiting Zealots. A guard lay tied and gagged beside them. When they had walked down the length of one street Peter suddenly found he was alone. He went to the house of John Mark's mother where some disciples were praying. He knocked on the door and a servant girl named Rhoda heard Peter asking to be let inside. Rhoda was so overjoyed she ran back without opening the door.

"Peter is at the door," Rhoda exclaimed.

"You are out of your mind," they retorted.

Rhoda insisted it was Peter and when they answered the door and saw him, they were astonished. Peter motioned with his hands for them to remain quiet and described how the Lord brought him out of prison.

"Tell Josephes and his brothers about this," he said.

Then he left for another place, a day's walk from Jerusalem. King Agrippa ordered a thorough search for Peter which failed to find him. Agrippa was furious and cross-examined the guards. They could not explain how Peter escaped and were jailed, and later executed. King Agrippa advised his palace staff to prepare for a stay at Caesarea for the harvest festival of Pentecost. The King had been in dispute with the people of Tyre and Sidon who had joined together and sought an audience with him. They secured the support of Balak Strauss, a trusted personal servant of the King to help with initial negotiations. The towns' population depended on the King's country for their food supply and needed to compromise with him over the price of goods and for greater trade between the two kingdoms. Balak informed his wife Salome, who in turn passed the news on to her brother Jesus. He passed the news onto his brother Simon.

"Agrippa staying at Caesarea, that is the news I have been waiting for," Simon said.

"You only have two weeks to plan the assassination," Jesus said. "The two schooners are moored at Haifa, ready to sail whether the assassination attempt fails or succeeds."

"Failing isn't an option," Simon said. "If the snake poison fails the Sicarri will strike."

"The King is well guarded," Jesus said, "that would become a suicide mission."

"So be it," Simon said, "we should have died on the cross years ago."

Jesus could never understand Simon and Judas' temperament, they were always willing to fight bloody battles and die for their cause. Josephes and Jesus preferred skilled negotiations and James was somewhere in between, he would negotiate and if that failed, he would fight.

The Zealots planned the King's assassination. Simon asked Barabbas, Theudas' son, to prepare a snake poison that could be mixed with wine and kill within six hours, without showing immediate side effects.

"You are not asking for much," Barabbas said, "however my father taught me how to prepare such a concoction."

"When can you have the poison ready?" Simon asked.

"I keep the snakes in a pit behind the hen house. The poison will be ready in two hours and maintain full potency for a month," Barabbas said.

Barabbas took a long rod with a simple hook on the end and selected the snake that stored toxins from the toads and beetles it ate. He hooked the snake, lifted it out of the pit, grabbed its tail and pinned the head to the ground, using the flat end of the rod. Simon marvelled at the speed and agility of Barabbas as he handled the deadly snake. Barabbas held the snake behind its head and handed Simon the rod. He picked up the body of the snake with his other hand and the two men walked to the barn.

Barabbas milked the venom into a small metal container and then chopped off the snakes head. He gave the writhing snake body to Simon to hold while he fetched sharp knives and several containers. Simon held the snake on the bench top while Barabbas sliced open the snake and cut out the liver and nunchal glands that stored the deadly toxins. He sliced the organs into small pieces and mixed them with a small amount of water. Barabbas stirred the mix and then pounded it to a paste. He added more water and placed the mix in the sun.

"Now we wait for the water to slowly warm and absorb the toxin," he said. "Come inside for a drink and tell me about your need for such a potion."

The men discussed the mission and sipped wine while two nurses volunteered to relieve the men of their pent up tensions. An hour later, Barabbas poured the fluid into the container holding the venom and slowly stirred the two liquids together. He poured the mixture into a container and covered the small opening with a waxed cork.

"The poison will turn clear overnight and can be mixed in juice or wine," Barabbas said. "There is enough there to kill an elephant."

"Or a tyrant," Simon said. "By the way, you haven't seen me in years."

Simon shook hands with Barabbas and slid a gold coin into his palm.

Herod Agrippa entered the synagogue hall at Caesarea with great pomp and ceremony. He was wearing royal robes and sat on his throne that was brought from his palace. He had twelve armed guards standing behind him and scores more guarding the entrances. He delivered a public address to the people inside and asked two officials, one from each town to join him for the signing of documents. Balak served the three men with tumblers of wine to toast the new agreement which still heavily favoured the King. The King did not praise God, or make a toast, instead he clinked his tumbler with the two officials and skulled the wine.

"Let that be the end of this matter," the King said as he stood and walked out of the hall.

Within four hours of the meeting, the men involved with the conspiracy rode to the port at Haifa where the two schooners were docked. All the families were waiting aboard, most would not step foot in Iudaea again. On board the vessels were Jesus, Simon, Josephes, John, Peter, Paul, Balak and their immediate families, everyone that had direct involvement in the plot. The remaining Apostles James, Matthew, Jonathon, Andrew, Philip and Thomas were not involved and would stay in Judea or Galilee and continue with their normal lifestyles.

The two schooners sailed to separate destinations. The *Accyrenia* sailed to Fair Havens on the Isle of Crete with Simon, Josephes and their families. The *Pollonia* sailed to Ephesus with Jesus, Peter, Paul, Balak and John aboard. Jesus asked Balak about the assassination.

"Did the plan work?"

"It went like a candle in the wind," Balak said, "still burning when I left, but most surely flickering by now and will be totally extinguished before midnight."

Salome hugged her husband who she fondly called Blastus and gave him a kiss on the cheek.

"That is for being so brave. Many things could have gone horribly wrong."

"May James rest in peace now that Agrippa has received his punishment," Jesus said.

That night Agrippa and the two officials writhed in agony for hours until they died. Agrippa told his guards at his bedside that he had been poisoned by the one of followers of James that he had beheaded, but didn't mention it may have been his trusted servant Blastus. Iudaea was left without a ruler until Rome received news of the assassination and a procurator could be appointed. Agrippa was so disliked most people regarded his assassination as a blessing and very little investigation for his killers occurred. Certainly no one was punished for the crime

The *Pollonia* docked in Ephesus at night and departed for Corinth as soon as the passengers alighted. Jesus and the Apostles stayed in Ephesus until they knew they hadn't been linked to Agrippa's assassination. While on board the schooner, Jesus wrote two short scrolls that he addressed to Mary and Gaius. He wrote under his code name *John* and asked Stefan and Alexis to deliver them to the house next to the synagogue in Corinth.

The scroll to Gaius mentions Jesus joy at hearing his children were walking in the truth and Gaius' faithfulness to him and the church. Jesus says he has much to write but would prefer to talk face to face. He sends his greetings and hopes to see him soon.

The scroll to Mary, was addressed *to the chosen Lady and her children,* Jesus makes it clear that he is coming in the flesh. Jesus wrote, *dear lady I am not writing a new command but one we have had from the beginning. I ask that we love one another. I have much to write to you, but I do not want to use paper and ink. Instead, I hope to visit you and talk face to face, so that our joy may be complete. The children of your chosen sister send their greeting.*

Jesus had let Mary know Martha and her children were safe without mentioning her name.

CHAPTER 9: The Word of God Spreads

Jesus left Paul and John in Ephesus to establish and build Christian communities in Asia-Minor. Jesus, Peter, Luke and John Mark, travelled to Corinth and visited Mary and Gaius. Mary was in her last month of pregnancy, carrying Jesus' fourth child. Luke delivered the baby, a healthy boy named Michael Joseph Justus, born on July 30th 44A.D.

Peter was introduced to Bishop Tertius from the Isle of Corfu and together they planned a trip to Italia and Hispania to establish Christian communities in those two countries.

The *Accyrenia* sailed from Crete and was at sea, heading for Naples when gale force winds blew the vessel off course. The crew dropped the sails, but the storm strengthened and pushed the schooner past the islands of Sicily and Sardinia. The schooner was taking in water so the men and crew threw the cargo overboard and plugged the holes in the hull with planks and canvas. On the sixth day of the storm, the winds suddenly stopped, but the clouds still looked menacing and surrounded them on all sides as far as they could see. The captain took his bearings and headed for the nearest port, Marseilles in Gallia.

The eye of the storm passed over them and hurricane force winds pushed the vessel towards the coast of Gallia. During the night the rigging failed and the masts crashed on to the decks, smashing the helm and leaving the schooner rudderless. The next day the hurricane crossed land at Marseilles and petered out. The strong *Marin* winds, blowing from the south-east pushed the stricken vessel to shore. The *Accyrenia* hit coastal rocks and lodged on a sand bank near the coastal town of Arles. All members of the crew and passengers managed to swim or hold on to debris to reach land.

The townsfolk of Arles welcomed the shipwrecked survivors and before the vessel broke up they salvaged as much as they could. Simon, known as Lazarus, his wife Martha, a disciple named Maximus and some of the crew stayed in southern Gallia. They preached to the community and many were converted to Christianity. Josephes helped Simon build a church at Marseilles and stayed until word of the shipwreck reached Jesus in Corinth. Stefan sailed to Marseilles the following year, trading goods from Corinth to Rome, and cargo from Rome to Marseilles.

Josephes and some of the crew from the wrecked *Accyrenia* joined Stefan on a voyage to Britannia. They traded goods at London, and before the *Pollonia* sailed to Bristol to buy tin, lead and iron ore, Josephes disembarked with three disciples. They preached in London for some years and baptised many people into Christianity. The druid King Aviragus Gwenivyth, known as King Arthur, summoned Josephes to his court to discuss the new religion. Josephes told the king about Jesus the son of God, the crucifixion, the resurrection and the Christian doctrine. The king was not convinced and remained a Druid. However, he did grant Josephes twelve hides of land at Glastonbury where he built the first Christian church in Britannia. Tradition says that Josephes trekked to the highest point of the land with twelve new disciples to spot a suitable site for the church. As he trudged up the hill, his entourage rested on a rocky outcrop near the summit. Josephes thrust his staff that he had brought from Iudaea into the ground. At the summit the clergymen spotted the best site for the new church and departed, leaving the staff behind. The staff sprouted, growing into a thornbush that blossomed twice a year, in winter and spring. The thornbush is unique to Glastonbury and grew on Wearyall Hill where the disciples rested with Josephes, the brother of Jesus who inherited the title Joseph of Arimathea.

Jesus remained in Corinth for many years and remained the spiritual leader of the Christian movement. The new religion spread rapidly among Diaspora Jews, Grecian-Roman pagans and other races. However, the sect was always in conflict with traditional Jewish Chief Priests and Roman authorities who wanted peace and order throughout their realm. Jesus travelled extensively, attending secret meetings in Rome, Corinth, Ephesus, Caesarea and Jerusalem.

Jesus attended a council meeting held in Jerusalem during the spring of 46A.D. In attendance were the Apostles Matthew, Jonathon, Andrew, James, Philip, and Thomas. They discussed the future appointment of Agrippa II as king and decided James, Matthew and

Jonathon should seek an audience with him and continue instructing Agrippa in the faith that Paul had begun with him in Ephesus when Agrippa was a youth. Jesus told the six apostles about the rapid expansion of the Christian faith. Mary and her disciples were spreading the word in Corinth, Simon in Gallia. Joseph in Britannia and Peter had gone to Rome.

Three of the remaining apostles wanted to spread the word outside of Iudaea. Andrew elected to preach in Mesopotamia, Philip in Africa, and Thomas in Babylon and India. James remained in Jerusalem as Bishop, Jonathon remained Most High at Qumran and Mathew was Appointed Bishop in the new capital Caesarea. James advised Jesus that Ananias was recently appointed as the High Priest of the Temple and was already acting aggressively against the smaller religious sects and gathering information about our genealogy. Jesus gave James the responsibility to destroy all the family records he could find and to sell the property at Ramah.

Jesus visited his mother and advised her prepare to leave with him within three months.

"I can't leave Ramah and leave Rachel by herself," Mary said.

"Judea is becoming too volatile," Jesus said. "Your sister Rachel is welcome to come with us, and you can visit Magda and the children in Corinth."

Mary agreed to be ready to leave Ramah with her sister when Jesus returned later in the year. Jesus took the scrolls of Mark, Luke and John and the family scroll with the Justus dynasty genealogy and travelled to Caesarea to visit Matthew. Using the four scrolls, Jesus and Matthew wrote out another scroll suitable for Matthews teaching to his Sadducee converts. Jesus under his alias of *John* also wrote a scroll to his children in Corinth and despatched it with a trusted courier, together with a verbal message that he and two chosen women would be home before the end of summer.

Jesus left the scrolls in the care of Matthew so that he could complete the book of Matthew and sailed to Corinth as planned. Mary Magdalene had walked down to the docks to look for incoming vessels with her four children for nine consecutive days. Sarah was now sixteen, Tamara thirteen, Titus ten and toddler Joseph two. They enjoyed the walk to the docks and had sighted many ships, but none carried the special cargo they were seeking. Today two vessels had docked, one carried cargo only, but the other schooner had passengers disembarking. Mary and the children waited until all the passengers had walked ashore, but Jesus wasn't among them.

"Tomorrow is the last day of summer, maybe your father will arrive then," Mary said.

"I want him to come home today," Titus said.

"Mother, there is another ship on the horizon, can we wait here until it docks," Sarah said.

"That ship may not be landing here," Mary said.

"Please mother, it might be father," Tamara said.

"You children share your father's strong faith in life," Mary said. "You wait here while I find a place to feed

Michael. Then we will have to go home for our midday meal."

The ship docked, and some crewmen jumped on to the dock to secure the vessel ropes to the bollards. Two other sailors placed the gang plank and came ashore. Then Tamara and Sarah screamed with joy as their father and grandmother appeared on deck, followed by Auntie Rachel. Jesus kissed Mary and Michael and then hugged Titius, Sarah and Tamara. Mary gave Michael to Rachel and hugged Jesus again.

"Don't you dare wander off again," Mary whispered, "I have missed you too much."

The family mingled, hugged and kissed, and laughed and chatted while they waited for their luggage to be unloaded. Michael was handed from one person to another and thought it was a great game. If he was in someone's arms for too long, he would lurch towards the next person, only staying quietly in the arms of his father or mother. They walked back to their house for refreshments and the midday meal. Everyone carried luggage, including young Michael who held on to Mary's robe with one hand and dragged a goatskin bag containing gifts for the children with the other hand. Jesus stayed with Mary and the children for three years.

Jesus' mother and her sister Rachel passed away within weeks of each other in the winter of 48A.D. The *Virgin nun* who had married the *Holy Spirit* passed away peacefully in her sleep at the age of seventy-two. Her sister Rachel died with a broken heart at sixty-nine.

The following year Jesus made a short journey to Ephesus where he met with the Apostles Matthew, Paul, John, Peter, Simon, and Philip. At the council meeting, they discussed the imminent appointment of Agrippa II and his twin sister Berenice who was already showing her dominance over her brother. Rumours were circulating about Berenice that contradicted Christian teachings. She had married two old men for their prestige and money, the second marriage was to her uncle. Both men had died and Berenice was reported to be in an incestuous relationship with her twin brother. The problem was Berenice was ambitious and influential among Herod's court, and wanted to become a queen. She had greatly admired the power and prestige of Queen Cleopatra and wanted to emulate her achievements. A mention was made of John the Baptist interfering with monarchy marriages and its dramatic consequences on the sect. The council voted five to two not to interfere with the incestuous affair because of lack of proof and voted unanimously to instruct Berenice and Agrippa in further Christian ideology before Bernice could be admitted as a member of the new party.

The Christian religion was being taught in most of the Roman Empire and the teachings needed to be uniform. The committee decided the four scrolls should be bound together in the new format called a book. The book would be called *The New Testament.* Matthew's gospel was decreed to be listed first because it dealt with Jesus' paternal genealogy from Abraham up to the resurrection of Jesus.

John Mark's gospel quoted a prophecy from Isaiah; *I will send my messenger ahead of you, who will prepare your way.* The messenger was deemed to be John the Baptist, who announced *the coming of one greater than myself, Lord Jesus.* Mark's version also ended at the resurrection and was placed second in the book.

Luke's scroll was a scribe's copy of the carefully worded account sent to the *Most Excellent Theophilus,* and was based on *Jesus' life, The Way Sect and Jesus ascension into Heaven (Qumran Monastery) near Bethany on the Jordan River.* Luke's writing was voted to be placed fourth in the book, but Jesus declared it worthy of gospel status and wanted it placed before his autobiography.

Jesus wrote his story using aliases, metaphors, parables and historic events concealed as miracles. He dedicated his gospel to John Mark, the disciple he loved during monastery incarceration, naming his gospel John.

Matthew Ananus and John Cleopas returned to Qumran Monastery where the scribes set about producing a bible called *The New Testament*. Twenty-three copies were made in the first year. Each Holy Bible had three hundred and thirty-six hand-written pages on thick paper. They were written in Koine Greek, the universal language of the times, and the final page number 336 represented the date of the crucifixion and resurrection, March 36A.D. Thirteen Bibles were dispatched to Jesus and the Twelve Apostles. Ten copies remained at the monastery and were diligently copied tenfold every year. The copies were sent out to disciples, churches, and presented as gifts to royals that supported the Christian movement.

The Christian movement grew rapidly and became popular at the very top of society and the Gentiles, especially among the poor and downtrodden. The middle class, especially the Jewish nationals and the Sadducee sect were at odds with the Christians, causing many religious disturbances in the towns and cities throughout the Roman Empire. The rulers supported the new religion because money flowed into their coffers, and they could use the religion to control the masses. The masses enjoyed the promise of a better life in the after-world, men and women were treated more equally, and anyone who believed in the Christian ideology could become a disciple.

The two main established faiths, the Sadducees that didn't believe in afterlife and the Pharisees that believed in afterlife, joined forces to combat the Christians. The differences were plentiful and irreconcilable. The established sects believed the Sabbath was the day of worship and no work could take place on that day. Only men could become priests. Priests could only be chosen from priestly heredity or royal families. They believed in strict observance to Jewish protocols, traditions and pomp and ceremony. They didn't believe Jesus was the Messiah and convicted him of blasphemy, crucifying him on the cross.

The Christians believed Sunday was the first and greatest day of the week, but could still work to provide food and essential items for their families. They refused to stop work on the Sabbath while their families suffered from hunger and poverty. The Christians didn't celebrate Jewish Passover; instead they celebrated Jesus' resurrection. The masses worshipped Jesus as they could relate with his persecution, discrimination, victimisation and suffering. Jesus became their idol and hero for triumphing over evil men and corruption.

The conflict between the religious sects heightened in the reign of Emperor Claudius and he decreed all Jewish citizens be expelled from Rome. The act was endorsed by the Senate, and the Christian movement grew in strength, only having the pagans as an alternate ideology. Paul travelled to Corinth to be present for Titius Justus' Bar-Mitzvah ceremony held at the age of twelve. Silas and Timothy came down from Macedonia and joined Jesus and his family and John Mark and Apostle John Cleopas arrived from Ephesus. Titius was confirmed the David Crown Prince and granted a ceremonial position at apostle council meetings. The men remained in Corinth for the wedding of Sarah that was held twelve months later, while they were there, they preached to the exiled Jews from Rome and the Athenian and Corinthians

The Christian preachers continued to have conflicts with other groups, but for some years they enjoyed relative peace and general acceptance within the community. Paul and Sosthenes the synagogue leader had a minor conflict with the Jews, which was referred to the proconsul of Achaia. Gallio dismissed the claims and told the Jews to settle the matter outside the court among yourselves. Gallio meant by negotiation, but the crowd turned on Paul and Sosthenes and beat them in from of the court. Gallio showed no concern whatsoever and did not intervene in the caning of the two helpless men.

"Do not be afraid," Jesus said. "Keep on speaking, do not be silent. For I am with you, and no one is going to attack and harm you, because I have many people inside this city."

Paul remained in Corinth for some time. He stayed with a Jewish man and his wife, Aquila and Priscilla, who had been expelled from Rome. Paul assisted them in tent making and preached to the Jews and Greeks at the synagogue on the Sabbath. Paul remained in Corinth for some time and attended the marriage of Tamara's wedding in the spring of 51A.D. Then Paul sailed to Syria with Aquila and Priscilla.

Paul did not see Jesus again for some time as he preached in Syria and Asia Minor, and strengthened the disciples' knowledge of Christian ideology and the congregation's belief. Paul visited Corinth again for Jesus' second son Michael's Bar Mitzvah in May 56A.D.

"Your family has been a big part of my life since you turned my life around," Paul said.

"I knew if I could change your faith, you would use your enthusiasm for greatness among the Gentiles," Jesus said.

"I hope I have repaid some of my debt to The Way sect believers I persecuted," Paul said.

"You were misled by the High Priests. At the time, you thought you were acting lawfully and doing your duty. You have been forgiven for those deeds and saved many souls since."

The men talked for some time. They spoke about what happened on the road to Damascus, Jesus' family, the girls' weddings and the boys' Bar Mitzvah ceremonies, and politics.

"We have had to deal with many tyrants since my father's time," Jesus said. "Herod the Great persecuted our family, as did Emperor Tiberius and King Agrippa."

"Caligula, called little boots, greatly harassed our cause too," Paul added.

"Yes, he would have destroyed our early momentum after the unsuccessful crucifixion of my brothers and me," Jesus said. "Simon arranged for Christian Praetorian guards to assassinate Caligula while he slept."

"Claudius replaced him as emperor and was fairly tolerant on religious beliefs," Paul said. "Unfortunately Agrippa II is weak and his sister Berenice is acting as queen," Jesus said.

Do you believe she is having an incestuous relationship with Agrippa?" Paul asked.

"I believe so. Berenice has lived with Agrippa for several years and neither of them has remarried," Jesus said. "Unfortunately Berenice is controlling the throne for her brother."

"Is it true that Emperor Claudius was poisoned by his wife after he raped her?"

"Yes. Agrippina poisoned her husband and Nero was appointed Emperor," Jesus said.

"That man is insane and corrupt," Paul said. "I believe he will cause misery and havoc."

Jesus and Paul discussed matters concerning the next council meeting in Caesarea.

"I have sent messengers to all the Apostles to meet for the twenty-fifth anniversary council in Caesarea in September 57A.D." Jesus said. "All apostles except for you Paul, I hereby hand your invitation to you personally. By the way, you must attend."

"I wouldn't miss it for the world," Paul said with a laugh.

***

Caesarea
57 A.D.

The meeting came to order. Jesus stood and looked around the table at the twelve Apostles.

"Welcome to the first council meeting with a full attendance since we separated after 44A.D." Jesus said. "I will give a short summation of your Apolistic activities before we commence the council proceedings. Please do not applause until I have read out the full list."

Jesus picked up a sheet of paper where the twelve apostles had written brief statements.

"Mary has established a church in Corinth. She is head of the female ministry in the Roman-Grecian regions and has converted many to the faith. Paul, John and Andrew have established several churches in Asia Minor. Peter has established churches in Rome and Corfu and ministered in Hispania. Simon and Martha have built a church in Marseilles, Gallia and have established the faith throughout the province. Josephes, under the title Joseph of Arimathea, has built a church at Glastonbury, on the island of Avalon in Britannia and has converted many druids to the faith. Thomas has preached in Arabia and India and has taught the word to many converts. Philip is preaching in Ethiopia and northern Africa. Matthew has established churches in Alexandria and townships along the Nile in Egypt. James is the Bishop of Jerusalem and with Jonathon now retired as High Priest is our eyes and ears of our homeland and an indispensable source for the political information and contacts with rulers that strengthen our movement."

The Apostles stood up and applauded Jesus' speech and the work of the other Apostles. When everyone was seated, James stood up.

"I would like to praise my brother Jesus who has carried out the David role with distinction and integrity since he inherited it from our father. Jesus has transformed the Galilean-Samaritan 'The Way Sect' into a worldly Christian faith that is taking the world by storm. Jesus is the true Messiah and our Lord. Amen."

The Apostles stood up applauded James' speech that not only heralded Jesus' achievements, but also James' acknowledgement that Jesus was the David and accepted Titius was the Crown Prince.

The council minutes were discussed. Some of the matters raised included: the continued unrest in Iudaea, Agrippa II and Berenice, Emperor Nero, the Pharisee, Essene and Sadducee sects, the Roman occupation, and the continued expansion and consolidation of Christianity.

The meeting ended, and they gathered at a nearby Inn for the midday meal, some wine and friendly chatter. Mary held Jesus by the arm as they walked down the esplanade.

"I didn't mention your most important achievement at the meeting," she whispered, "your ability to keep me very happy and satisfied even in your old age."

"I love you Mary and I will always try my best to comfort you, even though regrettably it is getting harder in my old age."

"Oh, I hadn't noticed that," Mary smiled.

Jonathon announced that he had arranged accommodation for everyone at one of Agrippa's mansions on the foreshore of Caesarea that would be vacant for three weeks.

"Anyone wanting to stay in comfort should follow me," Jonathon said.

The Apostles stayed together for two weeks before sea-faring schooners docked and departed, taking the

Apostles to their far away destinations. Johnathon departed for Rome with some priests to a prearranged meeting with Emperor Nero and the Senate. Paul wanted to give offerings to the Temple and visit some friends and family in Jerusalem. Jesus, Mary and many others advised him against travelling to Jerusalem, but Paul didn't heed their advice.

Paul was greeted warmly at the temple where he underwent a purification ceremony and stayed for seven days to purify others and hand out offerings. When the seven days were over Paul emerged from the temple and was seen by Jews from Asia who stirred up the crowd. They shouted for Paul to be stoned for interfering with their Jewish laws and customs. They shut the iron gates to the court so that Paul could not escape and tried to kill him. A Roman commander arrived on the scene and arrested Paul for his own safety.

Paul was imprisoned until the full bench of the Sanhedrin were assembled.

Paul stood and addressed the assembly.

"My brothers, I have fulfilled my duty to God in all good conscience to this day."

Ananias, who had replaced Jonathon as High Priest and wanted to destroy the Christian Sect ordered those standing near Paul to hit him in the mouth.

"God will strike you," Paul said. "You white washed wall! You sit there to judge me according to the law, yet you yourself violate the law by commanding I be struck!"

"You dare to insult God's High Priest?" those standing near Paul replied.

"Brothers, I didn't realise he was the High Priest, for it is written," Paul said. "Do not speak evil about the ruler of your people. My brothers, I am a Pharisee, the son of a Pharisee. I stand on trial because of my hope in the resurrection of the dead."

When Paul said that, a dispute broke out between the Pharisees and the Sadducees and the assembly became divided. The Sadducees did not believe in resurrections, and that there were neither angels nor spirits, but the Pharisees believed in all of them. There was a great uproar in the chamber, and the commander sent in troops to escort Paul to prison for his own safety.

The following night, Jesus stood near Paul.

"Take courage for as you have testified about me in Jerusalem," he said, "so must you testify in Rome."

The commander was advised there was a plot to kill Paul as he was escorted from prison to the Sanhedrin courthouse. He arranged for Paul to be transferred under heavy guard to Caesarea. Five days later, Ananias and Tertullus, a high court lawyer, brought charges against Paul. Felix, the Roman procurator heard the case and dwelt over it for two years without making a final decision. He didn't believe Paul was guilty of any crime punishable by death, but his wife Drusilla was Jewish and the Jews were pleased Paul was locked in prison.

Festus replaced Felix as procurator. When he heard Paul had been imprisoned for over two years he heard his case. The Jews brought serious charges against Paul and wanted him tried by the Jerusalem Sanhedrin. Paul appealed to Festus that, as a Roman citizen, he should be tried by Caesar's court. Festus consulted Agrippa II and Berenice who listened to Paul's defence. King Agrippa thought Paul had gone out of his mind, the great learning driving him insane. The king left the room with Berenice and the procurator.

"I do not believe this man has done anything that deserves death or imprisonment," Agrippa said, "he could have been set free if he had not appealed to Caesar."

Paul was sent to Rome by ship and after a harrowing trip the vessel sank off the Island of Malta. The crew and passengers, numbering two hundred and seventy-six in all, scrambled ashore as the ship broke up on a sand bank. Among the shipwreck survivors were Paul, still in chains, Jesus, Luke, Felix and Drusilla.

They stayed on the island until winter passed and then boarded an Alexandrian ship that took them to Rome. Paul was kept in chains and guarded by soldiers, but was allowed to live in a rented house and preach to those that sought his teaching. Paul stayed in the house for two years before being sentenced and placed in prison to await trial. Christian prisoners held on minor charges were judged and acquitted, or given forty lashes minus one, as the law decreed. Paul's case was so complicated that it was often deferred on technical grounds by either the defence lawyer or the prosecuting lawyer.

Jesus visited Paul in 62A.D. and passed on the tragic news that his brother James had been killed. The Pharisee Jews had surrounded James after he announced Jesus as the Messiah and stoned him, and then clubbed him to death with a fuller's club.

Paul was still in prison when the great fire of Rome destroyed most of the city. The prisoners were transferred to a smaller prison where they were so cramped they could only stand. The commander asked the senate if the prisoners on low grade offences could be pardoned and released. The senate conferred with Emperor Nero. He was under pressure from Roman citizens who accused him of starting the fire deliberately to obtain more land for himself. The emperor wanted to know what the prisoners offences were before he would grant any releases. Nero was informed that many prisoners were Christians that had been arrested for preaching on the streets and causing disturbances with passing Jews

Nero seized the chance to clear his name, accusing the Christians of starting the fire and condemning them to death without trial. Paul was dragged to the town square and beheaded in public near the *Tre Fontane,* the three fountains. Paul was saved the agony of being tied to a stake and burnt alive as a human torch in a public park because of his Roman citizenship. Thousands of Christians were rounded up and burnt at the stake. Luke managed to hide in the catacombs with Jesus, but the soldiers were searching everywhere for them, and it was only a matter of time before they too would be captured.

Luke addressed and dispatched his unfinished scrolls to Theophilus, no longer a High Priest, but now a confirmed Christian living at Qumran Monastery as Most High. The scrolls that Luke had written while staying with Paul continued the story of Jesus after the resurrection and the travel of Apostle Paul. It also mentioned the assassination of Ananias and Sapphira who were responsible for the imprisonment of Paul. Peter had summoned the pair over a small misdemeanour regarding sale of a property without the full entitlement being donated to the church. Ananias was offered a drink of wine while at the tribunal hearing and dropped dead in minutes. Sapphira was heard next, also offered wine and she too dropped dead. Peter and the tribunal had judged Ananias and Sapphira guilty of Paul's prolonged incarceration and his demise at the order of Nero, and inflicted swift revenge.

Nero widened his search for Christians when he found he had public support. He sent soldiers to Corinth and Ephesus to arrest two leaders from each city. They arrested Apostle John and John Mark in Ephesus and Crispus and Apollos in Corinth. John Mark was lashed, for being a Eunuch chariot driver that was caught in the company of Christians. He was exiled to the Island of Patmos with other criminals deemed to have committed minor offences against Rome. Crispus, Apollos and Apostle John were lashed and thrown into a deep hole until Nero's next palace festival. He planned to burn them at the stake to light up his garden while he sang and played his lyre in front of his distinguished guests.

Jesus heard about their capture and organised their rescue. They knifed the solitary guard and dropped a rope ladder down to the men. They climbed out of the hole and followed Jesus to the relative safety of the catacomb passageways. They planned to leave the city with a small group of disciples during the night, but their hideout was discovered by several soldiers that saw them entering the tunnel. The disciples protected Jesus by throwing broken bricks at the soldiers. The soldiers were caught off guard as most Christians surrendered peacefully, even knowing they would be whipped, imprisoned, exiled or executed for their beliefs.

Four soldiers died in the opening volley and the Christians fought with the three others who were using their shields to protect themselves from the hail of bricks. The heavily armed soldiers slashed their way through the group. Luke dropped to the ground and feigned death. When the soldiers passed him, he grabbed the sword from a dead soldier and stabbed two soldiers from behind. The last soldier turned and stabbed Luke in the stomach before being struck on the back of the neck by a brick. He fell to the ground and was beheaded with his own sword.

Jesus cradled the dying Luke in his arms, talking to him and consoling him. Jesus thanked him for being his lifelong friend, delivering his children, and for saving his life. He reassured Luke that his writings would be added to his previous work and bound in the next edition of bibles for the masses to read. Jesus and the disciples buried Luke and the other dead Christians in an alcove and used damp clay and bricks to entomb them out of sight of the Romans. Then they moved the dead soldiers to another catacomb tunnel.

Jesus was tired and cold, and felt weak. He washed the blood off his hands and face and stared at his reflection in the pool of water. He was seventy-one; his long black curly hair had turned grey years ago, now it was cropped short and was white as snow. It didn't suit his olive skin and his piercing dark brown eyes, but his voice and quick wit still remained. Jesus gathered his senses. He had to save these Christians who had saved his life. He had to keep his promise to Luke. He had to revenge Luke's death and see Mary one more time.

"It is time to fight fire with fire, an eye for an eye and a tooth for a tooth," he said.

"What can we do against the Roman wrath," one of the male disciples asked.

"Nero has decreed our Christian faith unlawful and punishable by death. He is seeking out our leaders and crucifying them in public squares," Jesus said.

"You know we will follow you Lord. Tell us what to do."

"We will organise a mass demonstration and attack Nero's palace in the dead of night," Jesus said. "Follow me and I will lead you to safety until we can regroup."

Jesus walked into an alcove and removed a stone from the wall. He reached into a hole and removed two sacks of coins used to buy food and supplies. He led the group of men out of the catacomb passageways and onto the dimly lit streets. He led them through the bushland and swamp until they reached the River Tiber. The men followed Jesus along the river bank where he found a wooden boat large enough to hold all of them. There were no sails or oars, but the current would take them away from the city and sixteen miles down the river to the port of Ostia. Jesus and the men found two long branches they could use to guide the boat. They left short forks on one end of each branch for extra drag to steer the boat and snapped the branches into ten foot lengths. The men untied the ropes, boarded and pushed the boat away from the bank. They kept close to the overhanging trees until they were well away from the city, and then they steered the boat into the faster moving current and disappeared into the darkness. They sat quietly, mourning the loss of Luke and their brave companions.

An hour after sunrise, Jesus asked the men to steer the boat onto a sandy stretch of land. The men stretched their legs and relieved themselves among the bushes. The men returned and sat in a circle to discuss the next leg of their journey and to share out the coins.

"There is enough money for everyone to pay passage fares," Jesus said.

"We will need to split up into small groups before we reach Ostia," Crispus said.

"We can enter the town from three directions," John said. "Some of us can be dropped off before Ostia, some at the wharf and the rest at the southern end of town."

"The last group can scuttle the boat," Apollos said.

"We will have to lay low for six months," Jesus said. "I suggest you choose a place where you are not known, each group should choose your own secret destination."

The fifteen men chose their groups and carried out the plan. They said goodbye to each other, knowing that they would probably not cross paths again for some time. Jesus, John and Crispus sailed to Malta. They stayed for three weeks and then sailed to Fair Havens in Crete. Here the three men split up. No one knew the final destination of the others. Crispus returned to Corinth and told Mary that Jesus was on the move, but fairly safe. Apostle John landed at Taurus and walked to Derbe to stay with relatives of Paul. Jesus went to the Island of Patmos to visit John Mark, his long-time friend and celibate companion until he married Mary.

Jesus landed on the Island of Patmos and was spotted by Prochorus who ran to John at the cave where twenty disciples lived and worshipped. John ran to the coast and saw Jesus dressed in a white robe with a golden sash around his chest: 'His head and hair were white like wool, as white as snow, and his eyes were like blazing fire. When I saw him, I fell at his feet as though dead. Then he placed his right hand on me.'

"Do not be afraid," Jesus said. "I am the first and the last. I am the living one. I was dead, and behold I am alive for ever and ever. And I hold the keys of death and Hades."

Jesus stayed with John for two months. He asked John and his scribes to write a general letter of greetings to all the churches of Asia Minor and enclose seven individual letters. Jesus dictated different messages to each church, depending on their response to Apostle teaching and Christian ideology. Jesus also instructed John to document the history of what he had seen, what was happening now, and what will take place soon. Jesus departed the island with the seven letters and he promised John the completed scroll would be added to the new Bible.

Jesus sailed to Ephesus to attend a council meeting. He gave the seven letters to the elders to distribute to the churches and submitted Luke's scroll, called the *Acts*, to be added to the next batch of New Testament Bibles. There was some at the meeting that disagreed to the book of Acts being included in the new Bible, but Jesus claimed history of the movement should be included, and that John Mark was producing a book of Revelation at his request.

The committee passed the motion that the two books would be added to the next edition and Titius was nominated to oversee the whole procedure.

Jesus and Titius travelled to Corinth and then sailed with Mary and the extended family to live near Simon and Martha and their family in Marseilles. Jesus and Simon talked about the tragic deaths of their brothers, Judas and

James, and the good times they had on the farm at Nazareth when they were young. They also planned a journey to Rome to lobby the Senate over Nero's cruel treatment of Christians.

In 66A.D. Emperor Nero was informed that the Galilean and Judean Zealots had revolted against the Roman procurator Gessius Florus over the massacre of hundreds of Jews. Berenice returned to Caesarea after the breakdown of her third marriage to Julius Polemo, the King of Cilicia, and as Queen appealed to Florus to cease hostilities with her countrymen. She was lucky to escape with her life when Florus turned on the Queen and angrily dismissed her. Agrippa joined his sister Berenice in Jerusalem and pleaded with the public to accept Roman authority and not to riot. The King and Queen were mobbed, and they fled to Rome for their own safety. The Zealots burnt down their palaces and attacked Florus' soldiers.

Nero sent the governor of Syria, Cestius Gallus, with six thousand soldiers to quell the uprising. He defeated the Zealots in Galilee and then marched to Jerusalem. He could not defeat the Zealot force barricaded in the walled city without a siege and withdrew. On the route to Antioch Gallus forces were ambushed in a sandy swamp near Beth-Holon and Gallus fled the scene with his body guards. Five thousand Roman soldiers were slaughtered, and the Zealots commandeered their horses and equipment. Nero was furious when he heard the news. He demanded Gallus fall on his own sword and sent his most experienced commander Vespasian with three legions and seven auxiliary forces to quell the uprising.

The Zealots seized the Herod fortresses at Masada and Machaerus by armed force, and congregated a large force in Jerusalem. Another group of Zealots built fortress strongholds in Jotapata and Gamala and prepared for war with Rome. Berenice and Agrippa returned from exile in Rome, and their loyal followers joined forces with Vespasian's army. Titus, the son of Vespasian, was commander of one of the legions that besieged Jerusalem for one thousand, two hundred and sixty days. He was besotted by Queen Berenice's beauty and her lustful sexual appetite, falling deeply in love with the woman eleven years his senior.

While the fighting raged in Iudaea, the aging brothers Simon and Jesus organised a mass rally of two thousand Christians outside Nero's palace. They stormed the palace gates at night and entered the palace. The praetorian guards had already deserted their posts. Nero panicked and committed suicide before the Christians could hand him a letter to sign, stating Christians could practice their religion in peace, and to decree public gatherings lawful. Jesus and Simon left Rome and visited John Mark on the Island of Patmos to inform him of the devastating events occurring in Rome and Jerusalem.

John was delighted to hear that Titius, alias *the Spirit of the Lord,* was betrothed and would marry on his thirty-six birthday, and that Michael the second son of Jesus had been anointed Most High at the Qumran Monastery.

Vespasian returned to Rome in triumph and became the fourth Emperor to reign during the year 69A.D. He was appointed Emperor by the Senate after the quick succession of Galba, six month reign, Otho three months, and Vitellius seven months, all of whom were murdered or committed suicide. Jerusalem fell to the Roman forces in 70A.D. after a forty-two month siege and the whole city, including the Temple was destroyed. The surviving Jewish citizens were expelled or forced to work in the sulphur mines.

In Marseille, Jesus and Mary prepared for Titius' wedding that would be held in March 72A.D. on his thirty-sixth birthday which indicated it was a royal dynasty wedding. The family were inside the church discussing the final arrangements with the minister when a loud commotion on the street caught their attention. Jesus went outside and saw a ring of angry men surrounding a beautiful, but frightened young woman. Jesus parted the crowd and walked inside the ring of men as he had done on other occasions.

"What sin has this woman committed to deserve stoning?" Jesus asked.

Jesus bent down and drew a long curve in the sand.

"She has committed adultery," the crowd yelled.

The woman looked at the old man and what he was drawing. She stepped forward and drew a long curve in the opposite shape of the one Jesus had drawn. The two curves, joined at the head formed the simple image of a fish, the sign Christians used to identify their faith to strangers. The words *Jesus Christ Son of God, Saviour* in Koine Greek translates into *Iesous Christus Theou Yios Soter.* The letters I-ch-th-y-s spells the Greek word for fish.

Jesus took hold of the young woman's hand and then stood up, he looked at the men.

"If anyone of you is without sin, let him be the first to throw a stone at her," he said.

At this, those that heard began to walk away one at a time, the older ones first, until only Jesus and the woman remained. Jesus told the woman that no one had condemned her and that she should go home and leave her life of sin.

Jesus turned towards Mary and smiled as his eyes met hers. He kept his gaze on Mary as long as he could until she faded out of sight. A Roman soldier standing nearby had witnessed the same deed in Jerusalem many years ago when he was a child and knew the man was Jesus. The revolutionary had a bounty on his head, wanted for the protests against Emperor Nero and Roman authority worldwide. The soldier had thrust his dagger into Jesus' heart and bent over the prostate Jesus to hack off his head. Mary screamed and the men, still with rocks in their hands, circled the soldier and stoned him to death.

Mary ran to Jesus and cradled him in her arms. Her tears fell on his face, washing away the blood from his mouth. She kissed him and ran her fingers through his white curly hair. Jesus drew on his last source of energy to open his eyelids one more time. He smiled at Mary and listened to her beautiful angelic voice as he drifted off to heaven.

"I love you darling," she said. "You are the light of my life. You saved the life of that lovely young lady. Rest in heavenly peace, with your father, mother, brothers and baby Miriam. I will come to your side in heaven. Our love will live for eternity. I love you darling. I love you."

Jesus was buried in a secret location high in the mountains. Only Mary, Simon, Martha and Jesus' four children attended the funeral. French tradition has it that Mary visited a cave in the hills near Marseilles for twenty years after the death of Jesus. Probably the cave her husband was entombed for twelve months, before his bones were placed in an ossuary. Most of Jesus followers believed he had died on the cross thirty-six years earlier and had already ascended into heaven. Jesus soul remained embedded in the Christian ideology and spread the word of peace, love and faith to billions of people of all races, all over the world. Jesus was the greatest man to ever walk the earth. His name and great feats will live on for eternity.

After Jesus was slain, Michael opened the seven seals in the council meeting held in Ephesus. Six months later Titus attacked and destroyed the Qumran monastery, Michael and his wife Greta, who had given birth to a son fled into the wilderness with their entourage. They were pursued by the emperor's soldiers but eluded capture by fleeing into the wilderness area of the Buqeia plateau and then migrating to Babylon.

The book of Acts covers the period from the resurrection in 36A.D to the trial of Paul in 64A.D. Luke died before completing his book, however, he wrote down some of the early Christian history, including Apostle Pauls' missions with Jesus often by his side. Titius and his brother Michael both had male heirs that continued the King David dynasty. Royal weddings continued throughout history and the royal blood of Jesus flows through many Kings and Queens, and many people of high and noble character. Titius added the two books of Acts and Revelation to the four gospels of Matthew, Mark, Luke and John in the year his father died, recording the Christian history over the life of Jesus.

John Mark wrote in Revelations that to unravel his words *'calls for a mind with wisdom.'* Revelation covers the period of 64A.D. to the marriage of Jesus Titius Justus in 72A.D. In his book John Mark wrote about *The Lamb* that was slain from the creation of the world, and the rider on the white horse, the king of kings and lord of lords. He wrote about the siege of Jerusalem that lasted one thousand two hundred and sixty days. The Holy city fell after forty-two months, conquered by the beast with ten horns, the three Roman legions and seven auxiliary units. The mystery woman and the beast were Queen Berenice and Titus, the son of Emperor Vespasian. *The woman and the Dragon* was Jesus' daughter-in-law Greta who fled with her infant son from Vespasian's soldiers. John used the phrase *two wings of a great eagle,* to conceal her name, Greta of Galee (Galilee). *Nero Caesar* was given number 666, derived from Greek letters with their Hebrew values for each letter added together.

Titius Justus was given the title of *The Spirit* and after the demise of his father *The David*. Titius, at the age of thirty-six had a dynasty wedding in 72A.D. as declared in Revelations, *The Spirit and the bride say "Come!"*

The New Testament was written in code form as the Roman Emperors were afraid of the power Jesus held over the world communities and wanted to eliminate him, his family and his followers. The military might of Rome failed to quell Christianity and three hundred years later it was declared a legal religious ideology.

The word of Jesus has spread and increased teaching most of the world population to love one another, embrace peace, share their wealth with the poor and repent their sins. Although the history in the New Testament referred only to events that occurred between 10B.C. and 72A.D. in the first century, the religious message is still relevant today. Jesus was known under several aliases, *as John, the light, the truth,* and *The Word*.

Many have undertaken to draw up an account of things that have been fulfilled and many have misrepresented *The Word of God*. The New Testament should be read after using aliases from this book, *then you will know the truth, and the truth will set you free.* John 8:32.

REFERENCES

LIFE OF JESUS - BIRTH TO CRUCIFIXION

In the beginning	John 1:1-2
Paternal genealogy of Jesus	Matt 1:1-17
Maternal genealogy of Jesus	Luke 3:23-38
Birth of John and Jesus foretold	Luke 1:5-25 1:26-38
Birth of John 28th Sept 9B.C.	Luke 1: 39-80
Virgin Mary conceived Jesus, July 1st 9B.C.	Luke1:35 1:42
Birth of Jesus 29th March 8B.C	Matt 1:18-25, Luke 1:26-38
Jesus Aries the Lamb	John 1:29
Jesus blessed by High Priest	Matthew 1:23 Luke 2:25
Escape to Egypt	Matt 2:13-17
Return to Galilee	Matt 2:19-23
Jesus Bar-Mitzvah ceremony	Luke2:46
Jesus leaves monastery life	John 1:14
John the Baptist sent by Most High	John 1:6-9 1:15
John the Baptist not the Christ	John 1:19-28

John the Baptist prepares the way	Matt 3:1-12, Mark 1:4 1:7-8, Luke 7:33
John calls Jesus the Lamb of God	John 1:29-34
Baptism of Jesus 29A.D.	Matt 3:13-17, Mark 1:9-11, Luke 3:1-2 John 1:31
John the Baptist testimony	John 1:26-34 3:22-36
Jesus begins to preach	Matt 4:12-17
The first disciples	Matt 4:18-22 John 1:35-51
Jesus marries on the third day of the week, March 29th 29A.D.	John 2:1
An eye for an eye	Matt 4:38
Jesus sends out the twelve disciples	Matt 10:1-6, Mark 6:7
Names of the twelve Apostles	Matt 10:2-4, Mark 3:13-19, Luke 6:12-16
John the Baptist imprisoned	Matt 11:1-3, Mark 1:14, Luke 3:19-20
Jesus worked on the Sabbath	Matt 12:1-14
Jesus a prophet without honour	Matt 13:54-58, Mark 6:1-6, Luke 4:22-24
Jesus' brothers and sisters	Matt 13:55-56 Mark 6:3

John the Baptist beheaded	Matt 14:1-12, Luke 9:7-9 Mark 6:17-28,
Jesus death threats	Luke 4:29-30, John 8:58-59 10:29-39
Jesus sends out seventy-two	Luke 10:1
Jesus says I am the son of man	Matt 16:13 Mark 8: 27-30
Jesus, son of the living God	Matt 16:16, John 5:16-21
Zachariah killed	11:51
Jesus predicts his death	Matt16:21, Mark 8:31, Luke 18:31-33
Son of man will be condemned	Matt 20:17-19
Plots against Jesus	Matt 26:1-5, John 11:49-50
Plot to kill Simon Lazarus	John 12:9-11
Jesus anointed by Mary Magdalene	Matt 26:6-13, Mark 14:1-9, Luke 10:38-42, John12:1-9
Judas agrees to betray Jesus	Matt 26:14-16, Mark 14:10, Luke 22:1-6
Titius-Justus Born March 21st 36A.D	John 19:26-27
The Lord's Supper	Matt 26:17, Mark 14:12-21, Luke 22:7-12 John 13:1-3

Jesus prays	John 17:1-5
Jesus arrested	Matthew 26:47-50, Mk 14:43-47, Luke22:47-53, John 18:1-10
Before the Sanhedrin	Matt 26:57-68, Mark 14:60-65
Before High Priest Ananus	John 18:12-14
Before Pontius Pilate	Mark 15:1-15, Luke 22:66-71 23:1-25, John 18:28-40
Jesus sentenced	John 19:1-16
Judas commits suicide	Matt 27:1-5,
The crucifixion	Matt 27:32-44, Mark 15:21-32, Luke 23:26-43, Jn 19:1-16
Jesus succumbs on the cross	Mt 27:45-54, Mk 15:33-36, Lk 23:44-49, Jn 19:28-37
Women witnesses	Mt 27:55-56, Mk 15:40-41, Lk 24:9-10, Jn 19:25-27
Joseph asks Pilate for Jesus	Matt 27:57-61, Luke 23:50-55
Jesus, Simon, and Josephes entombed	Matt 15:42-47, John 19:38-42
Guard at the Tomb	Matt 27:62-66

LIFE OF JESUS – RESURECTION TO REVELATION

The Resurrection	Matt 28:1-8, Mark 16:1-7, Luke 24:1-7
The empty tomb	John 20:1-9
Jesus appears to Mary	John 20:11-18
Jesus appears to followers	Matt 28:9-10, Mk 16:6-7, Lk 24:13-50-53, Jn 20:1 9-20
Jesus appears to Thomas	John 20:24-29
Jesus instructs the Apostles	Acts 1:2-8
Matthias chosen as 13th Apostle	Acts 1:12-26 (After Judas committed suicide)
Jesus taken to Qumran monastery	Acts 1:2
Luke's book to High Priest 37 A.D.	Luke 1:1-4 (Most excellent Theophilus)
Peter and John before the Sanhedrin	Acts 4:1-22
Ananias and Sapphira judged	Acts 5:1-11
The Apostles persecuted	Acts 5:17-42
Stephens speech'	Acts 7:51-53
The stoning of Stephen	Acts 7:54-60
Saul's conversion	Acts 9:1-19
Saul in Damascus and Jerusalem	Acts 9:19-31
Saul and Barnabas in Antioch	Acts 11:19-30
Apostle James Cleopas beheaded	Acts 12:1-2 (Herod Agrippa's orders)
Peter seized and freed	Acts 12:3-19
King Herod Agrippa poisoned	Acts 12:19-23
Saul anointed as 14th Apostle Paul	Acts 13:9 (After James the elder beheaded)
Michael Justus, born July 30th 44A.D	Acts 12:24

The council at Jerusalem	Acts 15:1-35
Titius Justus Bar-Mitzvah	Acts 16:7 18:7
Paul in Ephesus	Acts 19:1-41
Michael Justus' Bar-mitzvah	Acts 20:2-3
Paul returns to Jerusalem	Acts 21: 1-26
Paul arrested	Acts 21:27-40 22:1-30 23:1-35
Paul's trial before Felix	Acts 24:1-27
Paul's trial before Festus	Acts 25:1-22
Paul's before Agrippa II	Acts 25:23-27 26:1-32
Paul's voyage to Rome	Acts 27:1-31
Luke's unfinished book to Theophilus	Acts 1:1-3 Acts1-28:31
Michael Justus marriage to Greta	Revelation 12:1 (Greta's son born at Qumran Monastery)
Jesus visits John Mark on Patmos Isle	Revelation 1:1-22:21
Jesus slain 72A.D.	Revelation 5:6 5:9 5:12 13:8
Titius Justus Dynasty Marriage	Revelation 22:17

THE PROPHESISED SECOND COMING OF JESUS

Jesus released from tomb April 1ST 36A.D	Matt 28:5-6 Mark 16:6 Luke 24:1-10
Jesus talks to Mary April 1st 36 A.D.	Matt 28:9-10 Mark 16:9 John 20:14-17
Jesus speaks to his Disciples April 1st 36 A.D.	Matt 28-20 Acts 1:1-9 Mark 16:14-18 Luke 24:13-53 John 20:19-23
Jesus speaks to Thomas April 8th36A.D.	John 20:24-29
Jesus at Lake Galilee April 36A.D.	John 21:1-25
37A.D. Jesus autobiography	The Gospel of John
42A.D. Jesus converts Saul	Acts 9:1-7
42A.D. Jesus talks to Peter	Acts 10:13-15
43A.D. Paul made Apostle	Acts 22:3-21
44A.D. Jesus writes to Mary	John II
44A.D. Jesus writes to Gaius	John III
47A.D. Jesus writes to his children	John I
57A.D. Paul states Jesus is alive	Romans 1:4
58A.D. Jesus talks to Paul	Acts 23:11
60A.D. Paul states Jesus is alive	Acts 25:19
62A.D. Jesus sends greetings	Colossians 4:11
63A.D. Paul states Jesus free	Timothy II 2:9
63A.D. Jesus stands by Paul	Timothy II 4:16-18
64A.D. Jesus visits John Mark on Patmos Isle	Revelation 1:12-20
72A.D. Jesus slain by a Roman soldier	Revelation 5:6 5:9 5:12 13:8

IMMEDIATE FAMILY OF JESUS

Jacob	Paternal grandfather of King David lineage
Miriam	Paternal grandmother
Heli	Maternal grandfather of King David lineage
Salome	Maternal grandmother
Zachariah	Maternal Uncle
Elizabeth	Salome's sister
John	Son of Zachariah and Elizabeth (Cousin)
Joseph	Father of King David lineage
Mary	Virgin Nun of King David lineage
Rachel	Virgin Mary's sister
Jesus	Eldest son and crown prince
James	Eldest brother of Jesus
Josephes	Brother of Jesus (also known as Joses)
Mary jr.	Eldest sister of Jesus
Simon	Brother of Jesus
Miriam	Stillborn
Salome	Sister of Jesus
Judas	Brother of Jesus
Joanna	Sister of Jesus
Mary Magdalene	Wife of Jesus
Sarah	Eldest daughter of Jesus and Mary
Tamara	Second daughter of Jesus and Mary
Titius	Eldest son of Jesus and Mary Magdalene
Titius' Bride	Wife and children's names unknown
Michael	Second son of Jesus and Mary
Michael's Bride	Greta of King David lineage
Jesus' Grandson	Name unknown
Jesus Descendants	King David lineage (known as the Holy Grail), names unknown to history.

PROVINCES, KINGDOMS, COUNTRIES

Achaea	Southern Greece
Asia Minor	Turkey
Britannia	England
Decapolis	A province in Iudaea
Cyrenaica	Libya
Dalmatia	Eastern Yugoslavia
Egyptus	Egypt
Ephesians	Eastern Turkey
Idumea	A province in Iudaea
Illyricum	Eastern Yugoslavia
Iudaea	Kingdom of ancient Israel and Palestine
Israel	Promised land
Italia	Italy
Judea	A province in Iudaea
Galilee	A province in Iudaea
Galatia	Central Turkey
Gaul/Gallia	France
Gaulantis	A province in Iudaea
Germania	Germany
Hispania	Spain
Macedonia	Greece
Mesopotamia	Iraq
Noricum	Northern Greece
Perea	A province in Iudaea
Samaria	A province in Iudaea
Syria	Eastern Arabia
Thracia	Northern Greece

RELIGIOUS GROUPS

Christians
Originally called followers of *The Way,* this sect grew rapidly under the second coming of Jesus the Christ, becoming the strongest religion in the known world.

Druids
A Celtic religion in Britannia, Gaul and Germanic regions, whose followers believed in three specific dimensions in the cycle of birth, life and death. Druidism was an ancient religion that was replaced by the more popular Christian movement after the crucifixion of Jesus and his resurrection.

Essenes.
A breakaway group of the Pharisee sect, the Essene followers only ate white meat and vegetables. They followed Pharisee religious doctrine.

Pagans
The ancient Pagans worshipped many Gods including acts of weather, planets, stars, insects, animals, emperors and kings.

Pharisees
Their followers believed in one almighty God, heaven, life after death and received religious instruction through clergymen in Synagogues.

Sadducees
Members of the elite class that believed in the life of wealth and power over mortality, they did not believe in life after death.

Therapeuts
A sect were followers practised their religious beliefs in homes and used herbal medicine to cure illness.

The Way
Joseph Justus formed this sect in 6A.D. at the bequest of Pharisee and Essene leaders after the demise of the Therapeuts. Originally formed as an independent member for the religious council to replace the seat lost by the Therapeuts, *The Way* became a popular religion among the lower classes and grew rapidly under the charismatic leadership of Joseph, his son Jesus and John the Baptist. In 36 A.D. Jesus was crucified as the Christ and *The Way* followers became known as Christians after the resurrection of Jesus into *heaven*.

Zealots
National extremists from any Religious sect that would fight the might of Rome for the total independence of Iudaea. The sect was formed in 6A.D. after Herod Archelaus was dismissed by Emperor Augustus and replaced by a Roman Prefect to govern Judea.

GLOSSARY

A.D.	Years after Archelaus Herod's Dedication ceremony
Abstinence	Abstaining from pleasure etc.
Adhortation	Advice
Alias	A false or assumed identity
Amphora vase	Roman /Greek two handled vase
Angel	Monastery alias for Messenger
Apostle	One of the twelve chief disciples of Jesus Christ. (two apostles were replaced after deaths in 36 and 42A.D.
Aquarius	A person who is born while the sun is in Aquarius - Jewish month of Shebat
A.U.C.	Ab Urbe Condita - Latin for 'From the foundation of the City' (of Rome)
Bagel	A dense bread roll in the shape of a ring, characteristic of Jewish baking
Bar-Mitzvah	The initiation ceremony of a Jewish boy who has reached the age of 12 and is regarded as ready to observe religious precepts and eligible to take part in public worship.
Basilica	A large oblong building with double colonnades and a semicircular apse used in ancient Rome as a law court or for public assemblies

Ben in middle of name	Means son of
Blasphemy	The action or offence of speaking sacrilegiously about God or sacred things; profane talk
Blood Libel	An ancient Jewish ceremony where pure blood of young Egyptian boys was mixed with red wine in religious rituals, especially in the preparation of Passover, that was perpetrated though out the middle ages.
Blood Red Moon	Caused by dust or ash in atmosphere
B.C.	Backwards to creation
Bollard	A short thick post on the deck of a ship or wharf used to secure the vessel by rope.
Brails	Small ropes that are led from the leech of a fore-and-aft sail to pulleys on the mast for temporarily furling it.
Caesar	A title of Roman emperors
Catacombs	Underground passages and cemeteries consisting of a subterranean gallery with recesses for tombs.
Cavalcade	A formal procession of people walking, on horseback or riding in vehicles.
Chief Priest	Rank of Bishop or Holy Spirit
Christ	Essene God or Most High anointed with oil

Consort	A wife, husband or companion, in particular the spouse of a reigning monarch
Celibate	Person bound not to marry
Celibacy	Total abstinence from sex
Census	An official count or survey especially of a population
Cloud	Monastery name for an Elder
Coital	relating to coitus copulation
Crown prince	Second in line of The David title
Crucify	To be strapped to a cross or tree usually until death for committing a serious crime against state laws.
David dynasty	King David lineage
Denarius	An ancient Roman silver coin.
Disciples	A personal follower of Christ during his life
Dynasty marriage	Royal celibate male marries at age 36 to produce heirs
Emperor	A sovereign of an empire
Entourage	A group of people attending or surrounding an important person
Equinox- Vernal	First day of Spring in northern hemisphere equal day/night hours
Equinox- Autumnal	First day of Autumn in northern hemisphere equal day/night hours
Foresail	The principal sail on a foremast

Gates of Hercules	The strait at the eastern end of Gibraltar
God (Heavenly)	An invisible supernatural being.
Gods (Ancient)	Most High, High Priest, King, Emperor, Pagan beliefs of extreme weather conditions, e.g. Thunder or Lightning, Egyptian dung beetles, planets, stars, etc.
Gomorrah	Name for celibate women lesbian acts
Hallel	A portion of the service for certain Jewish festivals
Haroseth	A sweet, dark coloured paste made of fruits and nuts eaten at the Passover Seder
Hawser	A thick rope or cable for mooring or towing a ship
Heterosexual	Heterosexuality is romantic attraction, sexual attraction or sexual behaviour between persons of opposite sex or gender
Heaven	Opulent third floor monastery apartment
Hell	Enclosed dungeon in monastery with furnace were poor souls work until death
High Priest	Head of Temple proceedings second only to supreme priest (King or Head of country)
Holy Grail	The blood line of King David descendants

Holy Spirit	Monastery name for Bishop
Hyssop	A wild shrub of uncertain identity whose twigs were used for sprinkling in ancient Jewish rites of purification
Iscariot	Knife bearing assassin
Kislev	The third month of the civil and ninth of the religious year, usually coinciding with parts of November or December
Laity	Lay people, as distinct from the clergy
Lamb of God	Alias for Aries born Jesus, the son of Most High
Leprosy	A contagious disease that affects the skin, mucous membranes, and nerves, causing discolouration and lumps on the skin and in severe cases disfigurement and deformities, and death
Lords supper	Held on Jesus' 43rd birthday, last supper before his crucifixion
Lightning	Pagan god and monastery name for top ranked Priest
Litter	Light stretcher carried by two or four persons for carrying another person or goods
Martyr	A person who is killed because of their religious or other beliefs

Masada	A fortification in the Southern District of Israel situated on top of an isolated rock plateau on the edge of the Dead Sea
Matza	Unleavened bread traditionally eaten by Jews during the weeklong Passover holiday.
Messiah	The promised deliverer of the Jewish people prophesied in the Hebrew Bible
Most High	Essene God
Movaan	A three positional sexual act beginning with filatio then vaginal and anal intercourse
Mitre	A tall headdress worn by bishops and senior abbots as a symbol of office, tapering to a point at front and back with a deep cleft between
Mulsum	Sweet wine water and honey beverage
Nahal	Wadi with running stream
Neophyte	A person who is new to a subject or activity
Omen	An event regarded as a portent of good or evil
Ossuary	A container or room in which the bones of dead people are placed
Parchment	Material made from the prepared skin of an animal, usually a sheep or goat that is used as a writing surface.

Palanquin	A covered litter for one or two passengers consisting of a large box carried on two horizontal poles by four or eight bearers.
Parables	A simple story used to illustrate a moral or spiritual lesson, as told by Jesus in the Gospels
Paradise	Name of the Judean cemetery at Golgotha
Paschal lamb	A lamb sacrificed at Passover
Passover	The major Jewish spring festival which commemorates the liberation of the Israelites from Egyptian slavery, lasting seven or eight days from the 15th day of Nisan
Pentecost	Christian festival celebrating the descent of the Holy Spirit on the disciples of Jesus after his Ascension, held on the seventh Sunday after Easter
Preparation day	The day immediately before the Sabbath and other Jewish festivals.
Procurator	A treasury officer in a province of the Roman empire.
Podium	A small platform on which a person may stand to be seen by an audience
Provinces	A principal administrative division of country or empire

Prophetic years	Years where religious sects predicted a great event would take place. In Jesus life time the years were 3969 and 4000 from creation
Resurrection	Revival
Sanctify	Set apart as or declare holy: consecrate
Sanhedrin	The supreme judicial and ecclesiastical council of ancient Jerusalem
Seder	A Jewish ritual service and ceremonial dinner for the first night or first two nights of Passover
Shebat	The fifth month of the civil and eleventh month of the religious year
Silphiuffi	Giant fennel herb used for contraception and prevention of sexually transmitted diseases
Silver Shekel	Roman coin
Special Sabbath	Falling on last day of the quarter, e.g. 31st March in A.D.36
Sodom	Name for male celibate sexual acts
Solstice- Winter	The sun's furthermost point in the opposite hemisphere, it appears to stand still for a day

Solstice- Summer	The sun's furthermost point in the closest hemisphere, it appears to stand still for a day
Son of God	Male child of Most High or High Priest
Stoning	Killing by throwing stones at victim
Symposium	A conference or meeting to discuss a particular subject
Synagogue	The building where a Jewish assembly or congregation meets for a religious observance and instruction
Sabbath	A day of religious observance and abstinence from work, kept by Jews from Friday evening to Saturday evening
Tammuz	The tenth month of the civil and the fourth of the religious year.
Tilapia	Fresh water fish with large opaque scales
Tetrarch	The governor of one of four divisions of a country for province
Torah	The law of God as revealed to Moses and recorded in the first five books of the Hebrew scriptures
Thunder	Pagan god and name for monastery second ranked priest
Tirone	New recruit in the Roman army

The Lamb of God	Alias for Jesus
The light, The Word, The Truth and John	Alias' for Jesus
The Son of God	Alias for Jesus
The World	Alias for Roman Empire
Thornbush	Crataegus Monogyna Biflora a small thorn tree with white trunk that flowers at Easter and Christmas originally from middle east.
Unleavened	Bread make without yeast or other raising agent
Vernal equinox	The equinox in spring
Wadi	A valley ravine or channel that is dry except in the rainy season
Wrath of God	Roman enemy of Most High or High Priest
Years Lunar Solar Calendar years B.C.-A.D.-A.U.C. .	Several different varieties Based on 12 moon cycles approximately 354 days Based on sun cycle approximately 365 days
Years Hebrew	Years from Creation
Zealot	Militant extremist

www.ingramcontent.com/pod-product-compliance
Lightning Source LLC
Chambersburg PA
CBHW060654100426
42734CB00047B/1571